Music and the Historical Imagination

Music and the Historical Imagination

LEO TREITLER

HARVARD UNIVERSITY PRESS

CAMBRIDGE, MASSACHUSETTS, AND LONDON, ENGLAND 1989

Library of Congress Cataloging-in-Publication Data

Treitler, Leo, 1931–
    Music and the historical imagination / Leo Treitler.
        p.   cm.
    Bibliography: p.
    Includes index.
    ISBN 0-674-59128-3 (alk. paper)
    1. Music—Philosophy and aesthetics.
2. Music—History and criticism.   I. Title.
ML3845.T77   1989   88-18066
780'.1—dc19   CIP

Designed by Gwen Frankfeldt

For Mary Frank

Acknowledgments

This book bears the mark of countless hours of conversation with more friends than I can possibly mention here. There are several, however, whom I want particularly to thank for time and thoughts that they have shared with me over the years, and for whose generosity this book is the better: Buffy Dunker, Allan Keiler, Joseph Kerman, Jan Kott, David Lewin, Lewis Lockwood, Leonard Meyer, Nino Pirrotta, Charles Rosen, Peter Schickele, Susan Sindel, my daughter, Inga Treitler, who is my tipster about anthropology, and last but not least, my companion Mary Frank, who helps to remind me always of the continuity between thinking and being, and to whom I dedicate this book.

To Margaretta Fulton of Harvard University Press I am indebted for the idea for this book and for her patient encouragement and good advice during its preparation. And to Jennifer Snodgrass, also of Harvard University Press, I am grateful for expeditious and judicious editing.

Contents

Music and the Historical Imagination

Introduction

How is historical thought about music possible? That such a question would even arise is the fact that has motivated this book. Again and again music's demand for attention to its present beauty and to its power to move the human spirit has been worried over as an obstacle in the way of historical thinking, a condition that must be dealt with in special ways. But it is a theme of this book that music's insistence on its presentness is a benefit to the historical imagination, whose play over the field bounded by past and present is energized by that insistence. The meaningfulness of music through all its presents, from the moment of its creation to the historian's present, is the content of historical thought about it. And the presence of music in the historian's consciousness is the condition under which such thought can take place.

The essays that are collected here move through two planes. They move back and forth between acts of thinking about music historically and reflections about such acts; and they move through the circumstances in which they were written, some shifting, others continuous, over a span of twenty-two years. Collapsing that time into the simultaneity of a single volume creates a new environment in which their meanings are differently shaded—by the light of each on the other, but also by the character of present social and scholarly concerns in relation to the provocations and circumstances under which they were written. To say that underlines a belief that is a premise throughout this book, that the meaning of a text is not fixed within its boundaries but is ever contingent upon the interests and the circumstances of the community of readers or listeners.

Nowadays that thought constitutes the core idea of a current fashion of literary critical theory, in which a "text" is the meaningful item as a whole, not only its graphic denotation. A piece of music is a text, as is a painting, and one would say that the text is always subject to change. But I think there is little advantage in this over my initial formulation, and that may have something to say about the fashions of literary criticism—that at least some of the time they come down to new formulations of old wisdoms. Perhaps the elaborate superstructure that has risen above the basic idea about the "deconstruction" of texts in other than their original contexts of meaning would not have generated quite such an arcanum if it had not answered to the need for relief from the opposite dogma—that texts bear immanent and enduring meanings which it is the business of critics to reveal. To question this dogma is to recognize that meaning is a product of the interaction of present and past. But that is the core idea of modern philosophical hermeneutics as well.[1] All in all, the temptation among younger musical scholars to follow the recent interests of literary theory is not just a matter of fashion-mongering. It reflects internal needs in musical studies, a desire for versatility and freedom from the rigidities of inherited dogma.

Presenting material from the past is itself an act of history. It is bringing something before someone, into the presence of someone, making it present in respect of time and place, the here and now: *hic et nunc*. The phrase conjures an ancient musical and poetic practice with which I have been engaged during most of the long period represented by these essays, although it is not represented among their subjects. In the high Middle Ages the chanting of the liturgy in the Roman church followed a tradition of several centuries' standing. But there was a new way of "presenting" (accent on the first syllable) the ancient chants that reminds me of my task in these introductory pages. The chants sang Scripture, in selections and arrangements that had been made centuries earlier. In a practice called troping, poets and composers took to composing new verses to introduce those passages and elaborate upon them, to transform their meaning in favor of contemporary theological values and interests, to actualize them by connecting their meanings explicitly with the ritual meaning of the day on which they were chanted (introductory verses were often begun with the Latin word for "today," *hodie*: "Today we must celebrate in song the child whom the

Father begot before time . . . "). Not only the subject of the chants was brought into the present by means of these new verses but even the act of chanting them, often through hortatory language that called forth the chanting, or descriptive language that conjured it up—chanting that enacted its own subject matter: "Let our voice sound forth today in a melodic symphony . . . Let the ring of musicians now resound . . . " As I write these lines on the day after Christmas the third stanza of the carol "Oh, Come, All Ye Faithful" comes to mind:

> Sing, choirs of angels
> Sing in exultation
> Sing, all ye citizens of heaven above
> Glory to God
> In the highest.

Troping was a way of making ancient matter available for active engagement by the members of the community. I like to think of this practice in all of those aspects as the embodiment of a kind of "presenting," of actualizing, that is central to the idea of history as it is conceived throughout this book. Like the ritual art of troped chanting, history is a telling of the past in the light of present sensibilities. It, too, is ritual, like the chanting of epic and oral history, like the ritual performance of tragedy in the cultures of Greek antiquity, like the chanting of Scripture in the Judeo-Christian tradition (sometimes called "historia"). Therein lies the source of its capacity for the affirmation of individual and collective identity. In all such ritual acts the relation of daily experience to human self-awareness is illuminated. History has always responded to the need for the communal telling of past and present experience for its interpretation.

It is all too easy to forget about these associations of history, once the historian becomes caught up in the complexities of reconstructing a past that can be told. The despair over the loss, or more accurately the trivialization, of history is widespread. It can be felt in fields that have always had a historical dimension—first and foremost the field of history itself, but also art history, literary history, music history—and in fields that have long lived apart from history, such as anthropology and ethnomusicology. What it comes down to is a despair over the evolution of scholarship away from the opportunities for identification, away from the experience of the past and present life.

Musicology, as much as any research discipline, has its present character determined by the insulating distance that scholars aim to keep between their work and the conditions under which it is done. And the same principle is invoked to isolate historical objects from the life of past worlds. That stance never prevails entirely unchallenged, but the posture of aloofness from the conditions of the scholar's world as a principle of historical scholarship nevertheless reaches back again and again to form the attitude toward the historical object; it affects both the present and the past.

The influence of social context is rarely apparent in the questions we have been asking in musicology, in the ways we have of addressing them, or in the standards by which we recognize knowledge and truth. The correctness of this exclusion seems to be regarded as self-evident, even if we do not find it spelled out among musicology's axioms. If justification were asked it would be given in terms of the ideal of objectivity that is safeguarded by this stance and that provides the criterion for what can be known and what truth is. The attitude of detachment from the social relations of the world in which we work imposes upon truth and knowledge, and upon the methodologies by which we seek them, the requirement that they transcend the circumstances of their origins—in a word, that they transcend history. That seems a paradoxical condition indeed to place upon historical knowledge.

It is in the nature of things that the paradox does not normally enter our consciousness. We do not on the whole like to confront the historicity of the truths we hold or of the ways we have of coming by them. We do not like to acknowledge that, as historians, we are within history. We do not like to think that our choice of problems or our ways of identifying and evaluating evidence serve any particular ideologies or that they reflect the ways in which our worlds are structured, or that they would respond to change in the circumstances around us. That deepens the paradox: we hold our ways of coming to know things to be absolute, but we despise *a priori* knowledge. We do not approve of bias in scholarship, whether its source is scholarly or societal. Most paradoxical of all, this attitude prevents us from recognizing its own ideological base and its own historicity, except under extraordinary circumstances.

Yet if we look closely enough we can always find indications of *a priori* thinking in our work. As I now reread my own effort to show that in the fourth chapter of this book, I am struck by the way it embodies the very paradox I have been describing. There is talk there of the "trenchant criticisms," "sharp attacks upon tradition," "acrid exchanges" about the goals and methods of humane learning in general and musical studies in particular that were being aired in 1967, the year of its original publication. But it is written within a sharp boundary that excludes all mention of the conditions that had set the "skeletons rattling in the halls of humane learning" during that time. And it leaves no doubt about my own preference then for the more civil tone of the "reflective writing" and "serious theorizing" that one could also read, during a period that I chose to characterize as "a time of reflection" about what our discipline was doing and why. As I now see all that, it reflects my own sharing of the deep-rooted belief in the importance of protecting thought in and about scholarship from any confrontation with the conditions under which it takes place.

In 1967 Lyndon Johnson's escalation of the American intervention in Vietnam was two years old and had reached its peak, and so had the profound reactions and counterreactions in the United States. The race riots in the Watts section of Los Angeles were two years behind us. It was three years after the student riots in Berkeley and two years after those at the University of Chicago and Columbia University. By 1967 inhabitants of the Atlantic community had learned the paradox that our survival was assured by the capacity of our governments to set off a nuclear holocaust. Stanley Kubrick's film *Dr. Strangelove: Or, How I Stopped Worrying and Learned to Love the Bomb* had been released in 1964.

It is inconceivable that the consciousness of anyone who was at all conscious would not have been altered. It is no wonder that the historiographic mold inherited from the age of Enlightenment that cast history as a story of transformation toward the perfection of reason in man and society gave way to apocalyptic forms; or that accomplished American humanists would have come to question the very possibility of an authentic and morally legitimate humanistic study, to question the presumption of humanists to be the privileged purveyors of humane values. If Lyndon Johnson was at large, asked one, why were we not in jail? And if the executioners of Auschwitz were lovers of Goethe, asked another, how would our humanistic values protect us from the possibility of our own barbarism? Better not to think about it. To be sure there was a whiff of self-serving demagoguery about such slogans; it was an opportune time for opportunism. But there was no escaping the dilemma posed by students who could not easily integrate lectures on the forms of Haydn symphonies with their forced awareness that their presence in the lecture hall was a privilege granted them in a society that was just then making such a display of its barbarity.

That I would have written the essay of 1967—which raises fundamental questions about conventional reasoning in musicology—without taking any account of the social and political ferment that was so much in my own consciousness now appears to me as a clear manifestation of the divided consciousness that the god of objectivity seems to demand of the scholar, and of the suppression of the part that can be moved by *anything*—whether it is the expressive qualities of music or the suffering of human beings.

The same scruple that works to secure the scholar's study from thoughts about the surrounding life is also at work protecting the judgments of musicologists from the distracting influence of that love of beauty in music that drew them into musicology initially. That paradox helps to address the questions that must come up: Why is this whole matter of the context of scholarship even worth discussing? What consequences would it have for the practice of musicology if reason and sensibility were allowed to come back together? What if we were to work out of a consciousness that is not divided, that is vulnerable to those things in the world and in music that can move the scholar to feeling and action, without fear of the incapacitation of reason? Then the gulf between the scholar and the object of scholarship that has been thought to be the necessary condition of knowledge would close, and the exile of self-consciousness would terminate. For objective knowledge depends not on the unrealistic effort to ban the self altogether from participation in judgment but on recognizing its role in judgment. And we would put paid to the the scruple against the first person—literally and figuratively.

The ban against the writer's voice blows through our literature like the chill that blows through *Wozzeck,* from the moment when the Captain first addresses Wozzeck in the third person. *Wozzeck,* we might say, is objectivity parodied on the stage, a portrayal of the dehumanization entailed in the voyeuristic relationship of a subject who observes and controls, but avoids all identification with his object. *Wozzeck* displays the posture of objectivity as a perversity, but more: it shows the human cost. For the world of scholarship we must ask not only whether the goal of objectivity is attainable, but also whether the effort to attain it is worth the costs.

A conference on "The Future of the Humanities" sponsored in 1968 by the American Academy of Arts and Sciences brought me to some awareness of the sort of double life we were leading because of the division in our selves, and I tried to formulate something about that in an essay for the proceedings of the conference. I would like to cite its beginning.

These are the thoughts of a commuter between two worlds that often seem to exclude one another. They are the products of an earnest quest for standards that might serve a person in both worlds.

One of my worlds is the university, where daily we learn more about the impossibility of coasting along satisfactorily on habits and expectations formed earlier . . . But in my other world—the field of musicology—we are quite satisfied that the premises of our work are as correct now as when they were laid down. The difference has to be attributed to our isolation from things contemporary and to the absence of any habit for understanding even our distant objects in terms of their meanings for any society.[2]

The conference provided just the sort of extraordinary circumstance that forces recognition of the historicity of the principles of scholarship. Or, more precisely, it provided a focus for the extraordinary circumstances under which it was held, and to a degree that was hardly anticipated by the organizers and participants. What remains most memorable after twenty years is not transmitted in the publication of papers from the conference. The tone was set in the opening session: each of the participants was asked to identify himself and to make a brief statement about his hopes and expectations for the conference. The fourth or fifth speaker was Roger Shattuck, the critic, cultural historian, and French scholar, who spoke these words, more or less: "As I look around this table I see that we are all white, we are all men, all of us are wearing ties, none of us is bearded, and I do not have great expectations of this conference." The ensuing pandemonium that I see in my mental restaging of the scene is probably an operatic embroidery. But the remark certainly had an incendiary effect. It pierced the veil of civility that is the usual dress for such affairs; the conference proceeded not in tranquillity but in an atmosphere that was as though we were fiddling while Rome burned, and probably fiddling the wrong tune at that.

Why did Shattuck's remark have such an effect? The immediate impact was political: the conference failed to represent the legitimate interests in the humanities of groups who were excluded—women, members of racial minorities, those whose marginality would have then been symbolized by beards or open collars. That left no doubt about the link between knowledge and power in the institutions of academic scholarship. But the political point drove home an epistemological one. It was not only the interests of those groups that were not represented, but also their scholarly or philosophical vantage points. Judgments about the present and future of the humanities do depend on the identifications and beliefs and sensibilities of humanists. What could one expect from a conference that ignored that reality in its very makeup, other than the reaffirmation of established beliefs and standards?

Imagine this scene in different decades of recent history. In 1958 Shattuck's remark might have been regarded as cranky; in any case it would not have struck home. In 1988 he would not have had occasion to make it; such a conference without women and members of racial minorities would be unthinkable—mainly because of raised political sensitivities, not because we live by different ideas about knowledge and truth. (Beards and ties have by now become diluted as symbols of anything). The year 1968 was the optimal one for that scene, because of the insistent intrusiveness of the political and social events that eventuated in the heightened sensitivities of the present. Willy-nilly the conference had proceeded on the old premise that politics—not the politics of scholarship, but secular, mundane politics—stop at the gates of the academy. But the realities forced themselves inside, among them the reality of the scholar's subjectivity as a factor in judgment. Evidently only the political and social realities could break through the shield of theory and practice against this possibility. Yet today, as in 1968, the implication in the disruptive comment that there could be different standards of knowledge from male and female vantage points is likely to be resisted as unthinkable, although it touches one of the vortices, recognized or not, of current humanistic scholarship.

In speaking of objectivity I have referred to the attitude that in knowing we are guided by the qualities of what is presented to the mind and by reason, and we allow neither apprehension nor judgment to be colored by the state of our own minds or feelings. The mind is neutral, on this view, transmitting like a window what is presented to it. As the rules of reason are alike for all, knowledge shows nothing of the individuality of the knower, only the steadfast reality of the known.

In speaking of divided consciousness I have referred to the tendency in our culture to act separately out of two different kinds of awareness: the awareness called knowing, and the awareness of self as bearer of the flux of feelings, longings, fears, empathies, antipathies, images, and fantasies that make up the subjective life. It is only this identity that is individual, the seat of what we call character, the intimate self from which we look out. If the object of knowledge should touch this self, that would be irrelevant to our judgment of it.

Such restraint on the play of the subjective self, such reserve in encounters with the world, are often cited as distinctive features of the modern Western style of interaction—not only in science and scholarship ("scientific detachment") but altogether. Because that style has seemed so suitable to the pursuit of objective knowledge, there can be a temptation to think of it as a product of the emphasis that has been placed on objectivity in Western culture since the seventeenth century. But the idea that a culture would have developed such distinctive, pervasive, and deeply etched personality traits, which have after all to do with the individual's very way of being in the world, solely in response to the epistemological requirements of its science and scholarship seems hard to credit.

The alternative is to pay attention to the indications of strong historical and psychological forces in our culture that favor the development of a divided consciousness. That would change the status of objectivity from first principle to rationalization. It would shift the focus of attention from the illusory nature of the goal of objectivity to the cultural condition for which it is a rationalization, and it would allow us to think differently about the relationship of knowing. Although the attempt to maintain a detached and dispassionate stance has long been a dominant characteristic of the regime of knowing in our culture, it has not always been so, and it is not now so in many cultures other than our own. What would it be like to think otherwise about this relationship? I have received just an inkling from a report about the process of knowing in the culture of Laos that I want to share because the contrast with our own conception is so very telling.

In the language of the Lao the expression that corresponds to our verb "to know" is *khow jai,* literally, "to enter the heart." Knowing is an involvement of the knower with the known; to know is to be engulfed in and surrounded by the known (precisely what objectivity is meant to avoid). Knowing is a continuing relationship, not the product of a process of gaining control over the object. In preparing for knowing one gives oneself over to what one understands, and that presupposes an affinity for it. Understanding means being in harmony with one's surroundings.[3]

This Laotian conception of knowing as a bonding of the knower with the known rather than a separation has underlying affinities with Platonic, medieval European, and other modern oriental epistemologies. The very expression *khow jai* resonates with our expression for knowing something from memory—to know "by heart," which is a survival from medieval Latin. Aurelian of Réôme, author of the oldest surviving book on Gregorian chant, the *Musica disciplina* (ca. 850) wrote, "Although anyone may be called by the name of singer, nevertheless he cannot be perfect unless he has implanted by memory in the sheath of his heart the melody of all the verses . . . " As this was written in a time when musical notation was not in general use as a basis for musical performance, Aurelian's remark has the connotation that to know something well was to know it from memory, that is, to have it in one's heart.[4] Even in the modern Western tradition there is a vein of thought that emphasizes some sort of union between the knower and the known—from the nineteenth-century hermeneutic tradition of Dilthey to the philosophical hermeneutics of Gadamer in this century and the writings of scientists such as Michael Polanyi about what he calls *Personal Knowledge.*[5] The theme of alienation is not natural, and it is not objectively given. It is a product of a psychological dynamic that has received cultural reinforcement and epistemological rationalization.

About 400 A.D., Saint Augustine wrote movingly of his anxiety over the powerful feelings aroused by the sound of music:

I used to be much more fascinated by the pleasures of sound than the pleasures of smell. I was enthralled by them, but you broke my bonds and set me free . . . But if I am not to turn a deaf ear to music, which is the setting for the words which give it life, I must allow it a position of some honor in my heart . . . I realize that when they are sung these sacred words stir my mind to greater religious fervour and kindle in me a more ardent flame of piety than they would if they were not sung . . . But I ought not to allow my mind to be paralyzed by the gratification of my senses, which often lead it astray. For the senses are not content to take second place. Simply because I allow them their due, as adjuncts to reason, they attempt to take precedence and forge ahead with it, with the result that I sometimes sin in this way but am not aware of it until later . . . So I waver between the danger that lies in gratifying the senses and the benefits which, as I know from experience, can accrue from singing . . .

This, then, is my present state. Let those of my readers whose hearts are filled with charity, from which good actions spring, weep with me and weep for me . . . But I beg you, O Lord my God, to look upon me and listen to me. Have pity on me and heal me, for you see that I have become a problem to myself, and this is the ailment from which I suffer.[6]

If we, today, insist on restricting our accounts of music to its engagement with reason, and excluding from our account music's engagement with our senses and, through them, our passions, we are in the tradition of an ancient mythology that explains human consciousness as divided in two permanently antagonistic parts. The theme of the struggle between reason on one side and sensuality and passion on the other is projected early in the history of our culture through Plato's image, in the *Phaedrus,* of the soul as a chariot.[7] The charioteer, who is Reason, struggles to control the twin steeds of Passion and Desire, lest they run away with the chariot.

When we speak in the metaphor of knowing as enlightenment, we evoke the parable of the cave in Plato's *Republic.*[8] The material world that is perceived through the senses is but a shadow play witnessed by the unenlightened, who are chained in a cave. The way to true knowledge, an ascent toward the brilliant light of the sun into a realm of pure idea or pure form, must be accomplished against the pull of sensuality. The ascent to reason out of sensuality conveys a sense similar to that of the myth of the chariot. If we take into account Plato's association, in the *Timaeus,* of form and matter as the male and female principles, respectively, the ascent to knowledge takes on the aspect of a transcendence from the feminine into the masculine realm.[9] Knowing is embedded in a mythology in which reason and sensuality are mutually opposed, and that opposition is characterized as the duality of the masculine and the feminine.

This mythology is recast and given additional nuance in the retelling of the Genesis story in the first century A.D. by the Alexandrian Jew Philo.[10] The fall of man is the fall of reason, and the agent is sensuality, embodied as woman. But, Philo writes, "Just as the man shows himself in activity and the woman in passivity, so the province of the mind is activity and that of the perceptive sense passivity, as in woman." The paradox survives, mostly unrecognized as such, in our word "passion."

With Philo's elaboration of this myth—the woman as sensuality, active through her passive nature, the man as reason, fallen through his active nature—we can recognize the story of Wedekind's and Berg's *Lulu* as a modern telling of it. Lulu's passivity is stressed throughout the drama as much as her sensuality—her innocence, her childlike eyes, her Pierrot persona, her identification as Eve and as Mignon (the twelve-year-old child in Goethe's *Wilhelm Meister*), her self-identification as a prodigy of nature. Dr. Schön is the man of action, *der Gewaltmensch, der Tiger.* He is preoccupied with maintaining his rational life separate from his life of passion. He is obsessed with autonomy and the need to maintain control. The loss of his protective detachment is his Fall ("Jetzt kommt die Hinrichtung").

The wish to exclude subjectivity from the study of music and the wish for a disciplined study of music "that does not draw the blinds before music's expressive force,"[11] both take their place against the background of this persistent belief in its own deep division that has haunted Western consciousness since its recorded beginnings. The dilemma that is provoked by this belief is what Erwin Panofsky called "the curse and the blessing of art history" (see Chapter 4). But it does not affect only the study of the arts. The predicament is broad and deep enough to touch Saint Augustine, Dr. Ludwig Schön, and Professor Erwin Panofsky.

But modern history teaches that the threat of a Fall lies not only in the erosion of reason through the inroads of feeling. It lies also in the opposite, the anesthetizing of the self in the effort to leave reason free and clear (I want to emphasize the etymological sense of that word "anesthetizing": rendering the self without feeling, without aesthetic sense). The dream of pure rationality may turn out to be the nightmare of dehumanization, the scenario conjured up by Goya's *Capricho* "The Dream of Reason Produces Monsters" ("El sueño de la razón produce monstruos").

There is a morbidity underlying the steely confidence of objectivism and the divided consciousness by which it is supported that we repress both in our work and in our daily lives, because it is not pleasant to see. Nothing shows that more clearly, and in a matter that is of more vital concern to us, than the discourse of nuclear deterrence strategy. Its language is cleansed of all affective nuance and all hint of personal involvement. The reasoning operates on a sort of game-theory logic that is at bottom Machiavellian. There is a special technical vocabulary and special rules of reason that maintain the exclusiveness of the discourse as the preserve of professionals (politicians, generals, and their intellectual mercenaries, the "experts").[12] Nuclear strategists are notoriously intolerant of efforts to enter the discussions by people who would be affected by them but do not demonstrate their mastery of the discourse—sometimes called "Nuke Speak." That term is itself typical of a tendency to use benign-sounding language as a shield against an implosion of feeling, with expressions like "nuclear exchange," suggesting an exchange of gifts or greetings, or "mutual assured destruction" (MAD), with its implication that there is nothing to worry about. Even the names of the bombs that destroyed Hiroshima ("Little Boy") and Nagasaki ("Fat Boy") have an endearing quality, as Robert Jay Lifton has observed. The language is punctuated by numbers: megatons, millions of dead (but never millions of corpses).

Rationality is the basis of the discourse, and feelings (horror, fear) are rejected as irrelevant to it. In the projections of nuclear deterrence strategy the continued rationality of the players is a primary premise. No allowance is made for the possibility that presidents or party chiefs might be frozen by fear or grief, or motivated by the desire for blood revenge or ideas of national honor. Such factors are incalculable. They do not belong in the realm of the rational and therefore do not belong among the factors to be taken into account in planning national policies.

Sometimes high government officials leave office, and with their departure change their mode of discourse: they become open to their compassion for the victims and to their fears for the survival of civilization. Once detached from the power structure, they end their thralldom to its discourse and shift the grounds of their judgment. The outstanding case is Robert McNamara, who as Secretary of Defense presided over our nuclear strategy but since his departure from government has been a leading opponent of the idea of deterrence.[13] This phenomenon (Lifton refers to it as the "retirement syndrome")[14] leaves no doubt about the constraints that power places upon the exercise of reason, even by those in power.

This is hardly the only context in which the claim of objectivity is linked to the facts of power. For that claim comes down to a claim that things are thus and cannot be otherwise; and that is as much so for judgments about music and even for claims about objectivity as it is for nuclear strategy. In the politics of explanation those who stake their claims by right of objectivity wrap themselves in a mantle of absolute authority.

Separateness, detachment, a tendency to live a step apart from the other: these terms refer to a character trait in modern Western cultures that may be celebrated as individualism or deplored as alienation. Either way the correspondence to ways of knowing is unmistakable. Whatever works toward the insularity of the individual reinforces an epistemology that is based on detachment. This correspondence has an ironic side. In its prescription of detachment the objectivist epistemology entails a projection of a primary psychological condition. The window of the mind turns out to be a mirror. The irony is that this is precisely what ojectivism rejects: the imprint of the self or self-image on the process of coming to know. The robustness of objectivism, in the face of all continuing doubts about the verisimilitude of its portrayal of science and scholarship, can be understood only in light of its exact adaptation to this strong cultural trait. The dilemma of the knower and the known, in which objectivism represents one pole, is itself but a surface projection of a more profound dilemma of the self as being in the world. We can just begin to have some idea of its depth through awareness of its psychological and culture-historical foundations.

As children we learn to relate to others first through the mother, and we must learn to separate from the mother in developing a sense of self as distinct from other. The female child, however, identifies with the mother as another creature of the same type as herself, and that constitutes a handicap in the effort to differentiate a self. The male child has no such handicap to contend with; on the contrary, his identification with the parent of his own gender assists him in the effort to differentiate himself from the mother. And as his bond to the father is not so profound as it is to the mother his successful separation is more likely than that of the female child. In view of this early history the outlook for the female child is for continued bonding, whereas for the male child the outlook is toward separation. This fundamental difference, which has its roots in biology, is magnified by cultural patterns and social relations that stress autonomy for the male and merging for the female in the subsequent development of character. If such patterns and relations prevail, it is inescapable that an emphasis on detachment as a condition of knowing tends to identify the male personality as the ideal type of the knower, however implicitly and quite apart from the degree to which the culture may discriminate by gender in education, commerce, governance, the arts, science, scholarship, and so on. Such differentiation may be counteracted to the degree that cultures stress integration through their arts, rituals, and social institutions, and to the degree that they conceive of knowing as a bonding of the knower with the known.

It seems we have pursued ideals of truth and knowledge that are polarized according to gender. If that is the implication from the psychological point of view, it emerges even more sharply through attention to the history of knowing in Western culture. The rationalist model of knowledge of which Descartes is commonly regarded as the progenitor is based in dispassion and detachment. But that ideal of detachment leads to a peculiar sort of intellectual asceticism in which the knower deliberately turns inward. Here is a source it seems, of the rejection of worldliness in the pursuit of scholarship. [15]

Descarte's famous dictum "Cogito ergo sum" can be read as a measure of the extreme degree of epistemological alienation in his thought. "The fact that I think confirms *my* existence"; the unspoken question is, "How can I know that the world of which I am aware outside of myself really is, that the world of my existence is not a dream and that I am not completely within myself?" This is the ultimate nightmare, for Descartes, of a confusion between the inner and the outer sense, between self and other, the nightmare of an inability to differentiate between them. The defense against that confusion is the separation of intellect from the body and the withdrawal into the intellect as the reasoning part. And since, for Descartes, the body incorporates the senses as well as the imagination, the Cartesian withdrawal is protection from the threat that sensuality and imagination pose to reason.

What kind of world was it, and what was the nature of the human's relation to it, that Descartes' reconstruction amounts to a withdrawal from such a relationship? It was the organic universe of the Middle Ages and the Renaissance that had "beaten with the same heart as the human being . . . Before the scientific revolution the world was more like a garment [people] wore about them than a stage on which they moved. Compared to us [people of the Middle Ages] felt themselves and the objects around them and the words that expressed those objects immersed together in a clear lake of meaning . . . In [their] relation to [their] environment, [men and women] of the Middle Ages [were] rather less like islands, rather more like embryos." [16] In a word, the Cartesian separation is a parturition, "a defiant gesture of independence from the female cosmos—a gesture that is at the same time compensation for a profound loss." [17]

In the writing of Francis Bacon, a brief generation before Descartes, the relationship between reason and the world is imagined as a male-female duality. Bacon dramatized the relationship between the two in terms of the aggressive masculinity of reason and the passive femininity of nature: "I am come in very truth leading to you nature with all her children to bind her to your service and make her your slave."[18] The imagery survives in our conception of Mother Nature, and in the common talk of control in scholarly and scientific work (control of the subject, of the data, of the material, of the problem, and so on). In any case it is a relationship of control by the knower over the known—to put it bluntly, a relationship of power.

What this metaphor has in common with the metaphor of enlightenment is a conception of knowing not as a continuing process but as an end, and one of its attributes is the transcendence or mastery over a principle that is more or less explicitly identified as female. Knowing is embedded in a mythology in which reason and sensuality are opposed as masculine and feminine. The threat that sensuality poses to reason is a projection of the threat that woman poses to man in the transmission of that mythology through Philo and Wedekind. It is, after all, a product of the masculine imagination. In our modern evocation of these images the metaphorical sense has faded and the dramatization of the process of knowing as the triumph of masculinity has gone deep underground, but not so deep that it does not have surface manifestations.

Nino Pirrotta, who has made all musical scholars beneficiaries of his love of language, has intuited the essential manifestation in humane studies in general and musicology in particular, but he has composed his *aperçu* into a metaphor that plays against the others.

Musicology is a recent word . . . one many people are not too happy with. It is modeled, as others are, after the old and glorious name of philology. But whoever invented the older name set the accent on love—love of beauty in speech; every subsequent derivation has emphasized instead the logos component, with inelegant verbosity and, in the name of objectivity, with a detached, almost aggressive attitude toward its purported subject. Lovely and loving Philology was deemed by a poet the worthy bride of Mercury; I can think of Musicology only as a maiden, whose secret love for no lesser deity than Apollo will never have a chance until she gets rid of her heavy glasses, technical jargon, and businesslike approach and assumes a gentler, more humanistic manner.[19]

These lines issue from a belief that the human faculty of knowing is one, and they amount to a reassertion of its wholeness. *Sotto voce* they speak of the liberation of a repressed feminine mode of knowing and of its complementarity with the masculine. But perhaps it is time to take the still more radical step of purging our conception about understanding of the ancient and harmful idea that it has two modes, and of their underlying identification as genderized epistemological styles. If we can take that step we shall have in view the humanistic scholarship that has always been described by those voices in the humanities and in the sciences that speak of the interaction of the knower with the known, of knowing that engages both sense and sensibility, of connectedness and empathy, even when the prevailing epistemological winds have blown most stiffly in the opposite direction. Those possibilities have broad implications for the study of music and for the accessibility of the musical past in the present. Some of these are pursued in the following pages.

CHAPTER 1

History, Criticism, and Beethoven's Ninth Symphony

The purpose of this essay is to present a view about history and criticism, and especially about the relationship between them. I begin with some interpretations of aspects of Beethoven's Ninth Symphony in order to display the sorts of questions to which, in this view, criticism would be addressed.

The Ninth Symphony is a difficult work to begin in performance.

Of course the beginning is always a crucial moment for the way in which the listener settles into a piece, for it must achieve a reversal from silence to music, and with that a radical shift of worlds for the listener's consciousness. Beethoven followed different strategies in the symphonies. In the Sixth and Eighth there is an immediate engagement with a strong melody in *tempo allegro*. In the Third and Fifth there is a call to attention, wiping away the silence and announcing an event of importance. In the Fourth and Seventh a need is created for the beginning first, a deliberate disorientation for the listener that requires the beginning as a restoration of balance. The engagement is psychologically more complicated. The opening of the Ninth Symphony seems like that at first, but it turns out not to be.

Its beginning is difficult because the first sounds must be just a shade louder than silence. The silence is not broken, it is gradually replaced by sound. The listener is not drawn into the piece, he is surrounded by it as the orchestra fills and expands its space. Music is brought into hearing range, or it is moved from backstage to centerstage.[1] Or it is as though the music had always been going on, but the volume is just now turned up. The piece has really no beginning boundary, and the performance should reflect that. Countless electronic pieces begin that way (and most rock pieces seem to end that way). Recent instrumental music also makes much of the relation between sound and its absence, and of the possibility of the orchestra as a space. (One thinks of two famous and opposite modern openings: Ligeti's *Atmosphères,* where the sound moves in like a fog, and Boulez's *Pli selon pli,* where it hits like a solid wall. Those openings have become models for recent composition.)

Probably the sense of the cosmic and the infinite that has become a commonplace about the Ninth Symphony is a response to this condition of the opening.[2] There are hints about a radical sense of the time in which the piece exists. I can try to put it in two ways: (1) The time is circular, in contrast to the progressive or dialectical time that is the essence of the Classical sonata procedure. That itself has an expressive impact, for it is concretized as an inability to resolve and move forward. (One supposes that Beethoven meant something like that when he wrote in a sketch for the passage in the Finale in which the motto of the first movement is cited, "Nein, nicht dass, dass würde uns an unsere Verzweiflung erinnern"—No, not that, that would remind us of our perplexity.) The phenomenon is perhaps most evident in the music of Chopin (see the Mazurka op. 68, no. 4, for the extreme case). (2) The time is layered. The actual duration of the piece is a finite fragment of an infinite expanse of time. Or put it that the actual events of the piece are the foreground of a process that began before the opening. Both senses are reinforced by the subsequent progress of the piece. What I have tried to characterize here calls to mind an idea that became a topos of music-aesthetic discussions in Germany after the turn of the nineteenth century, the idea that music is capable of arousing an awareness of the eternal. (Carl Dahlhaus has convincingly argued that this idea is in turn a manifestation of the idea of absolute music.)[3] Is there a connection to be drawn? It would seem that as historians we would be obliged to consider the question. That means we must train ourselves to discover how such ideas might be concretized in music, if the historical context is not to remain closed to us.

Not only because of the quiet does the opening seem unlike a beginning, but also because of the absence of any movement. For the first two measures there is no time scale at all. The first evidence of a pace is given by the motto of fourths and fifths, which marks off four-measure phrases. There is a sudden intensification with the compression of phrase lengths to two measures each, punctuated by the successively higher entrances of clarinets in m. 5, oboes in m. 9, and flutes in mm. 11, 13, and 14. The rhythmic compression and the upward expansion of the sound-space are aspects of a very rapid buildup for the explosion of the principal theme.

But the harmonic circumstances are utterly static and anonymous. Only in m. 15 is there a shift of sonorities, from A–E to D–A; but that is quite surreptitious. It is accomplished simply by the flute's move to A and the bassoon's move to D, and the falling away of the E's. The flute's move is assimilated as a continuation of the upward expansion, so the new sonority is effectively dropped into place only by the descent of the bassoon in a subordinate rhythmic position. But the role of the D as root is dampened by the continued sounding of the A in the violins and cellos. The real harmonic event is the reidentification of the A, from generator tone to dominant. And it requires the D-minor theme (mm. 17–21) to do it. The harmonic reidentification is an aspect of an eruption that comes with little warning. It is in the interest of that effect that the actual shift of sonorities is done with such subtlety.

The announcement of the theme comes as the climax of a process in which an initial calm is very quickly ruffled. The theme is overwhelmingly forceful, owing to the sudden unison, the *fortissimo*, the dotted rhythm, and the precipitous plunge through the whole sound-space that had been opened up in the preceding measures. What it overwhelms is the opening motto. The theme is motivically descended from the motto, and the relationship of kinship and conflict between the two is itself *thematic* for the movement.

By the conclusion of the D-minor theme one knows one is firmly into the piece. But where is the beginning? Not in the beginning of the theme, for that is already a culmination. And not in the very opening. There is no hard-edged beginning. At first the opening seems like an introduction. But it is not that in the accustomed sense because each new "beginning," with the exception of the coda, is a return to the opening.

There is a revealing incoherence of detail in the preparation for the first return, mm. 34 and 35. The two groups of instruments arrive on the tonic at different moments (violin 2 and cello in m. 34, violin 1 and viola in m. 35). Literally that produces a simultaneity of tonic and dominant. But Beethoven fathomed that our ears can relate a single moment to two different time scales, resolving the inconsistency as a tonic that is and one that is to become (or better, perhaps, he taught us how to do it). The idea, evidently, is to get the *tremolando* on the tonic going in advance of the arrival of the other instruments, thereby creating the illusion that it has been going on right along. That matches the feeling one has at the beginning that there is a background of infinite spread from which the piece emerges repeatedly. But one thing more has to be done in order to make this juncture seem a continuation of the opening. The sound-space must be collapsed, and that is accomplished by the downward dash of the first violins and violas.

When the principal theme is taken up again in m. 50, it is with still greater abruptness. For after another rapid buildup the orchestra leaps in unison into B-flat major. It seems at the moment another irrational move, but one that again turns out to have a larger meaning. B-flat has a quasi-Neapolitan relationship to the dominant, in that it is fated to fall back through the half-step to where it came from. (The germ of that idea is in m. 24, where the bass G and the melodic B-flat are harmonized in a surprise move as the Neapolitan E-flat.) So that all of the brightness in the B-flat section, climaxed by the attempted heroism of the fanfare, is gone in a moment with the fall to the unison A in mm. 159–160, *pianissimo,* bleakly shaded by the low trumpet, once more rejoining what seems to have been waiting in the background.

Two measures later the E is put into place, and that sets up the replay of the entry into the piece. Beethoven had never before begun a development with such a strategy. In one way or another it had always been a step or a thrust forward, a dynamic moment in which the principal theme moves away from the dominant, as the decisive beginning of a process of retransition. Here there is a relapse. It does not seem as though there were a task of retransition to accomplish at all. The problem is rather that the music has been unable to pull away from its static point of origin. The solution is of a simplicity that signals a new atmosphere, oblivious to the suggested profundity of the exposition (rather the reverse of the accustomed relationship between exposition and development).

Before, the sonority on A was quietly replaced by one on D. Now it opens out to D major. The motto is given harmonic identification and hence motive force through the provision of the third. But the third is given to the bass, and the D major sounds immediately as a dominant. That finally propels the development on its way and, especially after m. 218, it proceeds in straightforward, busy, workmanlike developmental fashion: shredding down thematic material, making good counterpoint, and moving along from key to key. It seems, in fact, a little like genial busywork. But then quite suddenly at m. 301 the music stiffens. In retrospect most of the development seems suddenly like an unrealistic episode. Tovey wrote about this place, "the whole development is at once a thing of the past, a tale that is told."[4] The return he called "catastrophic," and so it feels. But why? It is the shock of *fortissimo* where we had known *pianissimo,* of the full orchestra where it had been the strings alone (not least the kettledrums shaking the ground), of the full triad where it had been hollow fifths, of D major when the preceding four measures had been preparing D minor. (There is no better display anywhere of the horrifying brightness that the major mode can have). It is, all in all, the shock of being now pulled into the opening with great force, instead of having it wash over us. Literally, the harmony in m. 301 is the same as that at m. 170, the chord that had launched the development on its way. But it is that harmony reconsidered: there the light of the triad showing for the first time in the setting of the motto, here that light magnified so that it blinds.

This moment of reprise constitutes a correction of the development, but an escalation, not merely a restoration, of the tone of the exposition. As the formal moment of recapitulation it is the antithesis of what that moment had been in the convention of the genre—a moment of arrival and resolution. The aggressive quality of the D-minor theme before has now advanced to the opening motto. The D-minor theme reacts by taking on an even more threatening tone. It is propelled by the greater eruptive force of the passage from motto to theme, of which these are the salient details: from the D-major chord the outer voices drop a half-step to F and A-flat (m. 312), defining a seventh chord in B-flat major. With the descent of the bass through the fifth to B-flat, that chord is reinterpreted as a German sixth chord of D minor; the resolution is to D minor at the end of m. 314, but without passing through the dominant. The important thing about all this is the rapidity of tonal action, especially the omission of intermediate steps, which yields great explosive power. It must be compared with the deliberately unobtrusive, almost hidden harmonic change in the parallel passage of the exposition. The effect overall is to make of the moment of recapitulation the high point of dramatic conflict and tension, rather than the moment of release.

The recapitulation concludes with a darkened reminiscence—of the fanfare, now cast in the tonic D minor. And in this atmosphere the coda is played out. That is, after all, a way of understanding the role of the coda in an extended sonata form: the main dramatic action is past, and traces of the thematic material pass in review as the harmony sustains the final tonality. The passage in which this is most apparent is the conversation among the winds over the second phrase of the main theme, against a dominant pedal in the strings, trumpet, and timpani (m. 469). (Tovey found in this passage "a tragic irony," the soundings of "a distant happiness." It seems to me that in music there is a quality of distance that is not specific as to whether it is of time or space. Mozart achieved a similar effect at the end of the first movement of the G Minor Symphony, with a conversation among the upper strings about the main theme, above a harmonically static bass on the tonic.)

There is one more such passage (m. 513ff). The tonic is held, but darkened by the chromaticism in the bass. Against that background, the sound-space (that is, the orchestral space and the pitch range) is expanded for what seems like one last time with a melodic derivative of the D-minor theme. It is a reflection on the past, and at the same time it sets the stage for the close, by climbing up for the last plunge through the D-minor theme. The upward runs in the midst of the theme this time (mm. 543 and 544) must be understood, I believe, as reversals of the downward run in the exposition five hundred measures before. This is said not in the sense of revealing a motivic identification, but as a suggestion about the purpose of the passage. The earlier run revealed a circularity about the piece by narrowing in on the point of departure again. These last runs prevent that emphatically by keeping the registral space open and full. The effect is to break out of the circularity and put a stop to the movement. (I say "stop" rather than "end," because "end" would imply a resolution that has not been accomplished.)

The Finale of the Ninth Symphony is paradoxical. It is the bearer of words, but it is composed as an instrumental piece, in the main. Its form is given by an extraordinary concatenation of instrumental genres.[5] For the remainder of this section I want to focus on the last movement, with particular attention to the matter of genre.

The main weight of the movement is carried in a four-movement symphonic form:

I. *Allegro assai,* m. 92ff
II. *Allegro assai vivace, alla marcia,* m. 331ff
III. *Andante maestoso,* m. 594ff
IV. *Allegro energico,* m. 654ff

At the same time, the overall dramatic shape of the movement describes a large-scale sonata form:

Exposition: first subject in D major, m. 92ff; second subject in B-flat major,
   m. 331ff
Development: m. 431ff
Recapitulation: m. 543ff

The D-major portion of the exposition, however, is presented twice: first by the orchestra, then by the chorus with orchestra. In this respect—that is, for the presentation of the thematic material—the movement adopts the rhetoric of the classical concerto opening.

But the thematic material itself is organized in the manner of a theme and variations: theme and three variations presented by the orchestra (m. 92ff), three variations presented by the chorus and orchestra (m. 241ff), together constituting the D-major portion of the exposition. The B-flat section comprises two variations. The development section of the sonata form is a fugue, and here the variation procedure is suspended. It is resumed with one final variation for the recapitulation (m. 543ff). The variations and sonata form are coextensive through m. 594, where both break off without closing the harmonic circuit to the tonic.

The paradigms on which Beethoven fashioned this movement are instrumental ones, and, as singers have often complained, the writing for the voices is instrumental. The text is incorporated in this giant instrumental conception as a sort of citation. The entire structure is framed, however, by two passages that are very clearly based on vocal genres: the recitatives near the beginning, and the very last section (m. 763 to the end), which has the gestural identity of an opera finale (say, the finale of *Fidelio*).

The operatic final passage does not come as a surprise. That is not only because the singers are already on stage, but especially because of the role that this passage must play vis-à-vis the whole symphony. The last movement must provide the resolution that never came in the first movement—Beethoven as much as says that in the beginning of the Finale, even before the high rhetoric of the review of the preceding "tones." The last movement *begins* with a resumption of the prevailing tone of the first movement, and with an indirect resumption of its main thematic idea. The opera finale was the preeminent medium of dénouement—not because it was so by nature, but because it would have been understood that way. That is an important fact about the communication value of genre.

But the recitative at the beginning brings a kind of culture shock (we might call it "genre shock"). It signals a breakdown in the purely musical means of expression. The aspect of the irrational, or the incoherent, which before had been a source of meaning, now forces a breach of the separation between music's precise but abstract expression and the concreteness of words. What comes is recitative in a deep instrumental voice, Sarastro-like, first caught up in the anger of the very opening, then dispassionate and benevolent. It breaks the ice for the ushering in of the voices and the Schiller text. But the question remains whether the unresolved "perplexities" of the preceding movements, which had been expressed there in music alone, can now be convincingly identified through the concreteness of words, that is, without really changing the subject, so to speak.

The question generalizes. How seamless is the synthesis of genres in the Finale, and does it all resolve as a new total form into which the individual components are assimilated? My perception is that each genre presents an association of conventions adapted for an artistic purpose. In each case the genre provides a clue to the meaning of the passage in the dramatic program of the movement, and in that sense genre presents a code to the listener who is entrusted with its conventions.

Consider the variations. The melody is unlike any heard before in the symphony: closed, balanced, symmetrical. It is mainly this feature that gives the melody its Apollonian quality. If the statement of such a melody is to be stretched out without unbalancing it, it can be only through repetition. And that is how it is presented, beginning in m. 92, the orchestra growing with each statement. The growth itself has a rhetorical effect. If one identifies "variation form" here, it should not be without recognizing the very particular expressive purpose to which this form is adapted.[6]

Consider the concerto procedure. The three instrumental statements of the theme are capped by a closing passage (beginning m. 198) that makes a transition to the dominant (m. 193). But this is interrupted before it can produce an A-major theme. It is not just the thematic *material* of the first movement that is brought across the border of the Finale, it is its thematic *idea,* the ruffling of peaceful processes, and that is what it is the business of the Finale to put down once and for all. The concerto arrangement is a way of putting this intensely expressive idea. Once the chorus enters in that same way it completes its exposition. That it begins a second transition to the dominant key but then turns instead to B-flat major for a second subject is a reference to the first movement—not simply for tonal unity but as another way of replaying the drama of the first movement and settling it in the end.

The fugue (m. 432ff) brings recognition that a sonata procedure is in progress. By virtue of its gestural distinctness as development, it has the effect of canceling in retrospect the diversity of the elements that have passed so far, and promoting instead the impression of a unified form. That is, the fugue functions as a sign of a sonata form. Another such sign is the joining of the Andante and Allegro themes (m. 655). It is the strongest moment of recapitulation, although it is, strictly speaking, outside the bounds of the "sonata form" proper. The sign functions in the absence of the thing itself.

That sort of separation became characteristic in the nineteenth century, and it is an aspect of the transformation and, in some cases, the dissolution of traditional forms. In Liszt's tone poems the meaning of a passage may depend upon its gestural identity as exposition, development, or recapitulation, even though the piece is not in sonata form. The appearance of such passages may not even be bound to the sequence that they would have in sonata form. Obviously a style cannot live forever on such borrowed meaning, and before long new means have to be invented.

This reflects a more general situation in the nineteenth century. To the extent that Beethoven exploited the genres in the Finale of the Ninth Symphony for their significative value, he contributed to a reduction in the distinctness of genres, that is, to a reduction in their capacity to act as codes.

Some very powerful general theories of art history have been generated out of such observations about the relations between the aesthetic transaction and the means that constitute artistic practices.[7] Their superiority over simple development schemes is owing to their dependence on critical encounters with individual works.

In 1912 Heinrich Schenker published a monograph on Beethoven's Ninth Symphony, dedicated to the memory of Johannes Brahms, "the last master of German musical art."[8] The subject was to be the work's "content": "the analysis of the contents gave me the desired opportunity to demonstrate the tonal necessities, hidden until now, that have made the contents what they are and not anything else." His slogan is "Am Anfang war der Inhalt." And probably we must be aware not only of the heavy portentousness of that quasi-biblical pronouncement, but also of the pointed perversion of the original: "In the beginning was the *Content,*" instead of "the Word." For it was Schenker's firm and central dogma that music's content is in no way, direct or indirect, verbal or literary.

The Ninth Symphony monograph is early Schenker. But the objectives and premises did not change essentially during the development of the analytical theories. Nor did the claims. In 1930 he sent forth his essay on the "Eroica" Symphony, "Beethoven's Third Symphony, Represented for the First Time in Its True Content."[9]

What Schenker meant by "content" is the *Ursatz* and its constituents. And the musical process, to carry out the biblical metaphor, is the process of transfiguration. The investigation of these things constitutes the proper study of music. As his model for what is *not* the proper study of music Schenker chose the section on the Ninth Symphony from Hermann Kretzschmar's *Führer durch den Konzertsaal* (Leipzig, 1888–1890), which he cites throughout his monograph. One sample from Kretzschmar will suffice to give a taste of the sort of *Schwärmerei* that Schenker aimed to replace: "The development unrolls the Faustian portrait still further: seeking and not attaining, rosy fantasies of future and past, and the fulfilled reality of a pain that now suddenly makes itself felt." Schenker's reaction is always as if to say, "If he would only just talk about the *music.*"

   This fuss of Schenker's over what is really in the music is more than a reaction of taste. It reflects a complex of attitudes that now have great influence in the practice of music analysis in general. A brief sampling of the discussion of the Ninth Symphony's opening bars will lead us to those attitudes. Schenker calls mm. 1-16 *Einleitung* (and mm. 160-79 *Überleitung*), characterizing those passages from the outside, so to speak, by their location in the sonata-allegro format. The introduction is the birthplace of the *Urmotiv,* and in that respect its task is to prepare the first two measures of the main theme. The material relationship between *Urmotiv* and principal theme is important to Schenker. The qualitative one is not. Because the introduction precedes the principal theme elsewhere in the movement, he asserts that it must be regarded as an integral part of the *Hauptgedanken.* But he raises no questions about the reasons for this unusual procedure or about its effects.

   In the discussion about the two opening sonorities Schenker observes that, because of the absence of the thirds, the listeners cannot judge the tonal identity of either, or the relationship between them—whether as I–IV or V–I. (The second, he says, will seem the more likely because it is the stronger progression. In a rare glance toward the affective he says that the uncertainty serves the *Spannungszweck* of the introduction.) But what sort of listeners are these? They are tacitly presumed to be at home in the syntax of tonal music. But they are not presumed to know any particular pieces from which they would have gained an internalized sense of the stylistic norms of the symphonic tradition—a larger musical competence, we might say, that would predispose them to hear the shift of sonorities as a V–I progression (not because it is "stronger" in an absolute sense but because they expect a V–I progression at that point), but that would also arouse their curiosity about why those chords are *not* explicitly spelled that way. When Schenker speaks about how the listener hears things, he really means to be saying how they *are*. His analyses concern the musical object and its relations to the system. The reactions of the listener play no formal role.[10]

With respect to the rhythmic subtleties, Schenker simply turns matters around and affirms that the descent of the bassoon to D in m. 15 on the second eighth-beat gives that beat a stronger accent because that is where the harmony changes. He does not ask why this shift is made in a normally weak rhythmic position, and why, in general, actions in this passage are conducted so much under cover.

In the discussion about mm. 34 and 35 Schenker explains the run in the first violins and violas as a portamento, composed out. He substantiates that with the observation that the flutes play the beginning and end tones of the passage. He observes, further, that the restatement of the principal idea begins before the conclusion of the run, in m. 35 rather than 36 (actually it is underway in m. 34), and he explains the overlap as a marvel of organic linkage. But why there should be so rapid a plunge through that great distance at that moment, and why a simultaneity of tonic and dominant harmonies should be tolerated on the downbeat of m. 35, are questions not asked. (There is any number of ways in which a smooth linkage could have been accomplished without allowing the dissonance in m. 35.)

What the restrictive definition of "content" amounts to, in effect, is that again and again individualizing features of the work are neutralized by placing them under general concepts that apply across the tonal system or the symphonic form, or both. The effect is to head off just those questions that can lead to an illumination of the qualities of the particular work. What is accomplished is the demonstration that the work exemplifies a system or a class, or a theory about one or the other. To put it quite simply, if one asks about *this* opening, "What is it?" and the answer comes, "an introduction," has the question really been answered?

In the explanation about mm. 34-36 Schenker evokes the standard of organic unity. That idea stands at the center of the premises that underlie his analyses. It entails the ideal that all aspects of the work should function under a single governing principle and that no aspect should be extraneous or dispensable. The work is regarded as complete, self-contained, and autonomous, and the grounds for analysis are immanent in the work. The organic idea is the background for Schenker's claim to demonstrate the *necessity* of the contents as they are. The claim that the way things are is the way they must be is common to organicist theories about any subject, and it reflects the deterministic nature of such theories.[11]

Schenker framed his case in a dichotomy, with the analysis of content at one extreme as the superior alternative to Kretzschmar's mode of interpretation at the other.[12] He thereby promoted an entrenched but misleading view of what the alternatives are in talk about music. We might call it the dichotomy of the "cool" and the "hot" approaches, but it has also sometimes been concretized as a dichotomy between the ideals of "absolute" music and its opposite (difficult to characterize in a word, but in any case music conceived as means for the expression of ideas, images, or feelings outside itself.) Schenker's quarrel with Kretzschmar is an embodiment of this debate. The idea of "absolute music" is a presupposition for Schenker's mode of approach, and Kretzschmar's notion of "musical hermeneutics" entails an attack on that idea.

H. H. Eggebrecht has documented this difference as it is manifested in approaches to Beethoven's music since the beginning.[13] Eggebrecht argues that certain constants in the responses to Beethoven's music, because of their persistence, have a claim to objective correctness in their assessment of what is in the music. The common element is the idea of Beethoven's music as reflection of human experience. Busoni's remark is representative: "Das Menschliche tritt mit Beethoven zum ersten Mal als Hauptargument in die Tonkunst" (With Beethoven the human condition enters into music for the first time).[14] Beethoven himself sometimes spoke of or at least hinted at the experiential content of his music, but cannot himself be regarded as the source of this idea, according to Eggebrecht, because it is evident in appreciations of his music that were written before his remarks on the subject could have been public knowledge.

In the 1920s, writes Eggebrecht, a reaction set in against the strong subjective element in Beethoven appreciation. It was manifested in a focus of attention on the "composition-technical," and in the denial that there was anything else to the music. But some of the same affective language crept back into the writing of even the purists, and Eggebrecht argues that therefore there is all the more reason to accept the

Rezeptionsgeschichte—the record of the reactions to the music—as an index of the durable reality of the contents to which it is a response.

The very inability of the purists to maintain their purity is a clue to the misdirected nature of the dichotomy, however much of a historical reality it is. For these conflicting claims about music's "contents" do not really mark out different fields of reference that are consistent and distinct. Schenker could write about the *Spannungszweck* of the introduction in the Ninth Symphony's first movement, and about character contrasts in the B-flat section of the exposition. On the other hand, there are "purely musical" matters (especially in the rhythmic and registral domains) that he left entirely out of account in his analysis. He had no singleminded idea about what kind of a thing the musical object is. On the other hand, the sort of interpretation that is attempted in the first section of this essay would be quite impossible without attention to "composition-technical" matters.

The difference is not between two conflicting notions about what a musical work is (for example, a constructive order versus a vehicle of expression). It is a difference of purpose that I have marked, a difference of *Erkenntniszweck,* to draw a term from an important essay to which I must return in the discussion of history.[15] Schenker's purpose was to demonstrate the unity of the work and the necessity of its constituent moments, and to display it as exemplification of a theory. This amounts to the *explanation* of the work in the strict sense that its events are seen to follow with the force of deductive logic. My purpose in the first section was the illumination of the work in its individuality. I take this to be a permanent difference between analysis and criticism.[16] The elucidation of the goals of criticism in view of this difference is preliminary to developing a view of the relation between criticism and history.

———————

Schenker's claim to give an account of the content of Beethoven's Ninth Symphony is as though someone were to claim to give an account of the content of *Hamlet* by analyzing its grammar and syntax without paying any attention to its meanings. That charge may seem unfair because we expect the literary analyst to deal with both structure and meaning, whereas we hold that music has no "meaning" in the lexical sense. It is praised and envied because its content is its form—"sounding form in motion," Eduard Hanslick said. But does music's "indefiniteness" (Edgar Allan Poe's word) block inquiries about music's meaning? Or does music, like literature, move also on levels of discourse that are not reached by structural analysis alone? There is a view of the relation between structural analysis and criticism in the study of literature that can be helpful to us in thinking about this question. It is presented by Jonathan Culler, in his book *Structuralist Poetics:* "Even in its own province the task of linguistics is not to tell us what sentences mean; it is rather to explain how they have the meanings which speakers of a language give them . . . Linguistics is not hermeneutic. It does not discover what a sequence means or produce a new interpretation of it but tries to determine the nature of the system underlying the event."[17]

Musical analysis is in a similar way with respect to music. My identification of the harmony in m. 314 of the first movement of the Ninth Symphony as a "German sixth chord" does no more than account for our ability to assimilate it into its context, to hear it as a coherent event. When I say that the dominant chord is omitted and the tonic chord is in the first inversion I make a similar kind of identification. I move to another level of meaning when I say that the inversion makes the tonic chord unstable, and that the omission of the dominant makes the return to the tonic abrupt. But I have not yet said what purpose this instability and abruptness serve in this place, or in the movement of the symphony as a whole. I address those questions with the suggestion that the sense of catastrophe that Tovey heard in this place is a consequence of such things, and with the interpretation of the movement's plan in the light of an escalation of dramatic conflict at the recapitulation. But the questions may not come to rest there, either. We may want to ask, "Why such an intensification here, where the genre has accustomed us to a resolution?" And that question might very well lead to Kretzschmar's sort of reading, but also into the realm of social and historical relations. For now we are talking about the event as a historical event.

The decision to establish a limit on the pursuit of questions of meaning at the boundaries of the work, and to restrict the language of that pursuit to the "technical" language of analysis, is an arbitrary decision that places severe limitations on the historical understanding. Analysis can lead to questions of meaning in a larger sense, but it cannot answer them. When I say "in a larger sense" I mean "What does it mean that *this* happens *here*?" That question, asked in ever expanding contexts, is what provokes criticism. And it may be asked of music as well as of literature. The answers will be interpretive transformations of the relations revealed by analysis, or hypotheses about the intentions of the work, or readings of the work as a system of gestures of particular kinds in particular circumstances, however one likes to put it. They will focus on the unique qualities of individual works, rather than on the system that makes the uniqueness of works possible. If we do not ask such questions, the music of the past can be only partly accessible to us.

The problem of the contexts of criticism has been framed by Culler in terms of the concept of competence. A fundamental strategy of structuralist analytical methods is the distinction between "competence" and "performance." For an analytical practice in the arts (I do not now mean the narrow sense of musical analysis) the distinction would be between a background system of options and constraints that could be described in a theory, and the individual productions that are concretizations of it.[18] For music the word "competence" can be quite literally appropriate in referring to the tacit mastery of the system by the listener and the composer or performer. One vantage point for understanding the absence of a tradition of music criticism is that music theory, in the academic and scholarly sense, does not constitute an adequate theory of competence for such a practice. But it is virtually the only sort of theory we have had for the close study of music.

Musical analysis has been a thing separate from criticism because it is mainly practiced by theorists whose ultimate concern it is "to determine the nature of the system underlying the event . . . The [theorist's] task is not to study [works] for their own sake; they are of interest to him only in so far as they provide evidence about the nature of the underlying system."[19]

What will be the terms of a theory of criticism? They must proceed from assumptions about the listener's competence quite different from those that Schenker made: for, to begin with, they will be the terms of style and genre. By "style" I mean those "systems of forms and schemata that are at once the basis of perception in art and the currency of transmission in the history of art."[20] Style is a premise for criticism because the interpretation of artworks "presupposes and is conditioned by the possession of a vocabulary of forms." But the artist "can no more approach the creation of a new work without the mediation of an internalized vocabulary of forms and schemata than can the audience find order in a canvas or poem or musical work with an eye or an ear that has no habits or expectations."[21] So the interpretation of art and the history of art proceed from the same grounds. Style is a concept of history, and criticism is an exercise of the historical understanding.

"Genre" is a concept that overlaps "style." The difference is the additional coordinate of function. The concept is well explicated in the theory of literature.

A genre . . . is a conventional function (it might be clearer to say "functioning") of language, a particular relation to the world which serves as norm or expectation to guide the reader in his encounter with the text . . . An account of genres should be an attempt to define classes which have been functional in the process of reading and writing, the sets of expectations which have enabled readers to naturalize texts and give them a relation to the world . . . The theoretical orders of poetics should be viewed, at any moment in their history, as essentially mental codes, with which the practicing writer comes to terms in his writing.[22]

But: "If a theory of genres is to be more than a taxonomy it must attempt to explain what features are constitutive of functional categories which have governed the reading and writing of literature."[23]

Meaning in music is a function of the engagement of codes or orders by the note-complexes of which the music is comprised. When we say of a musical event that it is of a certain kind, or has a certain quality, we locate it with respect to a classification scheme. Music engages multiple realms of order, and the meaning of a complex is not exhausted by relating it to just one realm. The meaning of the first sixteen measures of Beethoven's Ninth Symphony is not exhausted by referring them to the syntax of tonality or to the formal conventions of the symphony. But what other realms are engaged, and how will the critic set perceptual nets to catch them?

In the first section of this essay it seemed important to sort out the experiences of the Ninth Symphony with reference to the nature of beginnings and their consequences, the relation between silence and sound, the experience of time and space, the quality and pace of movement, the quality of immediacy or indirectness in the musical presentation, the compatibility between ideas—all of these being dimensions to which we were led by consideration of the "strictly musical" elements. There is a realm of quite concrete expression that is projected through systems of conventional reference descended from the rhetorical tradition: the heroic in the fanfares of the first movement, the religiosity of the great moment of release in the slow movement (mm. 133-36, accomplished through the organlike scoring and the generally *stile antico* evocation of the passage). But mainly the expression does not depend on such concreteness. It is achieved through the very abstractness and indefiniteness for which poets, especially since the nineteenth century, have admired music. (T. S. Eliot wrote of "feeling which we can only detect, so to speak, out of the corner of the eye" and which "only music can express.")[24]

Our only access to these realms is through the categories of style and genre. However, the burden of Eliot's apperception is that verbal categories alone cannot suffice to capture the qualities that the critic is after. There are realms of meaning to which only other works can direct the attention of critics and about which they can communicate only by pointing to other works. So the critic must operate with a synoptic sense of style and genre, with a conception of the *tradition* of music (such as Eliot formulated for poetry), in which all the works of a tradition constitute a simultaneous order wherein each work casts light on all the others. (I shall return to that conception of Eliot's in the next section.) From such a perspective, as Culler wrote, "one can see that it may well be misleading to speak of poems as harmonious totalities, autonomous natural organisms, complete in themselves and bearing a rich and immanent meaning."[25]

This characterization of criticism, not as the study of works as objects but in the context of the continuing exchanges among works and listeners, is not just a gesture toward the laudable sentiment that music is meant to be heard. It is a basic strategy that determines the nature of criticism and its sources. And it has strong implications for a conception of history.

The historian works in the face of a dilemma. On one side is the desire to explain the past, through attention to questions of origins, influence, trends, movements, development. The general form of such questions is "How or why did the past come to be as it was?" The general form of answers is such as to represent the past as the likely or necessary consequence of antecedent conditions. There is a mode of historical thinking—we can call it the diachronic mode—whose focus is this conception of the historian's task. Its characteristic features are the tendencies to represent the past in continuous narratives, and to make *change* and *novelty* the principal subjects of history; to hold past, future, and the passage between them as the primary categories for knowing the objects of history; to think of the past as prehistory of the present, and the present as consequence of the past.

The diachronic mode itself has a background of diverse sources and motives. Among them are the jealous wish to establish history as an exact explanatory science parallel with the natural sciences; the attitude that every event in the world belongs to a more-or-less concealed organic process, and that explaining the event is an aspect of revealing the process as a whole—an attitude which, carried out to completion, produces world-historical systems; the compassionate quest for an understanding of the meaning of human suffering in the past and present in view of the future outcome; the inherited Christian conception of human history as a story of salvation; an old epistemology in which knowledge of anything depends on knowledge of the stages through which it has passed; the modern positivist version of that epistemology in which knowing "why" is the only real form of knowing "what"; and the tradition and forms of storytelling.

On the other side is the impulse to seek knowledge of the past in its individuality and its particularity, in and for itself, "as it really was," in a famous and much misunderstood phrase.[26] Now historians are more inclined to ask "what" than "why." In seeking answers they aim to stop the past in its tracks and hold it still, as though it were a present. It is tempting to follow a terminological fashion and identify the historiographic mode to which this leads as "synchronic." But for the sake of the further development of the argument it will be more important to emphasize that *presentness* is the leading category for knowing the objects of history under this way of thinking. Historians usually follow both modes of thought, in different mixes. What creates the dilemma is that the diachronic mode brings with it an epistemology that frustrates the historians' desire to understand the historical object for itself, and as intimately as they might like. But the more they set their sights on the object itself, the more they—or in any case, their critics—may doubt that they are able to explain it, and indeed, doubt that they are practicing history.

There is a claim that the problem is more acute for historians of art because their attitude toward the object must be both aesthetic and scientific. Though artworks may be of the past they are directly given in the present and they require to be treated fully as apprehended in the present. They tend to disappear from view as artworks the more historians concern themselves not with the uniqueness but with the generalized and abstracted dimensions and categories of art that can readily be presented in continuous narratives. Major scholarly strategies have been thrown up in defense of the artwork against its dismantling by diachronic history: New Criticism, for example, and even the denial of a history of art and the separation of the critical from the philological treatment of artworks by Walter Benjamin—locking the artwork in its own keep.[27]

But this is not a conflict for art history alone. It has divided opinion about history in general for a long time. In his essay "On History" (1830), Thomas Carlyle wrote this:

As all action is by its nature to be figured as extended in breadth and in depth, as well as in length; and spreads abroad on all hands . . . as well as advances toward completion—so all narrative is, by its nature, of only one dimension; only travels forward towards one, or towards successive points; narrative is *linear,* action is *solid.* Alas for our "chains," or chainlets, of "causes and effects," which we so assiduously track through certain handbreadths of years and square miles, when the whole is a broad, deep immensity.[28]

Carlyle's target—the idea that the events of history are to be explained by showing their place in continuous bound processes—was the central idea in the historiography of the Enlightenment. But the idea has held its appeal, and we find Claude Lévi-Strauss challenging it as recently as the 1950s. In the chapter "History and Dialectic" of *The Savage Mind* he gave this sharp formulation of the historian's dilemma:

Biographical information is the least explanatory but it is richest in point of information, for it considers individuals in their particularity and details for each of them the shades of character, the twists and turns of their motives, the phases of their deliberations. This information is schematized, put in the background, and finally done away with as one passes to histories of progressively greater "power" . . . The historian's relative choice is always confined to the choice between history which teaches us more and explains less, and history which explains more and teaches less.[29]

It is the narrative impulse that brings the fictive element into history, for there is both too much and too little evidence for continuous narratives; the historian must both fill in and weed out.[30] The historian's claim to give an account of the world that is privileged because it is objective is therefore suspect. "Alleged historical continuity is secured only by dint of fraudulent outlines." Lévi-Strauss's analysis makes us aware of how ironic it is that the case for representing history in continuous narratives has always been linked with the claim that one could, and would, represent the world *objectively* in doing so. By the same token it is significant that the first great modern historian to abandon the idea of writing a narrative history of his subject, Jacob Burckhardt, should also have explicitly denied that his book on the civilization of the Renaissance in Italy was an objective or scientific—that is, explanatory—account.[31]

The difference in the two approaches to history corresponds closely to the difference between analysis and criticism as approaches to the musical object. In both cases it is a difference of objectives, from which the difference of methods follows. Musical analysis and diachronic history have in common the aim of explaining their objects and the tendencies to apprehend the individual event as part of an organic whole and to regard the particular as exemplification of the general. Musical criticism and the particularist historiography share the aim of illuminating the particular in itself. They may do so in a very broad context, but the focus is always on the particular. Wilhelm Windelband (see note 15) categorized these epistemological attitudes as the "nomothetic" (emphasis on the positing of *laws*) and the "idiographic" (emphasis on the elucidation of the *thing itself*). The correspondence that I note here is not a matter of chance coincidence but a fundamental agreement of aim and outlook. In the case of criticism and the particularist historiography the correspondence is of still a higher order: It will appear that criticism answers exactly to the description of historical knowledge given by the writers who developed that position.

The first order of business in the summary of their case must be an attempt to elucidate the central concept of "presentness," and especially to show the sense in the seeming paradox of the "presentness of the past."

Of the three categories of time in history—past, present, and future—only the category of the present allows us to think of time as stopped, standing still, apprehended in present consciousness. The category of the past reflects our sense of the evanescence of time; that of the future, the sense of the unknown. Our use of the word "present" entails the sense of "here and now" (not just "now"). "Present" can be rendered in German as *aktuel*. But that may be translated back into English as "actual" or "real," and that sense survives when we say that we "actualize" something; we concretize it, make it real. All this resonates with a sense of security about the present, a sense that what is present is what we can grasp and hold, believe and understand. If we take the word to stand for that sense we may aim to think, as far as we can, of the past as present. (That gives a better reading of Ranke's standard for history, to know the past "as it really was.") The work of the historian, in the view that I wish to describe, is to develop what is present in the past. The leading questions are, What is entailed in that task and under what conditions can it be carried out?

————————

The principal writers I shall cite are Johann Gustav Droysen (*Historik,* based on lectures going back to 1857),[32] Wilhelm Windelband (the essay cited in note 15, 1894), Wilhelm Dilthey (*Die Entstehung der Hermeneutic,* 1900),[33] and R. G. Collingwood (*The Idea of History,* 1956).[34] The considerable authority of this company is sufficient, I believe, to assure that the historian who takes a particularist approach can indeed claim to practice history.

What sets these writers apart from the philosophers of the Enlightenment and their modern descendants, who worked (and still work) at theories about the course of history and the nature of historical causation and explanation, is their focus on a theory of historical knowledge. Their emphasis is on history as a mode of understanding, and their discourse is descriptive rather than deductive.

Droysen wrote of the historical understanding as a faculty of mind developed early in life. Its manifestations are representations of the past (*Vorstellungen*) which feed, so to speak, on the actual residuals of the past, taking those as points of departure, building on them, and adjusting themselves accordingly. We might simply identify those residuals as the concrete evidence. But the special view taken about them is that they are in the last analysis always expressions of human will and thought, what Droysen called "formative power." The task is to understand the evidence, and in attempting to do that we reconstruct the act of will with the aim of representing it, in a synoptic view, as a whole.

Windelband put it that historical reasoning brings the event to full representation through the application of synthetic judgment. The historian seeks to understand the evidence as the listener understands a speaker: What does he mean? What is his intention, that he expresses himself thus? What is the *ich* in his utterances? These are the questions that direct the historian in the search for evidence and in its interpretation.

Dilthey emphasized that the residuals of the past are themselves isolated signs. They are the "outsides" of events, and the historian's task is to confer an "inside" upon them through a process to which Dilthey referred variously as *Nachverstehen, Nachfühlen, Nacherleben,* or *Nachbilden*. One must do so in order to complete one's perception of the residuals, for otherwise they are incoherent and unintelligible—one cannot really say what they are. The historian constructs a context of "psychic reality" for the evidence, and that is what is meant when we say that we interpret evidence.

Through such reconstruction historians develop a "historical consciousness" that enables them to hold the past present within themselves. Philology—the exercise of "a personal skill and virtuosity in the scrutiny of written memorials"—is Dilthey's designation for the practice of interpreting documents to that end. (Here Dilthey is closer to the older sense of philology as humanistic learning than to the newer one as the scientific study of language or texts.) And hermeneutics, which begins as the interpretation of Scripture and comes to mean something essentially like literary criticism in general, is the product of a union between a "virtuoso practice of philological interpretation" and "a genuine capacity for philosophical thought."

Collingwood characteristically gives the sharpest and most provocative expression to these ideas. He reads like a man with a chip on his shoulder. Yet if one is not thrown off at once by his claims, his arguments reach further and deeper than those of his earlier German colleagues. His basic proposition is that all history is the history of reflective thought, and that there can be no history but of that which can be described in those terms. (Reflective thought is conscious, deliberate, and purposive.) He wrote that an action is the unity of the outside and the inside of an event (he used Dilthey's language exactly), and that the inside, which can be described only in terms of thought, is something that the historian arrives at through its "reenactment" in his or her own mind. (Collingwood took this idea so far as to claim that history is the true science of mind. Dilthey had subsumed history under psychology. Such an idea, which must seem strange to us now, at least serves to underscore their very strong sense of history as a mode of understanding.) If historians are unable to stage such reenactments, if events cannot be made to resonate in their minds, they cannot have historical knowledge of these events.

In a discussion about causal explanation Collingwood claimed that when we know what happened we already know why it happened. To understand how he could make such a claim—it is a question of which Collingwood would have approved—we can simply turn it around. We cannot really know what without knowing why, in the sense of intention or purpose. We cannot have a complete perception of something—in Dilthey's sense, we cannot see it as coherent—until we have conferred an "inside" upon it. If we read a dialogue of Plato and do not know the argument that he was opposing, then we cannot claim understanding of the dialogue. Benedetto Croce claimed, in exactly this sense, that we cannot know the history of Hellenic painting. He would have had an even better case for saying that we cannot know the history of Hellenic music.[35]

Because all history is the history of thought, reenacted in the mind of the historian, Collingwood claims that all history is contemporary history. One cannot know what has passed. One can know only what traces it has left, and the context that one has created for them in order to understand them. But that is knowledge of things in the present. The implication is that so much of historical knowledge as the historians have, they have at once. Dilthey put it explicitly that "the historical consciousness . . . has enabled modern man to hold the entire past of humanity present within himself." (This line of thought leads to Lévi-Strauss's idea of "synchronic history." But that idea depends on the view of historical knowledge that I have been describing. The dichotomy of diachronic-synchronic history is therefore not the fundamental one and is, even in itself, of dubious value.)

There is a direct application of the idea of the simultaneity of history to the history of art in T. S. Eliot's famous essay, "Tradition and the Individual Talent": "The whole of literature has a simultaneous existence and composes a simultaneous order . . . What happens when a new work is created . . . happens simultaneously to all the works which preceded it . . . The past is altered by the present as much as the present is directed by the past . . . The conscious present is an awareness of the past which the past's own awareness of itself cannot show." [36] This viewpoint has the important implication that temporal order and the associated concept of change are not of the essence in historical judgment.

Perhaps the most extravagant sounding of all Collingwood's claims is that historical knowledge as he viewed it is certain knowledge. This seems to be of the same order as Dilthey's claim that historical knowledge, in his conception, would be objective. What *is* the status of historical judgments, from this viewpoint, so far as truth or validity is concerned? Collingwood denied that the reenactment of past thought is a passive surrender to the spell of another mind. There is no claim that the historian aims to bring about a *duplication* of past thought ("reenactment" is in fact one of the more misleading expressions in Collingwood's vocabulary). The claim of certainty is no more than a claim that one will have provided the most coherent context of thought that is consistent with all of the evidence. Collingwood's way of expressing it is that one will continue to put questions raised by all considerations that could possibly bear on the case, and when they come to rest the historian may hold the representation that survives with certainty. There is no claim that the historian will have duplicated the original thought, and there is no procedure for verifying that one has done so (criticisms of this position that point out the impossibility of knowing the thoughts of persons not living are really off the mark). But the "logic of question and answer," as Collingwood called it, certainly is subject to verification. It is only on this view of historical knowledge and certainty that Dilthey could claim that it is the aim of interpretation to understand authors better than they understood themselves.

––––––––––

For Windelband the ideographic nature of history was its defining characteristic. But Droysen, Dilthey, and Collingwood, too, can only have regarded the historical object as individual, for it is only individual actions that betray an intention (of a human agent, that is, not of metaphysical forces), that have an "inside," that can resonate in the mind of the historian. The whole movement entailed "the replacement of a generalizing consideration of the human forces in history by an individualizing one."[37]

Dilthey adopted Windelband's classification of history as a *Geisteswissenschaft* (in distinction to *Naturwissenschaft*). But he denied that "philosophy of history" (for example, that of Hegel) is a *Geisteswissenschaft*, because it loses sight of the individual. Evidently *Geisteswissenschaft* is the rendering into German of J. S. Mill's "Moral Science."[38] Droysen identified the "historical world" with the "moral world," and by that he meant the world of individual human action. Historical analysis which ignores the individual has no moral content.[39] Collingwood wrote that to understand the historical action is to criticize it. If the historian's aim is to display facts as the necessary consequence of a causal nexus, criticism of them is beside the point. An individualizing tendency in historiography makes value an issue. It is the conception of history as critical engagement with the object that directs attention to the individual and to the particular. It is not, as has sometimes been thought by critics of this position, a belief that history concerns unique events whereas science concerns itself with classes of events.

That the criticism of art is a form of historical knowledge, distinguished only by its subject matter from historical knowledge in general, was directly acknowledged by Droysen and Dilthey. In a discussion about criticism Droysen argued that the events or institutions of which historians speak—battles, councils, revolutions—are not matters of "factual reality" but are the products of a synthesizing historical imagination, bringing together countless isolated details under the organizing principle of an intention. He meant that to be a lesson from the way in which artworks are apprehended. Their "objective facts" are directly given, but they are intelligible only in the light of an interpretation which intuits the purpose or intention that they embody.

Dilthey wrote:

We must call *Verstehen* that process by which we intuit, behind the sign given to our senses, that psychic reality of which it is the expression. Such *Verstehen* ranges from the babblings of children to *Hamlet* and *The Critique of Pure Reason* . . . The orderly and systematic understanding of fixed and relatively permanent expressions of past life is what we call exegesis or interpretation. In this sense there is also an art of exegesis whose objects are statues or paintings.[40]

Dilthey's exposition on the foundations of historical reasoning in hermeneutics is in effect at the same time a propaedeutic for literary criticism.

It seems fair to say that modern historical musicology has in the main been dominated by the diachronic mode of reasoning, and that its explanations, even where the subject is quite particular, tend in the main to aspire to the nomothetic. But music history provides as rich a field as any for Carl Hempel's charge that historians rarely make good their use of words like "therefore," "thus," and "because" on any rigorous notion of causal explanation.[41]

The conception that I have summarized here about the historian's objectives and capabilities does not have built into it such a shortfall between aspiration and achievement. It shows the separation of criticism from history to be unnecessary and inappropriate. And on the contrary it shows that the music historian can be, by virtue of training, intellectual temper, and the needs of the discipline, the preeminent practitioner of musical criticism.

CHAPTER 2

"To Worship That Celestial Sound": Motives for Analysis

The line quoted in the title of this essay was suggested to me by Peter Kivy's book *The Corded Shell*.[1] Kivy is one of those philosophers interested in music from whom we hear now and then of their surprise at the way professional music analysis is conducted—in strict formalist fashion, as if to avoid the embarrassment of confronting that about music which Dryden, among countless others, praises most.[2] Kivy's book is a serious philosophical argument for the possibility of responsible talk about music that does not draw the blinds before music's expressive force. I chose that particular line from Dryden because of the striking way in which it resonates with a crucial passage in the musical work with which I plan to illustrate my arguments, Beethoven's Ninth Symphony.

In his propaedeutic to the members of a panel gathered, under his chairmanship, to review recent working methodologies in American musicology during the 1981 meetings of the American Musicological Society, Claude Palisca asked them to consider how those methodologies have "contributed to our *understanding of the music and musical cultures of the past*" (italics mine). This way of putting the question implies a new conception of the task of music history, a radical departure, in fact, from the program that Guido Adler had set upon our profession in 1911: to trace the development of musical style.[3] One hint of the newness of it is in the fact that as recently as 1972, during the Copenhagen congress of the International Musicological Society, the topic for one of the panel discussions was "Current Methods of Stylistic Analysis." Not only is the title significant, but also the fact that the panel ignored it, for the most part.

The simple formulation of our task as the understanding of the music and musical cultures of the past can be read without surprise, because it catches the spirit in which many musicologists are now working. As for Adler's program, it seems to function mainly in the textbook industry in this country, sustained more by the market than by a shared belief that it represents the appropriate goals for musicology today. There is of course the interesting question about how that squares with the teaching of analysis. I shall return to that at the end.

I see no way of discussing the fit of analytical methodologies to the task of understanding the music of the past without first taking a measure of the task itself. Does the wording suggest that the "pastness" of our objects distinguishes our kind of inquiry from that of other groups of scholars dealing with music? It quickly becomes apparent that all music, except that which has not yet been composed, or performed, or thought of, is music of the past. On the other hand all music, insofar as it is or might be the object of the historian's attention, is in the historian's present as tradition. But tradition is the transmission of music through a continuous succession of presents or contemporary contexts from the initial present of its moment of creation or first sounding to the historian's present. There is naturally a priority of interest in that initial present, and that is presumably what is meant when we say, simply, that we are interested in the music *of the* past. But that priority is not sustained. It isn't the pastness of our objects that distinguishes them as historical, or us as historians. It is our interest in them as objects (or acts) in tradition.

So, not music *of* the past, as a principle of selection, but music *in* the past, music in contexts, as a principle of knowledge. History is a discipline, not by virtue of a particular subject matter but by virtue of an epistemological stance. And the change in the formulation of the task of music history entails most centrally a change in epistemology, a shift of emphasis from the genetic to the ontological.

The difference turns on the question of what it is to *understand* the music of the past, particularly on the matter of context again. There is a causal sense in which music is understood as a precipitate of its context. And there is a hermeneutic sense, in which it is viewed as a meaningful item within a wider context of practices, conventions, assumptions, transmissions, receptions—in short a musical culture, which serves to endow its constituent aspects with meaning while attaining its own meaning from the combination of its constituent aspects. Like historians of literature and art, we are becoming more interested in contexts of meanings than contexts of causes. That has consequences for the role of analysis, both in its absolute importance and in its particular tasks, and for the methodologies that will be suited to them.

From this perspective analysis must be a central activity of the historian. The most engaged and engaging writing about the music of the past nowadays tends increasingly toward a comprehensive understanding. There is a tendency to want to understand not just the structure of the musical object but the meaning of its structure, interpreted as a conception against the background of norms and models, stylistic and semiotic codes, expectations and reactions, aesthetic ideals, circumstances of transmission and reception. Not just the score is evidence for such analysis, but also the scores of other music, manuscript traditions, evidence about performance practice, the writings of theorists and pedagogues— read in understanding of the nature of *their* tasks, *their* readerships, and the style of *their* reasoning—critical writing, chronicles, and more. What I am talking about is the crossroads of approaches that, in the nineteenth century, were called hermeneutics and historicism, before those words, especially the second, became accusations.[4] With such a notion about their tasks, historians will not sensibly tolerate the separation of "analytical" from "historical" methodologies, even in the sense of the sequence of investigative operations. As investigative procedures, neither analytical nor historical methods can be absolutely prior to the other. They inform one another in a continuous circle.

The polemical sense with which the term "historicism" is now loaded has several factors behind it. One of them is also among the issues that have divided analysis and history and their practitioners. It is the absolute priority that historicism once wished to give to the initial context of its objects in studying them. The nineteenth-century hermeneuts (specifically Schleiermacher and Dilthey) essentially accepted that notion. According to its original definition, hermeneutics is the art of clarifying and mediating by the interpreter's own efforts what is encountered in tradition. That meant bridging the gap between the familiar world of the present and the strange world of the past. The nineteenth-century hermeneuts held the interpreter's boundedness in his present as something to be transcended. Bridging the distance between minds meant shedding the interests and habits of the present in order to understand the subjective intentions of the persons who are involved in history.

In this century the philosopher Hans-Georg Gadamer and his followers have given systematic and reasoned legitimation for the reluctance of critics in all the arts to restrict their analytical categories to those that might be recognized by the artist, without opening the way to utter relativism.[5] The work of art is regarded not as a fixed and passive object of study but as an inexhaustible source of possible meaning. It exists in tradition, and the effort at understanding it is episodic; every understanding is a moment in the life of tradition, but also in the life of the interpreter. Like language, art bears the history of past understandings. The interpreter confronts not the work alone but the work in its effective history (*Wirkungsgeschichte*). The encounter is more a conversation with a respondent than an operation on a passive object. The knowledge and interests of interpreters are as much factors in understanding as are the meanings of their objects in their successive contexts. Understanding takes place in the fusion of the horizons of present and past.

I recently experienced so exact a demonstration of this point that I would like to tell it, by way of demystifying the general idea. I had been rereading *The Art of Measured Song,* a treatise written by Franco of Cologne about 1270, in the translation of Oliver Strunk.[6] As I read the eleventh chapter, "Of Discant and Its Species," something leaped out of the text that each time before had gone by without my taking any special notice of it. It is the use, three times, of the word "written" in the sense of "composed": "Let us speak of how discant ought to be written"; "Discant is written either with words or with and without words";

and "In the conduct . . . cantus and discant are written by the same person."

The word "written" had heated up for me because I have lately been thinking about the history of music *writing* in relation to the history of musical composition and transmission. The idea of "writing" as "composing" is a modern one. But I had recently come to the conclusion that the condition that made this linguistic usage possible—the entry of writing as a characteristic and necessary link in the chain of transmission—first obtained during the thirteenth century, and that is when Franco wrote his treatise.

To have my impression directly confirmed by this important text was exciting. But I thought it best to check the Latin text, and I found that it speaks not of discant being "written" but of its being "made." Presumably Strunk felt at liberty to use the more idiomatic expression because there was for him no context that was sensitive to the difference, as there is now for me. That he was so discriminating and cautious a scholar only reinforces the point. Differences or changes about what a text says are not necessarily to be charged against the frailties of interpreters; they can as well reflect differences or changes in the interests of interpreters. The idea that interpreters should shed their interests and read the "invariable" meanings of texts is, I think, not realistic. And if this is so of the interpretation of texts, with their semantic contents, it must be the more so of music, where semantics plays a relatively minor role.

––––––––––

Do we currently have, in musical analysis, methodologies that lead to the understanding of the music of the past?

Ian Bent has given us, in his fine article in *The New Grove Dictionary of Music and Musicians,* an overview of analytical methodologies, as well as a history of the practice of musical analysis.[7] On the history we also have a number of recently published separate studies, the most valuable of which is Ruth Solie's paper "The Living Work: Organicism and Musical Analysis."[8] And Allan Keiler is preparing a book on Heinrich Schenker and tonal theory. From all of this we can learn something about the historical and theoretical factors that underlie the characteristics of analytical methodologies as they are.

The analysis of music as such goes back little more than a century. Before then, concrete demonstrations about how things musical worked were conceived more as models for composition. Thus they had the aspect of taxonomies or inventories of correct practice. The philosophical pivot for the emergence of an analytical attitude was provided by the aesthetic idea, since the eighteenth century, of the contemplation of beauty for its own sake and without self-interest (especially in the writing of Immanuel Kant). In contrast to the tradition of cataloging correct practices, what characterized aesthetic writing in general and analytical writing about music in particular during the nineteenth century was a preoccupation that had two sides: reflection about the nature of the creative process, and the search for structural coherence in music. These were not abstract, scientific interests; they were motivated by ideologies about the human faculty of genius and the quality of greatness in music, for which structural unity was the sine qua non. There is an evaluative impulse in analysis from the beginning, and that impulse survives in the seductive pleasure that can attend an analytical closure and thereby distract the historian from the real task of interpretation.

The relationship between the ideas of genius and unity is this: Genius is the natural creative capacity of mind that provides the controlling force in the production of unified works of art. This doctrine was couched in terms appropriated from the organicist philosophy of the early nineteenth century, and the organic metaphor was applied to all the elements of it: the human mind, the capacity of genius, the creative process, and the analysis of music as the uncovering of deep-seated principles of organization on the basis of such a model: to put it in other words, the deductive explanation of the work from such a model.

The analytical methodologies that Bent surveys in his detailed review fall into two general categories. On one hand there are empirical, discovery-procedure approaches, such as the feature analysis entailed in Knud Jeppesen's *Palestrina and the Style of the Dissonance,* Jan LaRue's *Guidelines for Style Analysis,* and countless computer-assisted analytical projects.[9] And on the other hand there are the essentially deductive procedures based on models of structural process, such as Hugo Riemann's phrase-structure analysis, the various approaches in the tradition of *Formenlehre*, Rudolph Réti's thematic process analysis and its descendant serial analysis, and Schenker's structural analysis. It is the methodologies in this second category, which grew out of the organicist movement of the nineteenth century, that seem to predominate in the teaching of analysis today.

We can see in some of the most characteristic features of these methodologies, and of the analyses that they generate, the marks of their ideological origins. First, the point of view is holistic and unitarian. The work must be explicable in terms of a single principle, and every detail must be derivable from the idea of the whole. Second, the focus is mainly on pitch structures. It is in the analysis of pitch structures that theorists have most successfully demonstrated the properties of organic coherence. On the other hand other dimensions of music, in which organic structure is less handily demonstrated, have come in for relatively little attention: time, sound qualities (sonority, register, timbre), the communication between performing roles, the relationship between music and language where there is a sung text. Third, the analytical perspective tends to be from the inside out, or from back to front, rather than from beginning to end. Music is apprehended as synchronic structure. One who opposed that conception was Sir Donald Francis Tovey, whose view of music was "time-like" rather than "map-like." The difference is fundamental. Analysis whose center of gravity is a synchronic conception of pitch structure is little interested in the phenomenology of music. Schenker's synchronic conception was an important theoretical achievement—in a way the final unfolding, so to speak, of the organic principle. But it has meant that the point of view of the auditor has not been much of a factor in the practice and teaching of analysis in this country. And that fact is now registered in the notice of the absence of a tradition of criticism in musical studies.

Fourth, analysis tends to be of an a priori, rationalist nature. It proceeds from universals about how Music works, more than it seeks to discover how musics work. Finally, prevailing modes of structural analysis are antihistorical, in two respects: they decontextualize their objects in their rationalist treatment of them; and they are taught and practiced without notice taken of their own historicality or, in general, of the role that particular models play in the organization of understanding.

Now the one thing I do not intend with this characterization of analytical practice is that it should be taken as an indictment. That would be to fault analysis for failing to accomplish what it did not set out to accomplish. What I do mean to allege is that the two things I have tried to describe—historical understanding and formalist analysis—do not match very well. I think that is evident from a comparison of the descriptions in the abstract. But it is driven home by some accounts of music of the past that have been generated from the formalist point of view and that provide questionable or inadequate historical understanding.

One such account that has been of concern to me in my research is the general interpretation of the Gregorian chant tradition that is represented by the characterization of chants in a widely read book on the subject as "unified works of art, no less so than in the case of a sonata by Beethoven."[10] This attributes to a Romantic aesthetic conception of dubious relevance characteristics that are far better understood from the point of view of the context of generation, transmission, and function in which the tradition actually thrived. The misinterpretation here eventually touches all aspects of the subject.

Another is the succession of analyses of pitch structures in the second of Schumann's *Dichterliebe* songs to which Joseph Kerman called attention recently, in which three prominent analysts consistently ignore the fact that their object is a song, performed by a pianist and singer who respond to one another in particular ways that influence the perception of the pitch structure, with the singer singing a poem that itself has structure and meaning. The result, as Kerman showed, is an inadequate understanding, even of the pitch structure.[11] This casts doubt on the claim that formalist analysis can achieve even its avowed aims by restricting itself to operations on the notes in the score.

Still on the subject of the *Dichterliebe,* there is a published interpretation of the sixth song, "Im Rhein," in which the dotted rhythm of the piano figure is said to represent waves.[12] What is missed thereby is a reference to an item of a stylistic code—the grandeur of the Baroque majestic style—and the reflection through that, so to speak, of the image of the Cologne cathedral. And with that is missed an entry into the meaning of the song—a case of misinterpretation resulting from decontextualization.

The singleminded formalist habit of blocking out music-language relations brings me back to the music of the Middle Ages, which has suffered misinterpretation on a grand scale, in a way that is displayed in this representative statement: "Medieval composers had no direct interest in their texts; the correlation of tone and word remained haphazard. Almost any music could be composed to almost any words."[13] Virtually all the formalist attitudes are ultimately wrapped up in that assessment.

But more important than such gaffes—major or minor—are the blind spots of formalist analysis: *Formenlehre* in abundance, but little attention to time process and time sense; sophisticated theories of tonality, but little interest in the qualitative side of key relations, although this was an important instrument for the rhetorical and expressive functions of music in the era of common practice. But key relations in this qualitative sense have a sequential, narrative order that has to be played out in real time, even conceptually. It will not survive reduction to a synchronic representation. That means that what is a gain in theoretical understanding is a loss in historical understanding.

For Schenker, Gregorian chant and the music of Wagner were blind spots—he pronounced them both incoherent.[14] Here the analytical methodology constitutes a criterion for the admission of works into the canon. An interesting variant is presented by the case of Ockeghem. Judging from the language of much of the modern literature, his music, too, might be in danger of being declared incoherent (quoting from various textbooks and scholarly works): "Generalizations about [its] formal principles are difficult to formulate" because it "unfolds freely and in an ad hoc manner."[15] "Il n'a pas de système."[16] The music "avoids precisely those features that would enable the listener to grasp the details or the large structural units and to integrate them in his mind."[17] It has structure and order, but they are "disguised and often inaudible."[18] Or it is put the other way about: "there are masses with no consistent unifying devices at all," but "the coherent effect [they make] on the listener is the result of internal consistency of style and expression."[19] As one writer summarizes it, Ockeghem is "a difficult, even enigmatic composer."[20]

But Ockeghem's stature as a great master is a *donnée* that has come down through an almost unbroken tradition since his own day. How can that be squared with the fact that his music fails to meet the most important general criterion for greatness?

The historian's puzzlement over Ockeghem's music finally becomes transformed into one of its leading characteristics. His "far-reaching renunciation of rational organization" is the manifestation of a "musical mysticism." The suspicion that the image of Ockeghem as mystic comes, at least in part, as resolution of the paradox is fed by the fact that it is a response neither to concrete, positive features of the music nor to any documented connections between Ockeghem and traditions of philosophical or theological mysticism. The term "mysticism" used with reference to Ockeghem has not been given any content. And the suspicion is further reinforced by the fact that the emergence of this image coincides more or less with the forced abandonment of an earlier image of Ockeghem as paragon of the strict formalist art of imitative counterpoint.[21]

This story illustrates the episodic and contingent nature of historical understanding. It demonstrates the role that formalist analytical attitudes play in the formation of such understanding. And it shows that they continue to exercise the biases of their organicist roots even after those have gone deep underground.

The obvious conclusion from these brief citations is that historical understanding is neither the prime target nor the chief beneficiary of the discipline of analysis. As music historians we want analytical methodologies that are less normative and more phenomenological and historical; that take account of much more than pitch structures; and that concern themselves not with structures alone, but with the relations of structure and meaning.

To indicate what I mean I should like to continue here with interpretative reflections about Beethoven's Ninth Symphony that I began elsewhere (see Chapter 1). I choose that piece because, more than any other work of the tradition, it *demands* interpretation. It does so in and of itself because it blatantly confounds efforts to account for its events on formalist terms alone, but also by virtue of the interpretational, or hermeneutic, field in which it has been transmitted to us. No work of the tradition has generated more reflection about its meaningfulness, both in the language of critics and through the music of the composer's successors. Formalist analysis, like the New Criticism that it anticipated, declares that to be irrelevant to the analysis of the work. It is among my purposes here to argue for the dependence of understanding on the work's tradition—both the tradition in which it was composed and the tradition that it has generated—what Gadamer calls its *Wirkungsgeschichte* or "effective history."

It was my interpretation that the great scope of the work is supported by Beethoven's manipulation of a concatenation of traditional genres, and that its expressive force is largely a matter of long-sustained power struggles, extravagant gestures, the contradiction of logical musical process, the ultimate settling of issues. It presents the paradox of a symphonic work that achieves conventional closure, but that nevertheless suggests a time frame of infinite spread, and that in the end leaves a residual sense of the infinite.

I suggested that such an interpretation resonates with aesthetic ideals that were prominent in Beethoven's time, and I showed that it corresponds to interpretations that have come down with the work as an aspect of its transmission. We are not obliged to commit ourselves to those interpretations, but only to respond in awareness of them as aspects of the field in which the work presents itself to us. The critical task is to interpret the text again (and again and again) against that background and from our present point of view.

What I shall focus on here is the phenomenology of key relationships, regarded in the sense of a narrative. For key relations are essential among the concrete musical facts that feed those interpretations. And in view of the theoretical intent of this chapter, the pursuit of this aspect will provide an opportunity for displaying the shortcomings of organicist theory, which makes the strongest claim for its powers of analysis in the harmonic domain. For although organicist analysis has been successful in demonstrating the grammatical coherence of the harmonic events, it cannot cope with questions of motivation. That is, it cannot say how and why things happen when and as they do. It is a primary purpose here to argue that such questions must be asked and that the quest for answers can be conducted entirely in terms of the music itself.

A few preliminary remarks are necessary. First, for Beethoven, key is quality as well as structure, and as such it enters into qualitative as well as structural relationships. Often facts in the domain of key can be only described, not interpreted, if we regard key only as structure. Second, there is not always a sharp distinction to be drawn, in Beethoven's music, between being *in* a key or *on* it, or between those and just having present the sonority of its tonic triad. To be sure, any sonority is subject to explanation as a function of some larger tonal process, but for the moment it may insist on its own identity and what is important is its juxtaposition with other sonorities that insist on *their* own identities. (The outstanding case is in the passage *Adagio ma non troppo, ma divoto* of the Finale.) The difference between the naked juxtaposition of two keys and the logical progression from one key to another can itself be an important factor in the way a work progresses and the impressions that it creates as it does so. Often an unexpected juxtaposition of keys is followed by its explanation in tonal-functional terms; first the effect, then the logical connection. That fact is itself a reason for the insistence that Beethoven's manipulation of key exploits its character aspects. He composes with key as a dramatist composes with character. Beethoven's symphonies are both narratives and "frozen architecture," and to rest with the analysis of the structural aspects of key relationships is to close one ear, or two if we count the inner one. (What I have to say, and especially the reasons I wish to say it, will be much clearer if the reader will take the trouble to go through the passages at the keyboard or in a recording.)

The first sonority in the piece is tonally anonymous, spread out as a background on which the D minor of the first theme is imposed as figure. The theme progresses to the dominant and plays itself out on the tonic. Ordinarily that would be routine. But here what ensues is the return to the introduction rather than a reiteration of the first theme, this time on what we now recognize as tonic rather than dominant.

Before we follow the consequences of that we must attend to another thread of the tonal narrative that has its beginning before the point we have reached. At m. 21 the third of the motives of which the theme is composed begins to rise through the D-minor scale, arriving at the peak tone, B-flat, at m. 24. At first that note is harmonized in the most obvious way, as G minor (IV). But then there is a shift to E-flat major,

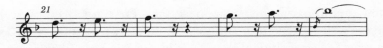

EX. 2.1

which brings out the B-flat while subduing the G. Harmonically this amounts to a plunge, deep into the flat side. At the moment it occurs it is the sudden flash of a new color, legitimized only after the fact as an inflection to the Neapolitan that then prepares a smooth return to the dominant. But it has long-range associations.

Replaying the opening on the tonic (m. 36) has the effect of forcing the restatement of the first theme out of the tonic. Exact analogy would have brought it back in G minor. Instead it comes in B-flat major. The real analogy, therefore, is with the shift from G minor to E-flat major in m. 24—here it is from D minor to B-flat major, with the same sort of effect, another sudden plunge deep into the flat side. Once again, after the fact only, the B-flat is interpreted in relation to D minor, by means of another scalar passage with first I^6 (mm. 59–60) and then V (m. 63) as goal. The prolongation of the V from m. 63 onward plays with B-flat first as an accented neighbor note (m. 67ff), then as prolonged passing tone from A to C as the bass establishes F minor, then F major (mm. 70-74). That is identified in turn as V of B-flat, and this entire passage since the V of D minor at m. 63 turns out to have been the transition of the exposition, and the now firmly established B-flat is the secondary tonality of the movement—rather than, as one might expect, the dominant or the relative major. Those would have been supporting keys. B-flat (and its relative E-flat) are in contrast, and that is instantly clear from the way both were first introduced.

It is good to recall what has forced this move to B-flat: the formal and temporal disjunction of the return to the introduction. The two phenomena are linked as the factors that set up the structural and expressive peculiarities of the movement.

B-flat is sustained through an abnormally long string of short thematic ideas, all in that key. A single theme would be likely to move out sooner in this style. As it is, more than half the exposition occupies B-flat. There is a brief effort to break out into B-natural, but that is just as quickly put down (mm. 108–115). Forty measures of buildup in

B-flat follow, led by a continuous ascent through the scale of that key in the bass. The climax is the unison fanfare in B-flat at the end of the exposition (m. 150). The departure from B-flat is even more abrupt than the entry into it—simply a drop from the unison B-flat to a unison A (m. 160).

Again the shift in tonal realm is also a disjunction in the time frame: back to the introduction. There is something illogical, eccentric, about these abrupt shifts between tonal and formal/temporal values, as though one were flung from room to room or from one state of consciousness to another. But once again, *after* the event, a logical connection is made. The next phase of the development section makes a progression down the circle of fifths on the flat side, from A minor in m. 160, to B-flat major at m. 232. The B-flat is interpreted as Neapolitan, and that prepares an exit via A minor (m. 255) to D major (m. 301). Such a steady, almost predictable progression has a humdrum quality, especially after the eccentricities of the exposition. It inverts the conventional expressive curve of the sonata form; instead of building tension through the development, it slackens because of the redundancy of what is going on. It is only just four measures before the recapitulation that the atmosphere becomes suddenly taut again, and the moment of recapitulation itself is the high point of tension, not its release as convention has it. The principal factor in that is the identification of the opening motto as D major, in an air of catastrophe. It is dampened quickly in mm. 313–314 through B-flat, which is interpreted subsequently as a German sixth chord in D major and catapulted directly to D minor without troubling about dominant preparation. The D major here actually picks up the harmony of the beginning of the development, which had been achieved there in an unprepared shift from the open fifth on A. There it was interpreted after the fact as the dominant of G, and that had launched the downward progression by fifths.

The shift to D major at that point opened up the development, correcting the implication that the piece would fall eternally back to the beginning, like the stone of Sisyphus. The fresh harmony, the inverted position of the triad, the *pianissimo,* gave a clear signal of some sort of forward motion. When the same harmony comes again at the recapitulation, now *fortissimo* with kettledrums pounding, the message is bewildering. For it simply asserts itself, not as a consequence of anything, not as a signal of what is to come: The crisis that its appearance creates must be put down and that is done by the B-flat that hands the piece back to its tonic, D minor.

There is no problem about understanding the D major in terms of the grammar of the movement's tonality, or about associating it with the D major at the beginning of the development. But neither of those provides the motivation for the defeat of every expectation at just this moment: fleshing out the opening motive with the full triad, the D major instead of D minor, the dynamics and scoring.

Sooner or later we come to understand the D minor–D major relationship in the sense of a drive to move out of the one and into the other. Eventually (of course with the singing of Schiller's *Ode to Joy*) it succeeds. And that is one of the main narrative lines of the work as a whole. The other, in the domain of key, is the attempt of B-flat to impose itself over the region of the tonic, and its eventual elimination from the piece. Both processes focus ultimately upon the *Ode* in the last movement: the D minor–D major process at its introduction, the B-flat story at its expressive zenith (to be identified presently).

There is of course a certain overlap between the two processes, and perhaps even a connection in history. In the Baroque era the sharp and flat keys were classified as two genera ("cantus durus" and "cantus mollis") contrasted in a distinct polarity of qualities identified as bright/dark, active/passive, tension/resolution, hard/soft. By the end of the eighteenth century the terms *durus* and *mollis,* or in German, *dur* and *moll,* were the names for what we call the major and minor modes. In other words the application of the terms was shifted from a polarity of transpositions to one of the octave species. The affective qualities that were associated with the terms before the shift remained with them afterward, that is, they shifted to the octave species. The shift left an area of overlap, for the most characteristic quality difference between major and minor is of course owing to the difference between the raised (sharp) or lowered (flat) third.[22]

Beethoven worked with all three sorts of situation: straightforward contrasts of sharp and flat keys, contrasts of major and minor keys, and situations that do not belong exclusively in one duality or the other. The passage from the end of the development to the beginning of the reprise is such a case. We would have to say that the harmony in the last four measures of development is dominant, A major, reached by turning a sharp corner from F major, the dominant of B-flat. But above the A major harmony strings and winds are playing in the scale of D minor, which leads us to expect that the dominant will resolve to D minor. When D major comes, it is with such exaggeration of the minor-major character contrast that it does not register in those terms. It registers directly as a blinding flash of brightness. We could say "D major," but what we are caught up by is the sudden assertion of that hard-edged F-sharp.

This whole invention of Beethoven's—the progression from an anonymous fourth-fifth configuration, to the juxtaposition of major-minor/sharp-flat sonorities, to the ultimate clearing away of everything but the major/sharp complex—worked free of its etymology in the key system and became a topos and a cliché for the nineteenth century. Composers elaborated it again and again. What its associations were can best be sensed through some of the pieces themselves: Strauss's *Also Sprach Zarathustra* (and Stanley Kubrick's assimilation of it for *2001: A Space Odyssey*), the *Prologo in Cielo* of Boito's *Mephistophele,* Mahler's Third Symphony, Bruckner's Seventh, and others. Nietzsche's meditation on hearing the Ninth Symphony gave it a concrete content that would even be translated into record-album cover designs: "The thinker feels himself floating above the earth in an astral dome, with the dream of immortality in his heart: all the stars seem to glimmer about him [that may even refer to a very specific moment that I shall identify later on] and the earth seems to sink ever further downward."[23] We can glimpse through that the Romantic idea of music as expression of the infinite.

D major breaks through on three subsequent occasions in the first movement, but always to retreat to D minor. First, the recapitulation of the second thematic group begins in D major (m. 345). But on second thought the beginning is taken over again in D minor, and that is the key of the continuation. The next occasion is the long dominant preparation before the last phase of the recapitulation. Mm. 369–73 are in D major, and mm. 387–400 seem to be dominant to D major. But then it turns out to be D minor, and that is how the recapitulation ends. The coda begins in D minor. In the midst of it the first horn, playing *piano* and *dolce,* sounds a tune in D major that is based on the tail end of the first theme (m. 469ff). But the strings, playing in D minor, take the moment away from the horn. Tovey spoke of this passage in the sense of a "tragic irony," "a distant happiness." He was no doubt responding to the associations that we have with muffled horn calls, and to the failure of D major. His language calls attention to something that happens here, if not for the first time, then in any case early in the history of a kind of musical treatment that became characteristic for the Romantics. It is the subjectivization of music, music interpreted by itself. The horn tune is a reminiscence, even a bit of nostalgia, colored brightly as it hadn't been before. The image is wiped away when the strings take over in D minor and work that tune into another rigorous developmental passage. Mahler created something similar, but made much more of it, in the long and deeply affecting post-horn solo in the third movement of the Third Symphony. And he wrote, quite explicitly, that the post-hornist should play "wie aus weiter Ferne."

One of the formal peculiarities of the Scherzo seems designed to stage a rather dramatic little scene in the D minor–D major story. The Scherzo proper, in D minor, is given a coda, coupled through elision to the beginning of the Trio, which is in D major. Following the playing of the Trio, the Scherzo is repeated and runs right through the elision into the Trio again, as though it would go round and round forever (shades of the first movement). But in mid-phrase the door is abruptly slammed shut, knocking the F-sharp right out of the tonality.

Even more explicitly and substantially than the Scherzo, the third movement is directed by these issues of key. Its formal idea is the presentation of two lyrical subjects, alternately in keys of contrasting color—flat keys, starting with B-flat major, and sharp keys, starting with D major. The movement begins in B-flat, in direct juxtaposition with the closing D minor of the Scherzo. Then come the second subject in D major (m. 25); first subject in B-flat again (m. 43); second subject in G major (m. 65); an invention on the first subject in E-flat (m. 83); first subject in B-flat (m. 99); and a continuation of the invention, moving twice to E-flat (mm. 121 and 131), the second time taking an unexpected turn to D-flat (m. 133), and returning finally to B-flat (m. 139), where it remains for the coda.

The D-flat is a surprise because it follows dominant preparation for B-flat. There are other special things about it: it brings a sudden change of dynamics and texture, counterpoint in large note values, and especially a change of scoring—for a moment the orchestra becomes an organ. The music assumes the gravity of a religious gesture in *stile antico*.

This interpretation opens onto a large domain, the atmosphere of religiosity that could infuse secular music in the nineteenth century. Beethoven himself provides the best term for it, in the directions for the section "Ihr stürzt nieder, Millionen" of the fourth movement: *Adagio ma non troppo, ma divoto*. Devotional music is what it is, climax of the intense lyricism of the third movement. Sometimes composers identified such gestures explicitly with performance indications, such as *divoto*, or very often *religioso* (for example, Berlioz, *Symphonie Fantastique*). Beethoven also identified such music with titles: "Hirtengesang. Wohltätig mit Dank an die Gottheit verbunden Gefühle nach dem Sturm. *Allegretto*" (Sixth Symphony); "Heiliger Dankgesang eines Genesenen an die Gottheit in der lidischen Tonart" (Quartet op. 132). Once again Nietzsche identified the current, speaking of "religious afterthroes": "However sharply one believes one has broken the habit of religion, it is yet never so much so that one takes no pleasure in the encounter with religious feelings and airs, for example in music."[24]

There is a hint in the biographical literature that Beethoven might have had a conscious belief that D-flat was the appropriate key for such a gesture *absolutely*. In 1824, the year of the Ninth Symphony, Beethoven's contemporary Friedrich Rochlitz published his book *Für Freunde der Tonkunst*, in which he reports on a remark that Beethoven made about the poet Klopstock: "He always begins on much too lofty a plane; always *Maestoso*, D-flat major, eh?" Nowadays Rochlitz does not have a very good reputation for the reliability of his gossip.[25] Yet this anecdote has appeal; one wants to believe it because it is so consonant with the character of that D-flat passage in the third movement. But do we really require it for an understanding of the passage? The move from F to D-flat is another thrust deep into the flat side, like that from D to B-flat. It is the newness of harmonic color thus exposed that Beethoven was after for this passage.

We see him using the third relation for that effect in an extreme form in the Scherzo. There is a long passage that comes after the two static blocks that are juxtaposed at the beginning, in D minor and C major. The passage opens out to some sort of development, and it does so by sprinting through great harmonic distances at lightning speed. The effect is kaleidoscopic, the chords plunging by thirds through a succession of always new colors.

From the second to the third movement the harmony steps from D minor to B-flat. From the third to the fourth movement it steps back to D minor, but retains the B-flat. Yes, that creates the dissonant shriek that is wanted for the opening, but its meaning is given, too, by this intensification of the confrontation of the two keys. After the review of the earlier movements the clash is repeated, aggravated by the addition of a full A-major triad to the D minor with B-flat.

The flashbacks to the earlier movements retrieve both the themes and their keys. The whole passage mulls over the issues of key as they had developed to that point, like the Count taking stock in Act 3, Scene 4 of *The Marriage of Figaro*: D minor at the beginning, A major in the recollection from the first movement, A minor in the fragment from the Scherzo, B-flat in the Adagio fragment, D major for the *Ode to Joy* tune. So when the bass sings "O Freunde, nicht diese Töne," he speaks both literally and figuratively.

The Finale turns once more to B-flat in the March, which constitutes the second subject of a large sonata form. It is led finally away from that key in the last stanza of the *Ode,* beginning "Seid umschlungen, Millionen." The stanza begins in G major (the sonata recapitulation had returned to D major and simply made a shift to G at the end). It moves down to F major, and thence to B-flat (m. 620). In the *Adagio ma non troppo, ma divoto* section ("Ihr stürzt nieder, Millionen") the chorus and orchestra begin an ascent in strong strides through chords on C, D, and E-flat. They just lift from one chord to the next, and each is functionally independent, without the mediation of preparatory chords, a change of color with each chord. The expression is of a most concentrated intensity. There had not before been so many such shifts in succession in this piece.

E-flat moves to E-natural, a diminished seventh chord is built on the E, E moves to A, and the chord has become a diminished ninth, with A at the bottom and B-flat at the very top. The text is "Über Sternen muss er wohnen," and the chord is set to shimmering. This, I believe, is the dénouement of the whole symphony. The ninth chord, of course, prepares the final return to D major. This moment bears a strong resemblance to an equally transcendent moment in Beethoven's Mass in

D, the *Missa Solemnis,* completed two years earlier. It is the setting of "Sanctus, Dominus Deus sabbaoth" (m. 27ff of the *Sanctus*), *Adagio mit Andacht*: A-major ninth chord, *tremolando, pianissimo;* then, "Pleni sunt coeli," *forte,* D major, *Allegro.* "Celestial sounds," surely.

But this draws attention to a strong similarity between the two works altogether with respect to their tonal schemes. The Mass, too, progresses through a network of keys headed on one side by D major, on the other by B-flat. How is this parallel to be interpreted? Perhaps Beethoven felt that this particular tonal configuration was exactly right for such pieces. But there is no corroborating evidence of that and in any case it would be an aptness that we could hardly appreciate directly. What we can say with confidence is that this network provided the basis for the kind of color and character contrast that Beethoven wanted for these large-scale tonal narratives. Whether consciously or not, this sort of thing does hark back to the Baroque idea of the *durus-mollis* genera.

Certainly the internal evidence regarding Beethoven's intentions with regard to key character and the character of key contrast is strong. They are centrally involved in the powerful drama and rhetoric of the Ninth Symphony. The external evidence is slim, but there is some, and perhaps one could find more.

In a sketchbook now in the Princeton University Library containing sketches for the Cello Sonata op. 102, no. 2, there is a passage in B minor which did not survive to the final version. Only the Bagatelle op. 126, no. 4 and the Agnus of the Mass in D are in B minor. In the margin next to this passage is the remark "h moll Schwarze Tonart." Anton Schindler, in his Beethoven biography, writes that Beethoven believed in the theory of Christian Schubart about the character of the various keys, but that his ideas did not exactly coincide with Schubart's (for the latter B minor is the key of "patience, of the quiet expectation of one's fate"; the reader is invited to compare Beethoven's two B-minor pieces to those characterizations of the key.)[26]

In a letter to his Edinburgh publisher, Thomson, Beethoven wrote that a certain Scottish tune marked *Amoroso* should not be set in A-flat, which key he characterized as *Barbaresco.*[27] But one would not say that the openings of the op. 26 and op. 110 piano sonatas, both in A-flat, have a *Barbaresco* character.

We know there was a contemporary doctrine regarding the character of keys, and on occasion, at least, Beethoven professed a belief in it. And however inconsistent he may have been in his explicit characterization of keys, his very mention of the matter confirms his attention to the qualitative side of harmony. But the best evidence for that is in the music, where character emerges from the relations of keys. He composed with keys, as a playwright with characters and plots.

———————

In the foregoing section I have tried to sketch an example of the kind of understanding of a work—I would call it historical understanding—that is not likely to be caught by the methodologies of formalist analysis being taught and practiced in North America today, even though the discovery procedures of those methodologies can lead to the threshhold of such understanding. But neither can it be caught by the notion of style history, with its roots in eighteenth-century Enlightenment historiography, that continues to inform historical surveys in our lecture halls and textbooks. Virtually all that these two overarching paradigms have in common is that understanding of the music and musical cultures of the past is largely beyond their reach. Their philosophical backgrounds, their goals, their ways of construing their objects, have little to do with each other. But these are the paradigms by which we prepare students for the study of music history, and that places on them an insupportable burden: to make a coherent synthesis of these paradigms in their own minds, and to take that as a basis for historical understanding.

We might make a better beginning by trying to teach analysis along historical lines—not simply arranging the music for analysis in chronological order, but deriving methodologies as needed from the coordinated study of music, music theory and criticism, reception and transmission, performance practices, aesthetics, and semiotics. Such an enterprise would in most cases require the confrontation and collaboration of historians and theorists, and that would do no harm at all. On the contrary it might foster a more critical habit of mind in students, and it might be an influence toward reducing the deplorable rift that now exists in this country between music history and theory.

CHAPTER 3

Music Analysis in a Historical Context

A spirited dialogue is underway about the need for criticism in history and the case for history in criticism.[1] I would suppose that the two questions are the same.[2]

The title of this essay could suggest a manual of instruction— *Vegetable Gardening in an Urban Environment*—or of description— *The Polish Peasant in America*. In that I read the title with a question mark I am bound to deny both implications, and the further suggestion that the author is a specialist. The subject is the concern of every member of this profession, for each of us acts on decisions about it, whether or not those decisions have been brought to consciousness. But to address it directly is to open a Pandora's box, and I can hope to do no more than consider some of the many divisive problems on both sides of the question that fly out as we do so.

I should like to frame the question first in the context of another art, by reading from two appreciations of Michelangelo's *Pieta*. The first:

To this work I think no sculptor, however distinguished an artist, could add a single grace, or improve it by whatever pains he might take, whether in elegance and delicacy, or force, *nor could any surpass the art which Michelangelo has here exhibited* [italics mine].

(Now the author expands on that word, *art*).

Among other fine things may be enumerated—to say nothing of the admirable draperies—that the body of the dead Christ exhibits the very perfection of research in every muscle, vein, and nerve, nor could any corpse more completely resemble the dead than does this. The limbs are affixed to the trunk in a manner that is truly perfect; the veins and pulses, moreover, are indicated with such exactitude that one cannot but marvel how the hand of the artist should in a short time have produced such a work, or how a stone which just before was without form or shape, should all at once display such perfection as *Nature* can but rarely produce in the flesh.

The author is Georgio Vasari, apprentice and biographer of Michelangelo.[3] He expresses an attitude that we may take to be Michelangelo's own in placing the highest value on the recreation of the intelligible world through the mastery of anatomy and perspective.

The second passage is from a study by the great German art historian Henrich Wölfflin, published in 1891:

I shall begin with the formal considerations. The first impression is always a sense of astonishment over the luxurious display of folds in the garments: the folds of the robe sinking between the knees, a piling-up of cloth over each knee, resulting in a kind of framing recess on the left knee, the same motive repeated over the left shoulder . . . Between the fingers of the limply hanging arm the artist has placed a single fold from the Mother's robe. There is something touching in that, as though a flicker of life were still playing about the corpse.[4]

The passages reflect a profound contrast in the standards from which these evaluations arise, one of them belonging to the artist's time, the other to our own.

The observations of both writers are accurate. With the exception of Wölfflin's last sentence they may be verified empirically. What is more, all the data gathered from both observations must have been available to each writer. Vasari, working in the Master's studio and having himself achieved some distinction as an artist, surely knew something about the planning of the formal arrangements. Wölfflin surely recognized the accuracy of the reproduction from life. The point is that each took for granted what was for the other most valuable.

We can readily understand why this should have been the case. What Vasari hailed as Michelangelo's great achievement represents a final triumph of the eye and the hand after long striving. Once achieved it could be repeated with relative ease, and it became a routine part of the artist's craft and the viewer's experience. In *Art and Illusion* Ernst Gombrich wrote, "The history of art may be described as the forging of master keys for opening the mysterious locks of our senses to which only nature herself originally held the key. Like the burglar who tries to break a safe, the artist has no direct access to the inner mechanism. He can only feel his way with sensitive fingers, probing and adjusting his hook or wire when something gives way. Of course, once the door springs open, once the key is shaped, it is easy to repeat the performance. The next person needs no special insight—no more, that is, than is needed to copy his predecessor's master key." What is true for the creative skill of the artist applies with equal force to the eye, or ear, of the viewer or listener.[5]

Wölfflin's—and our own—emphasis on form and its bearing on expression proceeds from quite another "discovery." This had already been enunciated by John Ruskin in 1857: "Affection and discord, fretfullness and quietness, feebleness and firmness, luxury and purity, pride and modesty, and all other such habits, and every conceivable modification and mingling of them, may be illustrated, with mathematical exactness, by conditions of line and colour."[6]

We may generalize from these passages that the analysis of works of art rests upon a *selection* from all the true things that may be said about them. And the evaluation of an analysis devolves upon the awareness and evaluation of the grounds—the standards—on which the selection is made. The question of the "correctness" or the "validity" of the analysis is, compared to that, trivial. In turn, we understand those standards best when we see them in the context of the history of aesthetic judgement. We ask about the meaning of the work. But we ask, too, about the meaning of the standards on which it may be judged. And each question illuminates the other.

This case suggests a complex of preliminary conclusions and premises that I should like to review before I proceed any further.

The notion of an "independent," "objective," or "contextual" analysis, based only upon observation of the work itself, and framed in categories and concepts suggested only by the work, is an illusion. The work of art has no existence apart from any interpretation of it.

The works we value most are those that continue to interest us through shifting interpretations. We cannot simply make a categorical decision for one kind of interpretation because it carries the authority of the artist's standards, or for another because it has the greater meaning—for us—of our own standards.

We are interested in the continuity of the work through a multitude of interpretations. This is a question of criticism, and of history, and of the history of criticism. In that these subjects constantly illuminate one another, no one of them can be pursued fully in the absence of the others. They constitute, then, a single broad subject.

———————

I should like now to approach the question of "Music Analysis in a Historical Context" from the standpoint of the purpose for which the analysis is undertaken, for each purpose will suggest its own criteria of value. I shall suggest four broad possibilities that do not necessarily exclude one another, but that differ in important ways as points of departure.

1. The establishing of the hard and irreducible facts about the musical work, the laying bare of its events. With this as a goal, the analysis of music may be said to be a search for consistency of practice. It would seek to distinguish the significant from the fortuitous; design from accident, or, as it is often put, from coincidence.

This is a safe formulation. It may be translated into a formulation that is, nowadays, far less safe: The analysis of music is the attempt to reveal the intentions of the composer. If we were to put it that way we should stand accused by some of having committed the "intentional fallacy," for, they would argue, the intention of the artist is in principle not available, nor is it relevant, as a standard for judging the work.[7]

But the two formulations are in essential respects equivalent, for in both the emphasis is upon consistency and design. The difference reduces to the question whether, having observed consistencies in the work, we care to attribute them to a human agent; or whether design in a work is taken to be the result of purposive behavior on the part of a human agent. This is probably what positivists call a "pseudo-question," like the question whether the rubber band, having been stretched, may be said to have recalled its original form, just because it has been observed to return to that form.

To telescope the argument: let us read, for intention, *significant design,* circumventing the unanswerable question of the agent. Then historical evidence is relevant to the determination of *criteria of significance*. If we can recognize, on whatever evidence, what the consistencies are, or are likely to be (what the composer is likely to have intended), then we shall have one kind of standard for the analysis of the individual work of music. In these circumstances the "intentional fallacy" charge loses much of its substance.

I should like to insert as one example of the possibilities the insights which Allen Forte has derived from the sketches for Beethoven's op. 109, in his monograph *The Compositional Matrix*. This is a promise of what lies ahead once the vast fund of Beethoven sketches is subjected to analysis. But Forte himself denies that even the sketches provide adequate background. He writes, "Any technical study of Beethoven's works must recognize that his compositional technique cannot be understood apart from certain concepts of musical structure which reached a definitive stage of development about a century before the composing of op. 109. Many of these concepts are expressed within the practice of thorough bass . . . Unless certain of the more basic concepts implicit in thorough bass are grasped it is almost impossible to cope with the complex structure of composed tonal music at any other than the surface level."[8]

In this study of a single work, the author appeals not only to the principles of order that are manifested in the work itself but also to evidence on two further levels that would direct us to a more sophisticated understanding of the functioning of those principles.

2. The interpretation of the musical work. With this as a goal, analysis is a search for the values and schemata that condition the apprehension of works of music, for values enter into the apprehension of facts just as facts enter into the determination of values. The interpretations of the *Pieta* demonstrate well enough the extent to which the reporting of objective facts, so called—in this case the physical characteristics of the sculpture—is dependent upon the values of the reporter. We find meaning, expression, and purpose in works of music through an interpretive transformation of facts.

If facts have to do with knowledge, values have to do with preferences. One deals with what is, the other with what ought to be. The determination of preferences provides another kind of standard for the analysis—on this level we might say "criticism"—of music. If the standard which conditions our apprehension of the work differs from that which conditioned its creation, we can hardly afford to ignore either one for the other. For each can be recognized and can take on meaning only in the context of the other.

3. The explanation of the musical work. With this as the goal, musical analysis is a search for the causes of works of music.

We seek a balance of understanding between the work considered in itself and the work considered as the resultant of a multitude of forces outside itself.

A truly discerning analysis, in the sense of the first of my suggested categories, is a manner of explanation, for it reveals the significant events of the work and the manner in which they are related to one another. Events and relationships may, then, be regarded as causes for the whole work which is the outcome. In this sense "explanation" may be read as "understanding."

But perhaps to the polarity of the significant and the fortuitous there ought to be added a third category, the normative. This would refer to those aspects of a style that may be found in every work belonging to it—hence that cannot be considered fortuitous; and that belong among the *données* of that style—hence that would be significant in the characterization of the style, but not so much so in the characterization of each piece. If we recognize such a distinction in principle, it can be given substance for any single work only by reference to other works of similar provenance, and to nonmusical documents that give evidence about what was normative.

Of course we do recognize such a distinction, but thereby we give ourselves the license to avoid the responsibility of understanding works in themselves and to explain them instead through the identification of conventions and antecedents. This has sometimes had two very serious and unfortunate effects: first, the acceptance of superficial resemblances as evidence for genetic relationships; second, the abstraction of conventions from the works themselves, and their reconstitution in the mystical notion of a "style" with a life cycle that follows its own immutable laws—from zygote to tadpole to frog. It has sometimes meant not explaining, but wholesale explaining away. This is surely one of the most sensitive questions bearing on the relation between criticism and history.

The misuse of the concept of the normative is responsible for the hostility that the study of conventions—indeed that the so-called historical approach itself—has engendered in many corners. Still, if our aim is the recognition of what is significant in individual works, it is difficult to imagine how we can do without that concept. To clarify my meaning I cite one illustrative example. In an essay on Dufay's tonal system[9] I called attention to one interpretation of melodic organization in the Italian monodic Lauda and the early two-part madrigals: "The orientation of each section of the melody toward a goal-tone and the ordering of those goal-tones in terms of one another—above all the dominance of final and upper fifth—give stable polar points toward which we can orient ourselves in the sound-space. Thus there is realized in the early two-part madrigals and the monodic Lauda an ordering of the sound-space that must be recognized as the basic form of tonality."[10] Now the features of Italian melody which are here singled out—about the description there can be no disagreement—are in general characteristic of European melody after the end of the first millennium. What is more, they are directly called for in expositions of the modal system from that time. In short they are normative in every sense. With the experience of the music of several intervening centuries behind us we may feel that we are witnessing in those repertoires the birth of tonality. But that would ignore the evidence of the theory and practice of their own time, which shows them to be fully developed specimens of a related, but quite different, system. It is one thing to recognize the caterpillar as that creature which will one day be transformed to become a butterfly, but it is surely quite another to mistake it, as it is, for a butterfly.

There is yet one more aspect to the problem of the illumination of works of music by historical information about norms. It is raised by music that, in some sense, incorporates common material: Christian chant, composed in many cases on established models or from a common stock of melodic formulas; liturgical and secular music of the Middle Ages and Renaissance employing an array of cantus firmus and parody techniques; music of the eighteenth and nineteenth centuries, where there may be a sharing of materials and techniques from the most specific to the most general. The study of one work in any of these categories informs the study of the other works of its kind.

In the first case—Christian chant—the composite character of melodies is of their essence; they cannot be regarded as though they had been through-composed, for the order of events in those melodies is to be recognized by reference to the strategic position of standard opening, extending, and closing formulas far more than from the persuasiveness of any inner logic or syntax.

In the last case, recurrent ideas are frequently those which lend a measure of referential meaning to the works in which they occur: the horn call at the beginning of Beethoven's "Lebewohl" Sonata, the sarabande rhythm at the beginning of his *Egmont* Overture, to cite two simple and obvious examples. Of course those clichés can and must be explicated in terms of the structure of the piece, but we lose a part of the meaning of the work if we ignore the reference.

Other works share modes of expression that are not nearly so concrete in their meaning, but that point nonetheless to vocabularies to which we can gain access only through the study of the several works which share them. One splendid example is the celebrated affinity, in manner and affect, between Mozart's G Minor Quintet (K. 516) and his G Minor Symphony (K. 550). In considering them together we can only gain in our sensitivity to their composer's expressive means.

While analysis deals, and must deal, with individual works of art in their wholeness and uniqueness, still there may be a sense in which each work is but a moment, frozen, in the creative life of the artist, and in that sense each work belongs to a larger whole. I do not see that it is necessary to regard these two points of view as mutually contradictory. Referring to his own practice, Picasso has remarked, "Paintings are but research and experiment. I never do a painting as a work of art. All of them are researches. I search constantly and there is a logical sequence in all this research. That is why I number them and date them." [11]

"Words to the public, of little use to the scholar," we might remark. Yet perhaps we behave on some such belief, all but the most pertinaciously new-critical among us.

4. The coordination of the musical work with the world of which it is a product. With this as a goal, musical analysis is an investigation into music's functions and environmental relations.

This statement of aims appears quite naturally to belong to the special discipline of ethnomusicology. But that impression is dispelled by Frank Harrison in the volume on *Musicology* of the Princeton Studies, "Humanistic Scholarship in America." Having made a strong appeal for the study of the institutions, the circumstances, and the beliefs that have nurtured and conditioned music, he wrote: "Looked at in this way, it is the function of all musicology to be in fact ethnomusicology." [12]

If we could believe that it were possible always to achieve the aims of musical analysis in the three senses to which I have so far alluded, then Harrison's suggestion would merely serve the filling out of the picture. But I strongly suspect that his conviction is born of long experience in the study of Christian liturgical music, and of the certain knowledge that analysis, even in the sense of laying bare the facts, is hardly possible without reference to the rituals which music served. Here, then, is at least one area in which the study of music's environmental relations is a crucial step in its analysis. But this must be the case wherever music has, by common consent, served some ritual or broadly defined expressive purpose.

Analysis in this sense would seek to comprehend tonality from the seventeenth to the late nineteenth centuries not only as the remarkable force for the creation of coordinated and directed musical structure that it is, but also as an instrument of a discourse of affects. It would seek to comprehend the rhythm of the Ars Antiqua, not alone for its achievement in imparting both vertical and horizontal unity to the polyphonic texture, but also in the light of the force with which the notion of "perfection" held the composers and theoreticians of that time. What in the first instance amounts to an aesthetic, in the second a metaphysical position, having called forth musical practices for their realization, must be regarded as clues for the understanding of those practices.

Now I must return to my first category, the analysis of music on the level of facts, for there is a point of view that I have so far left entirely out of consideration. It is that the goal of musical analysis is the conditioning of the listener for perceptive hearing. With this goal, musical analysis is the search for principles that will "codify previous hearing and extend and enrich the listener's perceptive powers by making listening more efficient and meaningful, by explaining the formerly inexplicable." (The quotation is from Milton Babbitt's review of Felix Salzer's book *Structural Hearing*.) [13]

This point of departure differs radically from all the others that I have suggested so far, for it recognizes as its object and as a unique mode of experience the response to the work of art. While I come to it last here, it is the first and usually the exclusive consideration when the analysis is pursued, so to speak, for its own sake and not in the context of a historical investigation. But are historical considerations irrelevant in such a case? Is it, on the other hand, an approach that is *hors de combat* where the historian is concerned? To phrase the question in the better-exercised battle terms, is there an antagonism between a "musical" and a "historical" point of view?

Such an antagonism would rest, presumably, on differences between the terms in which the work was conceived and those in which it can be most fully comprehended. As one such case I cite an analysis of Haydn's Quartet op. 76, no. 5.[14] In this analysis, all the progressions of tonicizations in the quartet are shown to be derivable from that of the opening passage by the operations of transposition, retrogression, and what is called "rotation" (the tonics of the progression are arranged in a circle, and one has the option of starting the process from any point on the circle).[15] Let us assume that the assertion is empirically verified. Even so, the analysis in its present terms would not have been possible, or, at least, it would have been highly improbable, before Schenker and Schoenberg. Is it necessarily irreconcilable with what *would* have been possible? Not, it seems to me, if we proceed with sympathy. Musical analysis is communicated in a conceptual language, but the modes of cognition of the composer at work may be quite different. The translation from one to the other is an ongoing process. The composer may hold all the aspects of his work in suspension in what may be quite abstract cognitions until he commits them to a score, where they continue to reside and await discovery. In far more colorful terms, but in a similar vein, the psychologist Rudolf Arnheim has written this:

Artists, in particular, have learned to tread cautiously when it comes to reporting the internal events that produce their works. They watch with suspicion all attempts to invade the inner workshop and to systematize its secrets. Surely, creative processes are not the only ones to rely upon impulses from outside the realm of awareness, but they are unique in that their results give the impression of being beyond and above what can be accounted for by the familiar mental mechanisms. To the artist himself, his accomplishment is often a cause of surprise and admiration, a gift from somewhere rather than the traceable outcome of his efforts. It is viewed as a privilege that might be forfeited like the golden treasures of the fairy tales, which vanish when curiosity ignores the warnings and peeps at the miracle-working spirit. The privilege and nuisance of relying on helpers who do not take orders require those abnormalities of behavior for which artists have been known: those fears of power failure, those irritations and despairs, the agonies of waiting, the manic delights of success, the elaborate rituals necessary to create propitious conditions.[16]

Simply stated, there are differences between the creative and the re-creative processes. There is no prior reason to expect that the thinking of the composer should resemble in form the thinking of the analyst.

If there is any question to be raised about analyses of the type that I cited just above, it is not about their anachronistic character—that is, about the inaptness of their terms for the period in which the work was composed—but once again about the significance of their observations. That is the question that suggests study beyond the single work in isolation.[17] On the other hand, if there is a residual—as there must be—when we measure individual works against contemporaneous standards, it begs the question to account for that residual with those popular paradoxes, composers ahead of their time and critics or theorists behind theirs.

We may ask ourselves how much we understand about the music of our own time, even when composers, in their new pedagogical roles, have given us more abundant documentation of their intentions than ever before in the history of music. Their lectures, journal articles, and program notes have left us in the main unsatisfied, if what we expect of them is guides for our hearing. More than likely that is not what they mean to give us, for they are understandably preoccupied with matters of technique; not with the thing itself, but with how it comes to be. And certainly not with how it may be comprehended! Future students of our music will have to read their writings with a sensitivity for their place in the total musical context of our time. In our search for guides to the music of the past we are obliged to exercise the same caution with respect to nonmusical documents. We must recognize, for example, speculative theory, which, as Guido of Arezzo wrote in the eleventh century, "is useful to philosophers, but not to singers," or practices which fail of recognition by theoreticians who, like medieval illustrators, copy not from nature but from their predecessors.

The true historical approach to music is, as it were, yesterday's musical approach, and conclusions from today's musical approach will add to the fund of tomorrow's historical knowledge.

I have taken too many twists and turns to offer a summary. But if my arguments bear on any single conclusion, it is what everyone knows: The analysis of music, like the analysis of anything, is best conducted in the context of all the information that relates to it. Polemics about the musical and the historical points of view would flounder if only we could agree upon the need for a sympathetic and canny, yet irreverent, approach to evidence of every cast.

CHAPTER 4

On Historical Criticism

There is a rattling of skeletons in the halls of humane learning.

It is natural that in the conduct of our daily work we avoid direct and interfering contact with its fundamentals. But it is clear, too, that there must come times of reflection about the goals that are defined and the ways that are marked. If sharp attacks upon tradition are symptomatic, then this is such a time.

The most trenchant criticisms have reached for the widest audience: the wholesale denunciation of humanities and humanists in William Arrowsmith's essay "The Shame of Our Graduate Schools"[1] and the radical curative proposals offered by Eric Larabee in his essay "Saving the Humanities" ("shattering the sanctity of jealously-guarded department boundaries, strangling the Ph.D. octopus, punishing pointless research, abolishing tenure, lowering inflated salaries . . .").[2]

In the field of musical scholarship acrid exchanges in the pages of *Perspectives of New Music* and the *Journal of the American Musicological Society*[3] have been only the sharp edge of a series that includes some rather more reflective writing.[4] The field of art history has seen some serious theorizing in the work of James Ackerman, E. H. Gombrich, Erwin Panofsky, and Meyer Schapiro.[5]

A recurrent theme in this new round of questioning and defining stems from a unique condition of historical studies in the arts. It is that the central object of study is an artifact born into a special, that is, an aesthetic, relationship with the culture of which it is a part, and which continues through its survival to be both a historical record and an object of aesthetic perception. It is a work of art, and the historian is obliged to come to terms with it as such; "the curse and the blessing," Panofsky wrote, "of art history."[6] There is a repeated show of concern whether we have met that obligation, whether our history is sound from the standpoint of what is called "criticism." Ackerman, Arrowsmith, and Kerman, especially, have argued that a more prominent place for criticism in our methodology is the most pressing need, and I shall take that assertion as a point of departure in the present essay. But I shall suggest that the diagnosis on which it rests can be misleading, that certainly in music-historical literature critical assessments abound, and that the issue is not how much or how central but rather what kind and on what premises. I shall offer an alternative view, not that history and criticism are too widely separated but that they have been, in a sense, too closely confounded. The cry for criticism has had something in it of the cranky, nagging child who does not articulate what it is he wants. We need to know what a critical account of an artwork may be, or what it may seek to do; and we need to know how it relates to a historical account.

I have already raised the first of these questions and attempted a number of formulations of the objectives of criticism, as the basis for a series of arguments for the relevance of the historian's evidence to the interpretation of musical works (see Chapter 3). I argued that in the analysis of artworks we seek to distinguish the fortuitous from the significant, and the uniquely significant from the conventional, and that the evidence of the historian is directly relevant to that task. This is the "historical point of view," in one sense of that expression.[7] My objective here is to explore another sense by asking whether there is a special "historical account" of artworks.

_____

How does the historian understand a work of art? To begin the investigation of this question I should like to set forth one point of view about how it is to be answered, a point of view that has had great influence on the discipline of musicology and on related fields. It distinguishes, first, between a commonplace meaning of "understand" that suggests a sense of empathetic or intuitive familiarity, and the scientific understanding of natural or historical phenomena: "I understand how you feel," as against "Learn to understand the principles of the internal combustion engine." In the second of these meanings—and it is only the second that is relevant to the systematic study of anything, according to this point of view—to understand something is to be able to explain it, and to explain a thing is to give its causes. Briefly, understanding is knowledge of causes.[8]

To complete the exposition of this point of view it is necessary to clarify what is meant by *causes*. They are of two kinds: precipitating conditions—conditions that must obtain in order for a given event to occur—and general laws under which the given event must occur whenever the specified conditions obtain. If I wish to explain some phenomenon, for example the production of ice cubes in my home freezer, I must show that certain conditions prevail—the tray of water has been placed in an enclosure in which a temperature below 32 degrees F is maintained—and I must cite a general law that is in effect: "At sea level the freezing point of water is 32 degrees F." It follows that the power to *explain* is tantamount to the power to *predict,* for, given the precipitating conditions, the general law tells us that the event in question will ensue. If I can explain my ice cubes, I can also predict that whenever I place another tray of water in the same enclosure under the same conditions I shall have more ice cubes.[9] Each case in which the same train of events is set in motion is covered by the same general law, and this paradigm for explanation is therefore known as the "covering-law model."

The general viewpoint that I have briefly outlined here is known as the neopositivist position. Its central thesis is that scientific study means systematic investigation of causes, in the sense of the covering-law model for explanation. While this doctrine took form earliest in the context of the natural sciences, its wider application to all fields of knowledge is the subject of continuing and urgent discussion. For the study of history the central neopositivist document is Carl Hempel's well-known essay "The Function of General Laws in History."[10] In his address to the New York meeting of the International Musicological Society in 1961, Arthur Mendel affirmed the correctness of Hempel's position and formally extended its application to the discipline of musicology.[11] In the course of his exposition Mendel distinguished, in terms of levels of generality, between two phases of the musicologist's work: his establishing of lower-order facts, such as the date and place of birth of some composer, and the relating of higher-order facts, such as musical styles. The first has to do with the treatment of evidence, the second with what I shall call, rather loosely for the moment, the writing of narrative history.

For the remainder of this essay I shall confine myself to the second of these subjects, and I shall raise these fundamental questions:

(1) Does causal explanation according to the covering-law model adequately represent what historians do when they explain historical phenomena?[12]

(2) What are the consequences of placing causal knowledge at the center of music-historical study?

It might be well to reflect first on the special problems that may be encountered when the historical facts we seek to explain are artworks or classes of artworks. If we wish to explain how it happened, say, that Haydn composed twelve symphonies for performance in London, we can readily refer to a chain of events and conditions that lead up to the fact in question. But suppose we seek to explain why it is that in the next to last of those symphonies (no. 103) there is a return near the conclusion of the first movement to the tempo and music of the introduction. Now we seem to enter a different realm, for it is hardly possible to imagine such an explanation in terms of precipitating conditions and covering laws. This would suggest that there are at least two kinds of explaining of artworks: explaining the *causes,* but also explaining the *quality* of their being.

In music history we often explain one work or style by reference to another, antecedent work or style. The establishing of the relationship of antecedence is a necessary and illuminating part of history writing, but as causal explanation it can, in most cases, hope to rely only on the thin paste of *post hoc ergo propter hoc.*

Another form of explanation frequently encountered in music history is that in which an individual work is identified with a class or type about which some general characteristic is alleged. As an example we may take the following sentence: "Four-part writing was of course no novelty *c.* 1300 . . . ; but its appearance in several English compositions . . . when considered together with the attempt at six-part writing in *Sumer is icumen in* . . . seems to show a predilection on the part of the English for greater fullness of sound . . ."[13] Associations of this type increase our power of understanding particulars. As soon as we are able to say that the particular in question is a such-and-such, we have taken hold of it. But we have by no means given a causal explanation of it.

Among the criticisms that have been raised against Hempel's thesis, some do not question the historian's interest in causes but nevertheless deny both the possibility of collecting enough information about the circumstances under which events took place and the possibility of formulating satisfactory general laws. With respect to conditions, in order to make a scientific explanation of Napoleon's decision to invade Russia historians would need to know far more about the emperor's public and private life than they could ever hope to learn (more, no doubt, than Napoleon himself knew). And with respect to laws in history, they must be of such generality as to be trivial, or of such specificity as to apply to only a single case.

We may take as an example the statement "Louis XIV was unpopular because his policy was detrimental to France."[14] The general law on which this explanation rests might take this unimpressive form: "Rulers whose policies are detrimental to their countries become unpopular." Or we might fill out the statement of the law with a complex of factors including Louis' expansionist foreign policy, his heavy taxation, and his religious persecutions. But as it gains in explanatory power it narrows in its applicability, until the conditions it specifies are met only by the case of Louis XIV. Then it might resemble general laws in form, but it would be, in fact, an explication of the particular case. And herein lies the thrust of an altogether different notion of explanation.[15] In this view the explanations that satisfy historians are indeed explications, detailed unfoldings of the case under consideration, in the context of all that can be discovered about the attendant circumstances. These may be related through an interpretative transformation of facts, so that they manifest a recognizable pattern or theme. In this view explaining is a kind of ordering process, like explaining the functioning of a sentence. To be sure, somewhere in the background there are ultimate regularities and correlations on which it all depends, but they are of an extremely general and fundamental sort, like the broadest generalizations about human behavior. It is not from these that the explanation derives its power. It is, rather, from the coherence of the pattern that historians have recognized. They are credited not with discovering that a particular phenomenon falls under a general law but with finding that a number of elements may be brought together into a single pattern in such a way as to be made intelligible in terms of one another. This view rejects the ultimate artificiality, the belief in the separability in practice of observation and theory—as Taine had it, "Après la collection des faits, la recherche des causes."[16]

These criticisms are made on logical grounds and from reflection about what historians in fact *do*. Others stem from consideration not of the truth but of the usefulness of the covering-law hypothesis. It is useful to pure scientists, for they are principally interested in the laws themselves; they value them because they explain. It is useful to applied scientists, for their chief business is making predictions. And it is useful to geologists, say, or to musicologists working with their evidence, for both are concerned in reasoning from present evidence through laws to past facts. But none of these statements describes the principal purpose of historians writing narrative history, for their objective is to establish connections among facts of which they are already in possession.[17]

The question of value may be approached from still another direction. The covering-law hypothesis, and indeed the general movement toward "scientific" procedure in historical studies of which that hypothesis is a late and quintessential manifestation, answered a pressing need. It was the need to bring to light the assumptions that are, as Hempel wrote, "buried under the gravestones 'hence,' 'therefore,' 'because,' and the like," and to erect a standard against which it would be possible to show that explanations thus offered are often "poorly founded or downright unacceptable."[18] It was to affirm that the responsibility for logical, deductive reasoning, to the limits of the evidence, was not to be circumvented by recourse to "intuitive conviction" and "historical sensitivity." I believe that Hempel's argument is best interpreted in that light, and not as a demand for strict adherence to the letter of the covering-law model. For Hempel himself recognized the impossibility of meeting such a demand in history; thus he spoke of "explanation *sketches,*" as others have spoken of "loose laws" and "probability hypotheses." [19] With this interpretation, then, the covering-law model is but a maximal formulation for the sort of reasoning to which historians are obligated, and for their recognition that events are orderly rather than capricious. The need for such an orientation is hardly to be denied.

It is in the leap from that emphasis to the central placement of causal knowledge in historical inquiry that the difficulties are to be located.

———————

And now I have returned to my principal subject. For it seems to me that in the practice of musicology explaining "what" has been heavily prejudiced by a preoccupation with explaining "why." The historian's account of what the work *is,* is conditioned by the habit of inquiring how it came to be. This is the second "historical point of view." The historical fact is understood principally through its antecedents and consequences, and the sequence of historical facts is linked in a genealogical chain of cause and effect. This view is supported, as we have seen, by the neopositivist approach to explanation. But it is also reinforced by a number of inherited beliefs about the nature of historical change and historical necessity that come, paradoxically, from another direction altogether. It is to those that I turn now.

We may begin by considering Guido Adler's propaedeutic postulate for musicology, given in his *Methode der Musikgeschichte:* "The task of music history is the investigation and the setting forth of the developmental paths of music." [20] The *Shorter Oxford English Dictionary* offers two families of meaning for the word "develop," as technical term in mathematics, photography, and warfare, and then this group: "To unfold or unroll, to unfurl, to unveil, to disclose, to bring out all that is contained in, to bring forth from a latent or elementary condition, to cause to grow what exists in the germ, to grow into a fuller, higher, or more mature condition." These definitions have in common the notions either of disclosure of what is already present or of realization of a stored potential. In either case a process is suggested for which the course is charted and the end point determined. Now the context for these definitions is largely biological, and we shall probably object that no such determinist ideas underlie our notions of development in history. Yet in the history of art, and in political and social history, there is a strong tradition for just such a concept.

It goes back, in any case, to Aristotle. He wrote, in the *Physics,* "Those things are natural which by a continuous movement originated by an internal principle arrive at some completion" and "Each step in the series is for the sake of the next." In the *Poetics* he wrote of the development of tragedy, "It was in fact only after a long series of changes that the movement of Tragedy stopped on its attaining to its natural form."[21]

From Leo Schrade's essay "Renaissance: The Historical Conception of an Epoch," we learn of the scheme of cultural development in terms of which the people of the fifteenth and sixteenth centuries saw their age.[22] Writers in all disciplines rejoiced in their participation in a "restoration," "renovation," "return to the light," "rebirth." The original or model was, of course, antiquity, in some versions together with the early Christian era. The two epochs—the original and the rebirth—had been separated by an "immense interval," a "lacuna," an "exile," an "abyss," a "dark ignorance," or "middle age." The rebirth was followed by a period of growth that, as Schrade observed, "stimulated the assumption of the biologic process of passing through the phases of infancy or youth, mature manhood, and old age. It seems but natural that the biological idea of an organic growth toward fullest ripeness suggested the principles of progressiveness and perfection to the summit of potentialities."

This scheme of history again held a central position in the self-image of eighteenth-century artists and scholars. Immanuel Kant wrote in 1784:

All the capacities implanted in a creature by nature are destined to unfold themselves, completely and conformably to their end, in the course of time . . . In man, as the only rational creature on earth, those natural capacities which are directed toward the use of his reason could be completely developed only in the species and not in the individual, for reason requires the production of an almost inconceivable series of generations in order that Nature's germs, as implanted in our species, may be at last unfolded to that stage of development which is completely conformable to her inherent design.[23]

(Hegel, not long after, took the same doctrine, and nearly the same language, as a central tenet of his philosophy of history: "The principle of development involves the existence of a latent germ of being—a capacity or potentiality striving to realize itself.")[24] In a work begun also in 1784, Johann Gottfried Herder put it this way: "As a botanist cannot obtain a complete knowledge of a plant unless he follow it from the seed through its germination, blossoming, and decay, such is Grecian history to us."[25] That this doctrine should find expression within the context of a discussion of Greek civilization is, of course, especially meaningful. For once again that civilization, at its height, represented for the second half of the eighteenth century a perfection, a standard that was to be emulated.

All this is explicit in the work of the influential archeologist Johann Joachim Winckelmann. In his monumental *History of Ancient Art,* published in 1764, he distinguished three stages: "The arts which are dependent on drawing have, like all inventions, commenced with the *necessary;* the next object of research was *beauty;* and finally the *superfluous* followed." Here is his summary of the course of Greek art:

The earliest attempts, especially in the drawing of figures, represented, not the manner in which a man appears to us, but what he is; not a view of his body, but the outline of his shadow. From this simplicity of shape the artist next proceeded to examine proportions. This inquiry taught exactness [and] gave confidence and success to his endeavours after grandeur, and at last gradually raised art among the Greeks to the highest beauty. After all the parts constituting grandeur and beauty were united, the artist, in seeking to embellish them, fell into the error of profuseness; art consequently lost its grandeur, and the loss was finally followed by its utter downfall.[26]

This evaluation is important, for it shows that "dread of corruption," as Gombrich has termed it, through which the new "classicism" of the eighteenth century was to be purified.[27] It implied an appeal for the perpetuation of ideal forms that Winckelmann had already made explicit in his *Thoughts on the Imitation of Greek Works in Painting and Sculpture,* published in 1755. The economy and incisiveness that are asked for here became and have remained, as we know, synonymous with both the notion of "perfection" and the concept of "Classical."

Just as our conception of the Renaissance as a historical epoch follows, and continues to reinforce, the self-image of Renaissance individuals, so our continued designation of the second half of the eighteenth century as the era of Classicism rests ultimately upon, and preserves, ideals that were given expression at the time. And a single view of history—the developmental view—underlies both cases.

The active role that this theory of history plays in the practice of musicology is most apparent in textbooks of music history, although these do not by any means constitute its only sphere of influence. I shall cite a characteristic passage, and let it evoke others like it. And by way of preface to all the quotations that follow, I should like to make it quite clear that it is not my purpose to take issue with them or their authors directly, but rather to relate them to a framework of theory.

Here, then, is a passage about *Euryanthe* from a widely read introductory textbook: "When Emma's spectral funeral music . . . announced in its transformation at the end of the opera that the sinner is redeemed, the seed was planted from which, at Wagner's hands, the whole form of Music Drama was to grow."[28] We may read this sort of language as literary gift wrapping, enclosing less theoretical meaning than appears on the surface. But here is a less picturesque statement by a different author which is, nevertheless, informed by the same doctrine: "Instrumental music in the early 17th century was in a different stage of development from vocal music. Vocal music had to assimilate the new technique of monody . . . but instrumental music for the most part had only to continue along the path that had already been marked out before the end of the Renaissance."[29] Here is the same view again, expressed in a more recent textbook of history, and this time stated quite explicitly as theory: "Musical materials have to be 'used up,' their potential fully exploited, before style can move ahead on the long line of history. As in a development section of Beethoven, the material already introduced has to be shredded down to its constituent fibers, all its meaning extracted, before new meaning will seem meaningful."[30]

There can be no question that the developmental doctrine is a prominent feature in the philosophical background of historical musicology. Before asking how it manifests itself in the evaluation of musical works I shall need to make one final digression.

The concept of historical development falls squarely in the field of a fundamental and recurring philosophical controversy, that between the positions of nominalism and realism. To the nominalist, categories of particulars are constructs: artificial, arbitrary, and practical. The general terms by which we designate them are *names* only, and the study of categories amounts to the study of the linguistic rules that govern the use of the terms that represent them. For the realist, particulars are grouped together because of properties held in common, and general terms derive their meanings from the real features of the objects to which they refer—not the other way about. For the nominalist, categories are hypothetical and are valued for their usefulness in the management of data. For the realist, the common features of particulars by which they are set off in categories are independently "true" and are to be discovered. Whether a particular belongs to a certain category is for the nominalist a formal question of definition, of the use of the terms in the case, but not so for the realist.

For a concrete example from music history of the approach to a single problem from these opposed points of view we may consider the controversy over the status of the concept "Baroque." The nominalist position was represented by John Mueller in his essay, characteristically entitled "Baroque: Is It Datum, Hypothesis, or Tautology?"[31] In answering the rhetorical question of his title Mueller treated the style-category of Baroque as an invention of historians, thereby denying the first of his alternatives, and then challenged its soundness because, he argued, the integrity of the category could not be demonstrated. But Manfred Bukofzer claimed for the Baroque the status of "period in its own right"—not a construct, but a collection of real attributes.[32] In the following statement by Paul Henry Lang the realist position is taken a step further, in that the particulars belonging to the category *owe* their characteristics to the circumstance of their having been born into the category: "The Baroque stands vividly before us for its power to mold all the arts according to its own eloquent spirit."[33] Here "Baroque" is no longer a designation for the common attributes of Baroque artworks; it denotes a distillation of these attributes in ideal form, a generative principle, an essence. Baroque works are no longer particulars that share certain properties; they are individual embodiments of a single essence. In the light of that distinction Karl Popper has introduced the term "essentialism" for this extreme form of the realist doctrine.[34]

The historical theory in which the causes of events are sought in developmental processes is an essentialist theory. For at the core of each process of development—whether it is of a genre, of a school, or of a technique—there must be something that is recognizably the same even while it changes with respect to its outer form. We affirm this in our willingness to name what it is that is undergoing development—"music drama" and "instrumental music" in the textbook passages that I cited above. Those names refer to essences or universals, and to trace the development of such genres is to follow the successive embodiments of their essences. But the study of individual embodiments is undertaken as means, not as end, for they reveal the different forms that the essence may take; that is, they reveal its *potentials*. Indeed, an essence may be regarded as the sum of its potential forms, and to really know an essence we must follow it through all of those forms. This is the sense, once again, of Herder's figure: "The botanist cannot obtain a complete knowledge of a plant unless he follow it from the seed through its germination, blossoming, and decay." From this point of view the study of anything is necessarily historical.

Goethe warned once: "Too much inquiring after the sources of things is dangerous. We should rather concentrate on phenomena as given realities."[35] What a curious and unexpected thing it is that an idealist position—"All knowledge is historical"—and one that arises from a positivist orientation—"All knowledge is causal knowledge"—should come together in the doctrine of historicism that is the antithesis of Goethe's meaning!

We can anticipate three characteristics in the approach to the musical work from the developmental point of view. It will be regarded as the embodiment of an essence; it will be understood in terms of its antecedents and consequences; and it will be seen in the context of a process that culminates in the fulfillment or perfection of the essence that it informs. The following selections of music-historical writings are all taken from a single field of inquiry, the study of music of the Classical era. This is done in the interest of maintaining a consistent framework, not because that field is unique in its theoretical bearing. And this time I quote not from general textbooks but from scholarly publications intended for a professional audience.

First, passages from an article on "The Symphonies of Padre Martini" (the title is significant, for its form suggests that the author means to give a general account of his repertory).[36] Martini's works are repeatedly considered in terms of their embodiment of the Baroque and Classical styles. Thus, "The first book of Sonatas marked Martini's farewell to the Baroque," and "The Symphony no. 2 illustrates Martini's approach to the new [i.e., Classical] style." In the following passages the evaluation of musical works depends upon a comparison with past and/or future counterparts: the slow movement of Symphony no. 22 is "retrospective, for it begins with the Baroque chromatic descending tetrachord in the bass," and "Oddly enough, Martini reverts in the late symphonies to the descending chromatic tetrachord," or "Martini disappoints us, for while the symphony dated 1736 is *au courant* with the conventions of the day his later stylistic progress is small, and does not keep pace with the important changes taking place around him." Finally, in the polarity of a "nascent Classical style" on one hand, and a "full-fledged Classical style" on the other, we have the familiar image of birth and development to maturity.

Next I quote passages from an encyclopedia article on the symphony.[37] Regarding the music of Florian Gassmann, "his orchestral treatment . . . points to the future," and regarding that of Mozart, "Although Mozart did not consciously seek new and surprising effects, he was a pioneer with respect to the greater independence of the winds." "Massoneau's *Symphonie la Tempête et la Calme* (1794) may be regarded as preparing the way for the *Pastoral Symphony*." These passages, again, make their reports in terms of past and future. Characteristic too is the tendency to make no distinction between forerunner and progenitor, that is, to require no further evidence that forerunner *is* progenitor. This tendency seems always to carry with it the attribution of the greatest significance to the earliest occurrence of a phenomenon or trait.

The growth image is projected in this passage: "In the early years of the [eighteenth] century the overture is important as the cradle of the new Classic tone language . . . With composers of the first generation the sonata form of the first movement is only rudimentary . . . The second generation of overture composers shows greater mastery of sonata form." In this last passage, too, it must be plain that "sonata form" is an ideal, an essence. For how is it otherwise possible to speak in terms of degrees of mastery of a technique that has nowhere yet been fully defined or worked out? Of course we know the experience of the conscious quest for the solution of an intellectual or artistic problem. We are unable to specify the solution while we seek it, but we recognize it once it is presented to us. What I wish to observe here is the tendency to assume such a structure for all historical processes, and to derive from it every judgment about works of art.

There is an apparent difference between these last quotations and the passages about Padre Martini. Those were phrased in a heavily value-laden language; these seem objective and noncommittal. We might say that the first are *interpretative,* the second *descriptive.* But herein lies an issue of the first importance. The single criterion of value for the interpretative statements is the same developmental framework that gives form to the descriptive statements. The question is whether a descriptive statement on these lines can ever be bare of value connotations. Can we say "ripe Classical style" without implying a higher order of musical achievement than is suggested by "nascent Classical style?" Surely not, for all statements of this type are supported by a theory of history that imposes a hierarchy on their subjects. Every stage in a developmental process is a step nearer to the realization of potentials, hence what *is* is an improvement over what *was.* That is the spirit in which Hegel could write "The real world *is* as it *ought to be*" (italics mine).[38] The only difference between the passages on Martini and those on the symphony is in the degree to which their assessments are made explicit.

Let us return to the encyclopedia article. In the treatment of Philipp Emanuel Bach the interpenetration of historical position and artistic position is complete:

Although he was among the most respected and influential personalities of the 18th century both as theoretician and composer, he did not always succeed in coordinating all the musical factors in the full Classical sense . . . A conflict arises from Bach's breadth of background in the traditions of the past, which is coupled with a striking futuristic tendency. He combined Baroque, Classic, and Romantic characteristics in a mixture that rarely resulted in a satisfying synthesis. In Bach's symphonies sensitive and striking details often interrupt the flow and balance of the over-all conception, which is evidence of the basic opposition between *Empfindsamkeit* and ripe Classicism.

The assessment of the man's position as an artist is truly indistinguishable from his location on the historical continuum. If his music is unsuccessful, it is *because* he occupies an awkward position historically. (We know of other composers, of course, whose mark of artistic achievement is their position not between, but in advance of, scheduled historical developments.)[39]

Finally I quote from a monograph on *The Symphonies of Joseph Haydn*. Once again, measurement is taken in terms of the past and future: "Thus, the Salomon Symphonies sum up and synthesize all [Haydn] has achieved in the field, and at the same time look far forward into the future, to the orchestral world of Beethoven and Schubert, of Mendelssohn and Schumann." Defined goals are achieved through a gradual development: "The first six [Salomon Symphonies] show a steady progress in the direction of the 'English Taste.'" And what lies at the end of the development is the perfection of the form, the full realization of its potentials; last is best: "As the London period progresses, this tendency [i.e., the dramatic function of the slow introduction] emerges ever more clearly, and by 1794–95 [symphonies no. 102–104] the formal and emotional necessity of the introductory slow sections is quite apparent. In no. 104 the profundity of the introduction reaches its height."[40] Given the now familiar theoretical framework we might have anticipated that judgment, if not its paradoxical wording.

In this philosophy art is a collective, impersonal enterprise—tracings of the passage of time, now more, now less distinct, now leading, now trailing behind. Artworks are but manifestations of an idea, like the shadows in Plato's cave, whose value is measured by the closeness with which they approximate their models, and whose necessities are imposed from without.

In our quest for the sources of art we neglect its quality. We do so to the disadvantage of our faculty for judging artworks, for our standards of judgment have little to do with the ways in which we apprehend works. Then we are left with a history in which aesthetics and hermeneutics play no significant part. But it may yet be that the same obsession with causality that yields such a curiously one-sided history is responsible also for distortions in the narrative for which so much is sacrificed; that our categorical prejudgments effect not only the interpretation and assessment of artworks, but even those matters that we take to be open to "objective," "scientific" treatment: the reading of artworks and the attribution of authorship, chronology, and provenance. That is a question for further inquiry.

CHAPTER 5

The Present as History

My subject is modern music as it falls under the eye—and the spell—of the historian. Ultimately the discussion will focus on four books in which there is a historical assessment of the musical present.[1] But I do not see any way of treating this subject in isolation. On one side there is no divorcing our view of the present from our habits in writing of the past. On the other side the historical mode has come to affect the writing of critics and the beliefs—even the composing—of composers. In fact historical assessments of modern music are the most acute and most easily recognizable symptoms of the conditions of historical thought. What is often referred to as a crisis in contemporary music will, on reflection, turn out to be a crisis largely in talk about music. Hence I shall ask the reader's patience through a sometimes necessarily loose-jointed exploration of the present-day historical state of mind.

I shall begin with an innocent statement about how the historian's task might plausibly be construed: "We historians are engaged in the business of finding out what happened, and of telling it as it was."[2] We say that if we can never quite realize that ambition, it is because what happened is over and done with and we can be observers only of the traces that have been left. To compensate, we have developed whole arsenals of techniques for forcing the evidence to reveal that to which it bears witness. Judging from the way we allocate our energies and resources, we evidently feel that if only there were more evidence, if only the evidence would reveal all, our job would be done; all but the writing up of what we have found out.

However, when we direct our attention to the present and to the recent past, there are fewer mysteries posed by lost documents and forgotten traditions. No longer alone in the silence that is the historian's normal environment, we are surrounded by witnesses creating a din of testimony. Mired hopelessly in the bog of evidence about modern music, we shall have to recognize that the historian's excuse for the imperfections of history—there is still so much we don't know—has been part of a grand self-deception. When the excuse about evidence is no longer available, we shall be closer to knowing why our histories must be revised than this reason, given by Richard L. Crocker in his preface to *A History of Musical Style:* "Our basic ideas about what happened in music history clearly need overhauling to make them accord with the facts brought out by modern research." For the historians who write it all up are like the witnesses to the rape in *Rashomon,* or those to the events in the Tonkin Gulf during the first week of August 1965. They leave us with a strong impression about the habits and passions that mediate their telling of the story, but not with a compelling sense of confidence that we have found out what happened. We are used to that, so far as *Rashomon* and the Departments of State and Defense are concerned. "Varieties of truth" is one way of saying what art and politics are about. But *history,* we hold, ought not to be about what might have happened, or about what the historian wishes had happened; it is about what happened. This belief represents what has been our guiding standard of historical truth. When we fail to agree we are inclined to blame the lacunae in the evidence, or to charge one another with an unskillful or prejudiced handling of the evidence. We might try, for once, blaming the standard itself. This is my purpose: to argue that the difficulties over telling what *is* have something important to teach us about our ways of telling what *was.*

There are a number of presuppositions underlying our standard of historical truth which control the forms of historical thought, just as they control the forms of scientific thought, and even thought about ordinary perception and knowledge. It is through the sharing of those presuppositions that musical scholars—historians and others—constitute a community. I shall try to describe some of those presuppositions, and in order to hold them in relief *as* presuppositions, and not as revelations, I shall try also to describe alternatives.

―――――――

"Tell what happened, and tell it as it was." All the presuppositions that I wish to describe will be revealed in expanding upon the two clauses of that simple instruction. The first—"Tell what happened"—represents what is commonly called the narrative view of history. History tells a story (Crocker writes of "the story of style") in which events (or pieces, or styles, or genres) are related in the order in which they occurred, and in such a way as to show how one led to the other. History relates events *sequentially* and *causally*.

Now this is a very old doctrine, but it remains as hardy as a redwood tree. Still, as though we had been about to topple it, the doctrine has been newly fortified from an unexpected corner: the philosophy of neo-positivism. It is held in that school that in order to give an account of anything—to explain it—we must show its causes. To do that we must show two things: what went before it, and how its occurrence is governed by general laws. With reference to the latter, this way of explaining things has come to be known as explanation according to the "covering-law" model (see Chapter 4).

This can be understood in a nontechnical way as the establishing of a logical connection between events. We say there is a logical connection in any realm when, given a set of premises, certain conclusions follow (that is, *must* follow). Drawing the conclusion from the premises is called *deduction*. In explanation according to the covering-law model the premises are (1) a general statement (law) that under certain circumstances some specified event will always occur, and (2) a statement that those circumstances obtain. The conclusion is the statement that the event has occurred in consequence of the premises. In explaining a historical event, we are told, our task is to establish such a logical connection between it and a set of premises, so that we may say it has occurred *because* the premises hold. In detail, the main business of the historian would be establishing the premises—research into the circumstances and the collection of evidence for the formulation of laws. (Practitioners and readers of history know, of course, that there is actually very little of the latter, but we shall see later that there are often suppressed premises of lawfulness.)

If a claim for a logical connection of this sort is made, it is at the same time a claim that things could not have been otherwise. This sense of historical necessity is what one has to buy along with the view of historical explanation that I have just described. The claims that are made by historians and composers about logic and necessity in the history of music will have to be understood in this light.

With the emphasis on either the sequential aspect—as of old—or the causal aspect of narratives—as of late—the understanding of the subject of a history must, in this view, entail knowledge of its antecedents or its past. In view of the centrality of that premise, I shall refer to this general position under the term "historicism." (In view of the ambiguity in the general use of this term, I shall apply it consistently to the epistemological view in which things are to be understood in terms of their past and future.)

Historicism insists upon locating the objects of its study in an eternal process of change. To contemplate something is to stop it only momentarily in its tracks; and to ask what it is, is to ask what it has been and what it will be. To consider a thing apart from the ceaseless flow is really to threaten its existence. Historians fire on moving targets; they cannot take aim without plotting their course. If the subject is art, its history is like a cinematic film, and individual artworks are like single frames. They are removed only provisionally, and at the risk of rendering both film and frame meaningless. The historicist can answer the recurring question, "Who are we, and what do we stand for?" only with reference to the past and the future.

The artist navigates the river of time; nothing is worse than the threat of empty sails. "If [advanced] music is not supported," wrote Milton Babbitt, "music will cease to evolve, and, in that important sense, will cease to live." And from the other side, John Cage: "I'm devoted to the principle of originality. Not originality in the egoistic sense, but originality in the sense of doing something which it is necessary to do. *Now obviously, the things which it is necessary to do are not the things that have been done, but the ones that have not yet been done* . . . that is to say if I have done something, then I consider it my business not to do that but to find *what must be done next*" (italics mine).[3] This remark calls attention to something that I hope to make quite apparent in this essay: actors in history who adopt the beliefs of historicism place themselves under the compulsion to act in accord with their understanding of the historical process. Historicism is not merely a mode of understanding; it is also a standard for action.

It seems to me that two opposite qualities are conveyed by both of these remarks from leading American composers. One is expressed nicely by this image: "I have often thought of living art as a bus rolling down a long boulevard. We run to catch it. It does not stop . . . If we do not board it, it gradually draws out of our sight . . . But if we board it . . . we can enjoy the landscapes as they open up on each side and still look back comfortably, from our position, on the art of the past."[4] The other is conveyed by the medieval legend of the wild hunt, in which "The souls of the dead keep marching to nowhere all day and all night at top speed. Anyone who drops out of line from exhaustion instantly crumbles to dust."[5]

Such remarks, of course, are made to the press, and they are calculated to make a certain impression on the public. However they work on the public, they are heard with the greatest attentiveness by journalistic critics who take it as their first duty when confronting new works to locate them in the stream of things. But are the same attitudes manifested in the professional literature, when the public is out of earshot? They are, but in a different context.

References to history in the foregoing sense are pointedly avoided for the most part, but then a historicism of quite another sort is embraced. Leonard Meyer and others have observed that from the point of view often represented here, musical compositions are regarded as solutions to problems, or even as propositions about how certain problems might be solved. This implies an objectivity on the part of both the composer and the students of his work to which I must return in later sections of this chapter. The analysis of a musical work, from this point of view, entails the explication of this nexus of problems and solutions. It becomes a *necessary* companion piece to the work itself.[6] While the journalistic critic issues what is essentially a pedigree for the new work, the analyst issues a certificate of workmanship (or perhaps something closer to a patent application, in which it is stated what the invention proposes to do, how it proposes to do it, and that it has not been done before). Both critic and analyst work to bestow significance upon the new composition.

I count the analyst's approach as historicism because of its implication that what the work *is,* is of little interest—and may not even be knowable—apart from the history of its making. This implication is not challenged by composers who provide such information in their program notes. That this is prevalent, rather than the feeling that the work must be allowed to fight free of its history, is a conspicuous mark of the current and general historical frame of mind: the process overshadows the product.

Material bearing on the problems which composers pose for themselves and the means through which they seek solutions is adjacent to information about solutions attempted and rejected and about sources of ideas and methods. Together these categories constitute an important and inseparable part of the composer's biography. In another sense, they offer an approach to the work through the composer's intentions. There is irony here, of course, because nowadays that approach is felt to be quite irrelevant, and quite often in those circles where it has been allowed to sneak in through the back door.

Now the alternative case. In stating it I shall have to draw from a range of ideas and hope that they will cohere in answering to the different faces of historicism.

It will be important, first, to consider the proposition that in order to claim understanding of something we must show its causes, and that showing cause comes down to a demonstration that the thing to be explained is the inevitable consequence of circumstances and laws. There is an approach to the problem of explanation in which an explanation begins with a question and ends when there are no further questions.

We seek explanations when we are puzzled about things, and we feel we have got them when our minds are more or less at rest about them. Having reached that stage, we say that we *understand*. Note that nothing has been said about how we shall know when we have reached that stage, or about the form that satisfactory explanations must take under this criterion.

I shall try a simple example in which causal explanation is sought, but demonstration of inevitability is inappropriate. If I report that my dog has fallen into a manhole and broken his leg, it might be asked, "What was he doing near the manhole?" (that is, why he was there). I might answer, "He was chasing a squirrel," quite to the questioner's satisfaction. He might then ask, "But why did he fall in?" If I were suddenly to adopt a new mode of reply and cite the law of gravity, he might well think me perverse. To be sure, in giving a full account in that style I would also cite laws about balance and friction, and specify all the conditions that place the case at hand under those laws. As I proceed in this way the questioner is likely to become more and more impatient with me. But if I had answered the second question thus: "He heard another dog approaching from behind, turned his head, and plunged in," my questioner would probably have considered that a sufficient explanation; for that is the operative part of the story. *Of course* nothing falls unless the law of gravity applies. My questioner knew that all along, but it hardly answered the question. As for the rest of the information (the squirrel, the other dog, the glance over the shoulder), it is hard to imagine the laws that might be formulated about it without giggling (dogs chase squirrels if they detect their presence, and so on).

In this little story it is left in the end for the questioner to judge whether a sufficient explanation has been given. And the judgment will be made on this basis: whether the explanation makes the outcome appear not *inevitable* but *plausible* in the light of the circumstances. Now it must be the case that only one explanation for any event can satisfy the inevitability criterion, whereas several explanations may be tenable from the viewpoint of plausibility. We shall recognize the importance of this difference at once if we turn to the analysis of music, which is, after all, a kind of explanation. Here the opposing views would be (1) that there is a single correct analysis of a work which shows every event in the piece to follow inevitably from what has gone before, and (2) that there may be several analyses, each of which shows aspects of the work to be plausible in the light of some schema—each of which, in short, shows some coherence in the work. The second alternative suggests an attitude toward analysis to which I shall return later on: musical analysis is not the attempt to pry from the piece secrets about how and why it works, but a way of placing its events under general concepts, of looking at them from certain points of view.

The issue over necessity as against plausibility is a most crucial one, and I want to pause over it for a while longer. Of things that happen sequentially—in nature, in history, in novels, in music—it has ever been the ambition of the inquisitive Western mind to achieve understanding by stripping them down to their essential processes, to their *Urlinien*. To *understand* has been to isolate a central thread of events and to separate off from this those details that are superfluous, extraneous, tributary, tangential, foreground—in any case not essentially contributory to the final outcome but only decorating the main events. For both nature and art, germinal formulations of this ambition are owing to Aristotle. For natural processes the aim expressed in the *Physics* was to show that "Each step in the series is for the sake of the next." The neopositivist version of scientific explanation is really just the latest inheritor of that ideal. For art the aim is *unity,* as that is defined in the *Poetics*: "In poetry the story must represent one action, a complete whole with its several incidents so closely connected [as a series of probable or necessary stages] that the transposal or withdrawal of any one of them will disjoin and dislocate the whole. For that which makes no perceptible difference by its presence or absence is no real part of the whole." It is no new thing to lead the quest for order and necessity from nature into the sequences of things that men do.

Consider this passage from Crocker's book:

The main lines of development in the 1900's were by now clear. Schoenberg and Webern had been right all along—or, at any rate, more right than Sibelius or Hindemith. Furthermore Schoenberg, and especially Webern, had been right back in 1913. Was the Parisian experience, the whole output of Stravinsky up to *Agon,* the whole output of Bartók (except as it could be interpreted as twelve-tone music)—was all this a lie, a timid expedient, a cynical compromise with the mass audience? To say "yes" would be to miss one of the basic features of stylistic development.

Musical materials have to be "used up," their potential fully exploited, before style can move ahead on the long line of history . . . Schoenberg and Webern had moved in the right direction, but too fast—not just too fast for the audience, but too fast for the nature of the stylistic material. There was still much to be done with triads, and Stravinsky showed what to do; there was still room to move within broadly dissonant expressions of key, and Bartók showed how. Until these and other things were done, the novelties of Schoenberg and Webern could only seem arbitrary and isolated. But once these things were done definitively, then the prior achievement of Schoenberg and Webern made further delay impossible. Music must move beyond the triad into a twelve-tone space. That these things had to be was simply a matter of historical continuity.

And now consider this passage from Meyer's *Music, the Arts, and Ideas*: "The past is distinguished from the present in this: that an event is considered to be past when, on a given hierarchical level of events its implications appear to have been realized and its consequences on that level are known."

There is, of course, an important epistemological difference, for Crocker tells us that a style must be played out before art "can move ahead on the long line of history," whereas for Meyer that condition merely determines when "an event *can be considered* to be past" (italics mine). I shall come back to that difference later. But note that in both passages history meets Aristotle's conditions for the unity of a story; we are interested in the connection between present and past events in terms of implications and their consequences, in terms of the realization of potentials. When one thing happens after another under these conditions, each stage is a probable or necessary consequence of what has gone before and is for its time the summation of a cumulative process up to that stage, like each move in a chess game. The connection between events is a *logical* connection in exactly the sense discussed earlier. When one event follows out the implications of an earlier event, the two events are related as premise and conclusion. When the events are musical works or styles, the composer is, in effect, *deducing* the consequences of an earlier premise. The historian who brings the connections to light is, in similar fashion, working deductively. We shall see how very close to this formulation Crocker's exposition of the history of musical style lies.

For Crocker all historical relationships are of this sort. For Meyer this turns out to represent just one of three categories of relationship between the stages of a history, and the only one that is linear. He calls it "developmental change," and defines it as the realization of "the potential inherent in a limiting set of preconditions." At the opposite pole from this is "mutational change," which is an alteration in "some aspect of the material, formal, syntactic, or other preconditions of a style." Between the two lies "trended change," which "takes place within a limiting set of preconditions, but [in which] the potential inherent in the established relationships may be realized in a number of different ways and the order of the realization may be variable." The second and third categories recognize the possibility of histories in which one sees the outcome without feeling any obligation to show that "these things had to be."

As an example of such a history Meyer calls up the sequence of Picasso's styles, in which there are "significant differences . . . without there being a linear trend, much less a development or an evolution." The example is tossed off during a rapid sprint, so it is necessary to fill in the assumed details of the argument.

We can suppose that Picasso's style changes are said not to be linear or cumulative because there is no observable gradation from the Blue period to the Rose period to the Cubist period. Paintings do not become less Blue and more Rose, then less Rose and more Cubist. Because of this appearance it is concluded that Rose was not a potential of Blue, and Cubist was not a consequence of Rose. The progression is not *logical;* Picasso has proceeded willfully, not by following out the implications of each stage. But this is only the other side of Crocker's *ex post facto* confidence. We don't know at all that for Picasso the Rose period was not a "necessary" transition between the Blue and the Cubist periods. Meyer's distinction rests on the assumption that the logic of the sequence should be apparent, and deducible, from a gradation in the look of the paintings.

The difficulty stems, on one side, from the insistence upon importing into art and history a concept of necessity that does not belong to them. Think of *Crime and Punishment.* We respond at each stage in the story of Raskolnikov to a new and fresh situation which is nevertheless seen to be right, to make sense in the light of the preceding stages. We have a sense that the alternatives for Raskolnikov are steadily diminishing, yet if we were to lose interest in any stage because we had expected it as the most likely outcome, the novel would have failed. There is this paradox in art that science will not allow: the sensation of a directed motion and the mystery about where it is leading (the paradox holds even if we have read or heard the work before). We must feel of each stage that it was an *appropriate* consequence of what preceded it, but that does not entitle us to claim that it was in the cards, that it was necessary, or that we could have predicted it. ("Appropriate" is a vague word. The argument requires that it be left that way, to be concretized only in particular cases.)

In this, history lies closer to art than to science. Art historians or critics must show wherein lies the sense of Picasso's stylistic development, no matter whether it appears logical or not. They must show not why it was necessary but why we should believe it.

On the other side the difficulty stems from the characteristic historicist confusion between what a work of art is and the factors that have conditioned its making. The premise, again, is that each stage in a development is a summation of the preceding stages and will therefore betray its background. This has been the leading premise in the analysis of what is called "influence." Since that subject has lately been treated in the field of comparative literature in a far more critical way than ever in musical studies, I should like to synthesize a brief outline of a position that has been taking form there by citing just a few passages.

From René Wellek:

The work of art . . . is totally distinct from the mental processes of the author at the time of composition and hence of the influences which may have formed his mind.[7]

From Claudio Guillén:

The value of an influence is not aesthetic but psychological . . . the realm of the aesthetic is to be kept apart from the domain of influence . . . where value is concerned . . . An influence need not take the recognizable form of a parallelism, just as every parallelism does not proceed from an influence . . . The impulse for a work does not necessarily leave tangible traces in the work. On the other hand, parallelisms may not be in the central stream of genetic development.[8]

From Henri Peyre:

An influence is almost never manifested through imitation . . . Studies of countries and of relations between two or more writers would be well advised to give up in most cases the search for causes or influences, and to engage in the exploration of families of minds [a translation of the art critic Henri Focillon's *familles d'esprits*] and of fortuitous analogies linking authors who had no awareness of one another.[9]

From Guillén again:

Comparative studies may refer to an entirely a-temporal perspective, seeking patterns or aesthetic orders.

This new orientation in comparative literature has a direct counterpart in some recent writing about the historian's task. It has sometimes been suggested that when the historian asks, "How can I understand this?" The question is not at all "How (or why) did it come about?" but "What kind of a thing is it? or "What patterns does it make with other things?" (chronological continuity might be one kind of pattern, but there can be many others; more of that later). In William Dray's expression, the subject is placed not under covering laws but under covering concepts.[10] And in Maurice Mandelbaum's formulation, "The relationship which I take to be fundamental in historiography is the relationship of part to whole, not a relationship of antecedent to consequent."[11]

What is it to understand something by placing it under general concepts, or by viewing it as a part in relation to a whole? Again musical analysis is a realm of knowledge in which we can see that the idea is familiar. If we explain an extended passage as a prolongation of the dominant triad, we place it under the general concepts "prolongation," "dominant," and "triad." We view its details in the context of a pattern defined by those concepts, ordered as parts in what we regard as a coherent whole. This act of ordering under general concepts serves to put our minds at rest, at least with respect to some aspects of the passage. We can claim some understanding of it, or we can claim to have explained it.

Historians have interpretive concepts that function in a similar way to organize events in patterns; for example, the concept "revolution" for certain patterns of disruptive social, political, or military events. By virtue of having subsumed the events under the concept, historians will certainly feel that they have understood something about them, and politicians may even determine their course of action according to a decision about the applicability of the concept. Three things must be observed about this notion of historical understanding. First, there are no criteria that definitely fix the limits of applicability of general concepts (are the events in Vietnam understood as civil war, revolution, or invasion from without?). Therefore, the application of a general concept is itself saying something new about the events that are subsumed under it. Second, it must be reemphasized that this general notion of understanding is an *alternative* to historicism, and not in support of it. Saying "revolution" does not necessarily send the historian scurrying to the archives in search of documents showing that the French Revolution was a cause of the Russian Revolution, and so on. In other words, showing the applicability of a single general concept to different sets of events (example: "sonata") does not suggest anything at all about any genetic relationships among those sets of events. This seems obvious and trivial, but it is often forgotten in the practice of music history. And third, placing events under general concepts is saying that the events may be understood in terms of the concept, that they become coherent under the concept, but *not* that they *are* that concept and that concept exclusively (these events make a kind of sense when they are regarded as a revolution, or as a prolongation, but they make another kind of sense when they are regarded as something else; more of that later).

I am afraid that in none of this has there been any offer of reliable tests for the rightness of an explanation, for the appropriateness with which a general concept is applied, for the degree of illumination that follows from its application. It lies within this set of attitudes that there can be no such fixed and external criteria, that an explanation or an analysis is worth what we can get out of it in view of the questions we ask of it.

Of course it is just such reliance on "subjective" standards that the nomological model for explanation (causal explanation in terms of general laws) is designed to circumvent, and against which positivism in general directs its rich glossary of invective. Reliance on such standards would foster a "relativism" based upon "empathetic familiarity" instead of theoretical understanding. Such standards can only be communicated "intersubjectively" through language that is "emotive," "evocative," and "metaphorical" (all of which adds up to "meaningless"). But these words (except, of course, for "meaningless") do not necessarily have pejorative connotations for everyone. And that reveals the nature of the disagreement: by following strictly the axioms and definitions of one position no one will ever be led to the other. There is no way of evaluating the explanations offered in the foregoing example except with reference to the presuppositions of one or the other position. Against this last assertion, the charge of relativism can again be leveled. But it can be answered with a countercharge of dogmatism. And so on. Hence the emphasis I placed at the very beginning on the mere *possibility* of stating alternatives.

The alternatives to historicism amount to nothing less radical than the suggestion that we can achieve understanding apart from any process of change. On reflection this will seem a bizarre assertion, for it is made against the habit of many centuries of thought. One senses that fear in Meyer's new book. There the central thesis is the diagnosis that we have entered a period of cultural stasis, and that the arts have begun a course of steady fluctuation after a long history of cumulative and directional change.

Anticipating a natural resistance to the very suggestion that such a condition is conceivable, Meyer presents a rather lengthy argument with the purpose of persuading his readers that the terms in which they habitually think of the history of art (development, evolution, and so forth) represent constructs that sometimes do, and sometimes do not, accurately describe the history of art. They do for Western art between the Renaissance and World War II; they do not for the art of many non-Western cultures, and for pre-Renaissance and post–World War II Western art. He writes, "If the suggestion that the West faces the prospect of stasis in the arts appears remarkable and perhaps even bizarre, it is because we have become so accustomed to change that it seems almost a law of cultural life."

I shall try to make Meyer's point even sharper than he would perhaps be willing to do. Historicism places its object in a pattern of temporal succession in order to see it. That pattern is a construction placed upon a number of objects; it is a human invention. And it is no more natural, or exhaustive, than an alphabetical arrangement of the same objects according to the first letters in their names. The chronological and alphabetical patterns place the same objects in different lights; they show different things about them, each showing something the other cannot. Which pattern informs our point of view from time to time depends upon the questions being asked, not upon some absolute criterion. Chronological patterns will usually answer more of the historian's questions than alphabetical ones. In the same way, the chronological arrangement of the book stacks in the Royal Library of Stockholm according to the date of acquisition is likely to strike most visitors as an uncharacteristic failure of reason. But when historians restrict themselves to chronological patterns alone, they leave many questions unanswered; or, what is more common and more misleading, they respond to one question with the answer to another.

My reference to alphabetical patterns will have left the reader skeptical about the alternatives to chronology as an organizing principle for the historian. But I can suggest two cases that are less distant. Both have to do with the history of what is called "tonality."

The first is the suggestion that the general notion of tonality that is owing to Heinrich Schenker—"directed motion within the framework of a single prolonged sonority," together with the corollary principles of the integration of vertical and horizontal dimensions and hierarchical or layered structure—provides analytical concepts for the study of medieval and Renaissance polyphony, as well as the music of the eighteenth and nineteenth centuries for which it was formulated.[12] Naturally, this suggestion cuts across the commonplace distinction between modality and tonality and substitutes instead a single set of concepts that offers a way into certain aspects of the organization of a wide variety of music covering an extensive range of time. The advantage of using such a basis of comparison resides in the opportunity to observe the interaction of that fundamental principle of tonality with the conventions of style. In the end a historical concept is enlisted for the understanding of the uniqueness of individual works—a curious idea, since we have grown so accustomed to the generalizing function of history. The point is that historical generalization—the discovery that a number of works may be regarded from a single point of view—is not the end, but really the beginning of the historian's task. It is only when that point of view is chronology or genealogy that there seems to be nothing further to say.

Here is the second case. David Lewin has written about the sense of "tonal center" and "harmonic area" exemplified in some music of Arnold Schoenberg.[13] In general, "one can fix any one of the [inversions of the total chromatic onto itself] and regard the total chromatic as 'balanced' with respect to that inversion." (For example, the configuration in the Fantasy op. 47 in Example 5.1 is balanced with respect to the axis of inversion, C–C-sharp, F-sharp–G). "The 'balance' of the total chromatic induced by the functioning of such an inversion was treated by

EX. 5.1

Schoenberg, throughout his career, as something quite analogous to the balance induced by a tonal center."

There is a background discussion of the extent to which "the sense of 'tonal center' is itself already dependent on notions of inversional balance." First the treatment, since Rameau, of the tonic as center of a balance between dominant and subdominant; then reference to Schoenberg's "Chart of Regions" in *The Structural Functions of Harmony,* which suggests the extent to which Schoenberg "conceived of a 'tonic' as a fulcrum about which all else balanced"; finally, by way of illustration, an interpretation of the tonal action of the development section in the first movement of Beethoven's First Symphony in terms of an inversional balance of E-flat major and A minor about C minor–C major.

Background can be found well beyond Rameau, indeed in medieval melody, of which I offer a specimen (Ex. 5.2). How is a sense of "tonal center" secured here? The sound-space and phrase structure are arranged *as symmetrically (inversionally) as they can be* about G, given that the tone system is strictly diatonic and the tritone is devilish. Such an interpretation is easily borne out by the ways in which medieval theorists discussed the structure of the modes considered as abstractions: as the conjunction of two nearly equal segments (pentachord and tetrachord) that may be disposed with either one above the other, and in terms of the intervals that the "tonic" makes with the notes immediately above and below it.

Back in the twentieth century again, there are tonal polarities in Bartók's music that can be interpreted in much the same way: the tonal structure in the Fourth Quartet, achieved in ways remarkably similar to those of Schoenberg's Fantasy,[14] or the heavy anchoring of the first movement in the Music for Strings, Percussion, and Celesta, with imitative entries launching out in a double cycle of fifths upward and

EX. 5.2

downward from A, ultimately to converge on E-flat in the climax, where the texture congeals into a unison and after which the tune is turned upside down for the return to A. What is striking in all of these examples is the way that tonal centers function literally as *centers*.

Now we can reflect upon the status of these two general concepts and upon the consequences of their application. Two ways have been suggested of viewing tonal organization in a wide range of music that make pieces of quite disparate styles, given other points of view, commensurable with one another. This should serve not to divert attention from the differences but rather to bring them more sharply into focus. As it happens, it was the study of recent music that suggested both ways of viewing older music (I shall return to the significance of that in the next section). The concept of tonal balance does not translate to the concept of prolongation, but the two do not exclude one another. It would seem, rather, that they ought to be included among the conceptual paraphernalia of any exposition that claims to treat "the history of tonality." Should we be surprised by the connectedness of such a diversity of musics in terms of these concepts? Have we made a discovery? And must we now return to the archives to find documentary evidence about the causal threads that tie it all together? Was Bartók influenced by Schoenberg? Was Beethoven a closet medievalist? It would be nice to know; but one can be a historian without even caring. Finally, having drawn connections among works in terms of those two related concepts, we are not prevented from finding still other connections for some of the same works. There is no theoretical limit on the number of connections that can be drawn, and there is no fixed point at which we can claim to have tucked a work or an epoch away in our understanding.

These observations will call down a harsh judgment upon the models that we have commonly adopted for detailing histories of art: chains, streams, organic developments, evolutions. Several related characteristics are shared by them all. They single out genetic continuity as the foundation of all forms of connectedness, and as *the* historical concept; they make no allowance for discontinuities; they recognize only the connection between each event and its immediate successor; and they emphasize something like the centrality of tradition—"the mainstream of development."

Alternative models would need to take into account the interconnectedness of artworks from many different points of view, they would have to accommodate the idea that there is no *permanently* central connection, and they would have to be able to deal with continuities and discontinuities at once. These are not easy conditions to meet.

One such model is offered by Meyer: the familiar concept of hierarchical structure.

The length of time an event remains in some historical present depends upon the duration of the highest hierarchic level of which it forms a part—upon what might be called its historical "reverberation time." As a result, two events may be simultaneous and of roughly equal durations—say, a bridge game and the premiere of a new symphony. [Croce offered the charming comparison of the flight of a mosquito with the expedition of Xerxes.] But the consequences of the bridge game are short-term . . . The symphony, on the other hand, . . . has implications extending over a considerable period of time . . . "Importance" is defined by the highest hierarchic level on which an event is thought to exist . . . Insofar as recent events are conceived to be implications or consequences of earlier events, the significance of those earlier events is altered and the structuring of historical hierarchies is modified.

Wittgenstein suggested a model for continuity of meaning in the use of language that can be well adapted for history. Think of an unbounded number of such lines of connection among artworks as I suggested just a bit earlier as fibers, twisted about one another in a thread: all manner of lengths, taking up and leaving off in a multitude of places, an undetermined number of fibers passing through any single point in the thread's length, no single fiber running the entire length, unlimited points of contact and crossings-over among fibers, all of them contributing to a special kind of overall continuity.[15]

I do not mention these models in order to propose necessarily that we adopt them universally. I do so, first, to suggest that the models to which we have been committed for so long are models, and only models, and, second, to show how confining those models are compared to our needs and to the possibilities.

———

Come back to my initial proposition about history. Its second clause, "tell it as it was"—"wie es eigentlich gewesen"—expresses the hope and the standard by which historians have long worked. I shall refer to it as the standard of objectivism. And although I discuss it here under a separate heading, there is a great deal about the attitude of historicism that depends upon its tenets.

The fundamental proposition of objectivism can be put in this way: Of the things we say, the only statements that can be counted objective (and hence representative of proper knowledge) are descriptive statements about objects and events, or those that are analytic statements about the relations among objects and events. "Relations" in this context means logical relations, and they can be determined either through deduction or by convention (the latter to take account of definitions, which are normally regarded as objective statements).

Naturally, this proposition embraces the view that objects and events *can* be described directly and independently of the state of mind of the person (subject) describing them. Facts, under this doctrine, are descriptive statements, and they are functions of the properties of objects and events, not of persons; hence they remain the same, no matter who determines them. There is no excuse for disagreement about facts so long as everyone is looking at the same things, knows how to be a good observer (knows how to read evidence, and so on), and is not prejudiced (subjective).

Objectivism is a standard of truth, and it has built-in criteria of truth that can be easily drawn out: for descriptive statements, verification; for analytic statements, the rules of deductive logic and the conventions of language. Statements are either true or false on these criteria, or they are meaningless.

If *facts* are descriptive statements, analytic statements are categorized as *theory*. They are facts connected with what Norwood Hanson has called the "cosmic glue" of cause and effect. The purpose of theory is to *explain* (or predict) facts. Theory has nothing to do with the determination of facts. This establishes a certain order in the acquisition of knowledge: the facts are determined first, the theory is formulated afterwards. The priorities that have governed the practice of music history reflect that order: complete the factual research before attempting theoretical or critical studies (the piano teacher would say, "Learn the notes before you put in the feeling").

In talk about art the doctrine of objectivism is reflected in the belief that a clear distinction can be drawn among *description* (what is there), *analysis* (what is there, explained in terms of schemata), and something beyond analysis, like *criticism* (how you feel about it). The distinctions between form and feeling, and between form and content, are simply versions of the same basic reduction of the response to art down to the objective and the subjective. Just as, in history, theory is not supposed to enter into the determination of facts, so criticism is subjective and is not supposed to enter into objective descriptive and analytical formulations.

There are parallel objectivist attitudes about musical composition. One is the conception of composing as problem-solving already mentioned. This pointedly cuts out of the picture the composer as anything but a ratiocinating agent, involved with the logic of the problem, and it demands an appropriately objective response from the student of the composer's work. "I like it" is not such a response. The other, still purer objectivist attitude to musical composition is that which seeks in various degrees to disengage the composer from the selection of the elements, events, and orders of the work. Both attitudes are components of what Meyer calls the "New Ideology."

Finally, the old claims of logic and necessity in history provide the basis for claims of an objective *historical* role for the composer: to grasp what is the necessary consequence of the inherited historical development and to be midwife to it. Naturally the historian plays an equally objective role in bringing to light the deductive-logical nature of the relationships between the successive stages of the history. I shall return to the paradox of this common conceptual ground between the old history and the "New Ideology."

In accordance with the objectivist doctrine, questions in the history of art tend to be formulated in such a way as to call for answers about which one says "true" or "false." What I want to consider now is whether such questions can even be answered, given the objectivist criteria of truth. I begin by citing a recent formulation of a central, broad question.

In the introduction to a long book, Thomas Munro writes, "This book will ask again the question of whether the arts evolve."[16] Of course an affirmative answer is taken for granted in most books of music history. The evolution or development of music is the subject of such books. That this is the proper and true subject of history is a belief held with the force of religious belief—like that not of the proselyte who has deliberated and chosen to believe, but of those born to belief, who do not know the possibility of disbelief. From this point of view Munro's question is not even to be asked; the only questions are about the details of the evolution. Leonard Meyer *does* raise the question and, what is more, he answers it in the negative so far as the foreseeable future is concerned. In doing so, he places himself outside the tradition of orthodox music history. Earlier I made reference to his long argument in defense of that negative answer, which constitutes his central thesis. It begins with the assertion that history is a construct, that is to say, an invention. This drastically alters the status of all such concepts as "evolution" and "development" and disqualifies the form in which Munro cast his question. For the term "evolution" would then stand for a model, not a discovered and verifiable process, and the questions to be asked about it are not of the type "Is it true?" or "Did it happen that way?" but "How cohesive and intelligible does it make the evidence appear?" and hence "How illuminating is it?"

If historical concepts are human inventions, then they must be subject to the conditions under which humans invent them. This introduces a new aspect to the relationship between present and past, as Meyer makes clear. We have always understood that what the present is, is conditioned by the past. But objectivism has prevented us from recognizing that what the past is, stated through our historical constructs, is conditioned by the present. This important idea has been expressed before by critics and historians outside the field of music, and Meyer cites two of the most prominent among these. T. S. Eliot: "What happens when a new work of art is created is something that happens simultaneously to all the works of art which preceded it." And André Malraux: "It is not research work that has led to the understanding of El Greco; it is modern art." The study of Dufay in Chapter 8 exemplifies this idea.

What it all suggests so far as the doctrine of objectivism is concerned is this: as long as we regard art history to be more than the documentary history of art and artists, its data cannot conceivably be fixed, and its task cannot simply be to "tell what happened and tell it as it was."

These are all arguments that Meyer makes directly, or with which he would seem at least to be in sympathy. The trouble is that his main thesis fails to heed them, and instead falls back into the old faith. He yields to orthodox history the assumption that music has until recently followed a course of cumulative development. ("There is a clear line of development from Aeschylus to Shakespeare to Joyce, from Phidias to Michelangelo to Picasso, and from Monteverdi to Beethoven to Stravinsky.") But he ventures the prediction that music's present pluralism will hold it in a condition of static flux that will prevent further development for some time to come.

Here, again, is the question: Is music's past development a discovered process or a historian's construct? Are we to ask about whether and how music will develop in the future, or about how future historians will construe the evidence? If "history is a construct," what is to prevent future historians from placing certain familiar constructions on music from 1900 to 2200? What is to prevent them (if historians have not yet tired of the game by then) from constructing a genealogy that traces the descent from Wagner through Schoenberg through Webern through Boulez through ———? The answer might be given that such a construction would ignore the present multiplicity of aesthetics and styles; it would leave out of account Ives, Russolo, and Cage; Shostakovich, Britten, and Barber. But we have well-used concepts for accommodating such figures and their music: "novelties" and "experiments" which "did not of themselves result in new shapes for music" on one hand, "stylistic nostalgia" on the other. (The reader knows that I am not making this up. Crocker's book, from which I have been quoting here, is only one among many in which such a history of modern music is presented.) Those who have had the opportunity really to familiarize themselves with the full range of the musical repertories of any period in the past will know something of the multiplicity of styles, of the retrospective and peripheral practices that our history books have had to reduce in order to yield their clear lines of development.

Meyer might argue that through the pluralisms of the past there rose up common practices, essential agreements about what composers were to be taught, manifested in treatises of musical theory, whereas there is today no sense of a common practice. But, even disregarding the evidence about past quarrels, think what our age will leave to future historians: *Perspectives of New Music, The Journal of Music Theory, Die Reihe . . .* Will we fault them from our celestial observation posts if they find in them evidence of a common practice? Crocker knows more about our present multiplicity than will be apparent in the twenty-third century; yet the phrases "Toward a common practice," "A classic style?" and "the main lines of development in the 1900's were by now [mid-century] clear" are entered in his book with no apparent sense of hesitation.

Then perhaps the real force of Meyer's prediction is this: no matter what constructions we place upon them, the styles that music follows will not change appreciably in the foreseeable future. But how shall we say what is changed and what is the same? How shall we even decide whether the differences among the works of Schoenberg, Webern, and Boulez are more significant or more directional than could have been predicted merely from knowing that the man Boulez is not Webern, who was not Schoenberg? Meyer himself tells us that there are no fixed criteria, that it depends on the hierarchical level on which one is looking. History offers many confirmations of this. From time to time a close observer has reported a change in style or technique so radical as to signal the demise of music. Regarding these declarations from a distance, however, we must sometimes strain to see what the polemic was about. All cocker spaniels look alike, except to a cocker spaniel.

I imagine Meyer and Crocker on a stroll through wooded countryside. "We have passed through the forest," says Meyer, "and now we are lost in a multitude of trees, with no prospect of finding our way out." "This is no multitude of trees," replies Crocker, "it is a forest like the last one. And if you will just follow me, I shall show you the path into the next forest." Who is right? The answer can be given only in the words of Pirandello: "Right you are if you think you are." There is no fixed answer because there is something wrong about the question.

Disagreements about the course of modern music will not be settled without more clarity about the nature of course-plotting: how much is it a process of discovery, and how much of invention?

This shows, too, the failure of the objectivist insistence that only empirical or logical statements can communicate knowledge. Conflicting statements about the course of modern music, like those about forests and trees, cannot be resolved by the test of verification. But they cannot be resolved with reference to convention either, for, as the adage has it, it depends upon what one *sees*.

If we are really to believe, with Meyer, that formulations about the past are constructs, shapes in which we receive our multiplicities of evidence, gestalten that make the evidence coherent, then we must see the present scramble as a search for concepts or shapes or models. In this connection it is most instructive to study the apportionment of general history texts among the historical periods with which they deal. *The College Outline History of Music,* perhaps the most elementary of them all, devotes roughly twice the number of pages to the twentieth century as it does to the next most fully covered period. Perhaps this can be understood to reflect a special interest in recent history. But more likely it shows that the evidence about our century has not yet been organized into configurations as streamlined as those for the previous centuries. It is like blocks that will fit into a small box if one knows the pattern, but that require a larger box if one does not.

The problem of the present in musical history is a formal (linguistic, epistemological) problem, rather than a research problem. By reflection, this might suggest that the problem of *past* history is far more a formal problem, and far less exclusively a research problem, than we have generally allowed. And what that suggests, in turn, is a reversal of the objectivist priorities. It is problems of theory and interpretation that most urgently require our attention.

But I am committed to describing alternatives. After the foregoing I can attempt a straightforward answer to Munro's kind of question: whether the arts evolve depends on the existence of art historians who arrange artworks according to the model of evolution.

That answer, taken seriously, stands for a whole network of beliefs about factuality and about the relation of fact to theory that constitute an alternative to the dogmas of objectivism. That alternative has been best expressed in several recent expositions about scientific knowledge.[17] This is both ironic and instructive, for to us "scientific" and "objective" have always seemed to be synonyms. I shall try a very brief description of what an alternate theory based on those expositions might be like.

The world "out there," if we wish to talk about it at all, can be regarded only as a "blooming, buzzing confusion," in the words of William James. It is not a neat place, like a garden, from which we pluck facts as though they were flowers already grown. "Facts" come into being only at the moment we assimilate them, for they are orderings of our perceptions, meant to give them coherence. There is therefore no distinct boundary between facts and theories, only lower-order and higher-order facts. Our traffic with facts is always "theory laden," as Hanson put it. You may feel confident in your possession of a lower-order fact—say the date of Mozart's birth—and argue that it is incontestibly true quite apart from your knowing it. But that is because the signals are clear, unambiguous, and nonconflicting.

In this view "establishing the facts," or coming to know things, is an active, creative business. It is not a passive registering of things as they impinge on us; it is putting things into matrices or patterns. How we do that depends on a multitude of factors that constitute the premises of our knowledge. These may be sorted into such categories as innate structures, earlier knowledge, habits and skills, desires and beliefs. We become aware of them only through the knowledge which they inform, and when we abstract them and organize them into some sort of coherent system, we refer to them as theory. The distinction between theory and fact (or between analysis and description) is a conventional one, but it does not describe the process of coming to know things.

Similar to this distinction is that between concept and percept. According to tradition, percepts are formed independently of concepts, as facts are formed independently of theory, and afterward become organized according to concepts. In the alternative view that I am describing, conscious knowing of any kind is already conceptualized. (In the aesthetic realm the issue is over the distinction between "seeing" or "hearing" and "seeing as" or "hearing as." In the alternative view it is a conventional distinction that does not correspond to human experience. We always "see as" or "hear as"; the question is, "as what?")

With such a view of knowing as active and, in Polanyi's expression, "personal," the idea of *commitment* assumes great importance. If I were merely reporting "objectively" on what is "out there," plucking flowers, the suggestion that I had brought in the wrong flower would send me back to the garden for another one. But if what we call facts are made by us, products of the activities of ordering and assimilating, I will not give mine up so readily, for I am committed to them by the investment of the activity.

Of course, this runs counter to the dictate that all meaningful statements of fact are either true or false, judged by the criteria of verification and convention. Under that rule a person who clings to a demonstrably untrue statement can be dismissed under a variety of charges (lunatic, simpleton, spoilsport). But there are aspects of experience that stand against reliance upon that rule, even by reasonable people. First, we may know things with conviction and yet be unable even to *say* them (what a clarinet or an octave sounds like; how to keep your balance while riding a bicycle; many aspects of our competence in language, as linguists have been showing lately). Second, we may hold things to be true that have not been, and in some cases can not be, empirically or conventionally confirmed (the General Theory of Relativity, statements about the quality or value of a work of art or a bottle of wine, statements about evolution in the arts). Third, we may continue to insist upon the truth of a proposition even while being confronted by evidence that contradicts it (showing that we sometimes value criteria of coherence, adaptability, and suggestiveness, and even beauty, above those of "truth"). The word that characterizes the process underlying a change of commitment far better than "proof" is "persuasion."

This could be a frightening view of things, for it says that certain external sources of support have given a false sense of confidence, and that we are thrown back upon ourselves. It very much alters the status of our particular problems, and thereby it calls for different criteria for recognizing solutions. And it suggests some rather different priorities. If theory of all kinds is to be the endpoint in the analysis of percept-concept complexes, then historians will be called upon to study the forms of historical knowledge that they have embraced so far with only the most limited awareness, and perhaps to invent new forms. And in the aesthetic realm, the study of artworks would proceed not up the ladder from the factual (description) to the conceptual (analysis) to the critical, but from the inside out—from an elaboration upon an aesthetic apperception.

After so much of showing the cards on both sides of the table, it is time to come down to cases. The main themes have been brought up, and it will be necessary now to show them as central issues in discussions about our age as an epoch of history. It seems most reasonable to take up the four books under review in their order of publication.

Jacques Chailley's title, *40,000 Years of Music*, never fails to send a titter through the house. The books asks no more than an inch of shelf space. How is it possible to sift through forty thousand years of music and come away with a sample contained in so few pages? Furthermore, as everyone knows, there *isn't* any music for the first 37,500 or so years. What is the man up to?

The easiest part of the question first: A celebrated cave painting at Ariège (the cave of the *Trois Frères*) shows a man in a reindeer mask apparently playing music upon a bow, probably in order to charm some genuine reindeer. By estimation it was executed some forty thousand years ago, and if the man is indeed playing, the painting marks the beginning of recorded music history.

For the more difficult part of the question, a clue is provided by the obverse of this passage: "It is useless to study the past if the standards applied are those of today." Considering how much of the past he has bitten off, and assuming that people do not willingly pursue what they proclaim to be useless, it must be that Chailley hopes to find in the past a standard for the present. And if there is any remaining doubt, here is a sample of what the author thinks of the standards of "today." Webern's op. 18, no. 3 is characterized by "the donkey's bray style, from which we are periodically requested not to remove the faded label 'Avant Garde' attached to it nearly half a century ago."

Obviously we need a stage direction to instruct us how to read Chailley's title with the proper expression. It must be read with the air of a father looking upon the wreckage of the family automobile recently done in by his son, shaking his head from side to side, saying slowly, lamentingly, "Forty thousand dollars!"; "Forty thousand years of music!" That figure gives the age of the tradition that composers of the "avant-garde" have chucked (the constitution of that group is a matter of virtual agreement among all our authors, as we shall presently see). It also measures the length and weight of the club Chailley wields in the polemic that is the clear purpose of his book.

If Chailley issues his decrees about what composers ought *not* to be doing in the name of history, then he legitimizes the claim of his opponents that it is they who are acting in that name. For the really critical thing about his decrees—and this is central to so much talk about modern music in general—is the underlying proposition that composing music is a historical act, to be understood principally as that. And if he recommends "a more humble approach to those who, on the strength of a few hasty historical deductions, imagine they are in a position to predict the future from what they know of the past," then he softens the impact of his own attack from the vantage point of history (the advice is just as sound if "few" and "hasty" are replaced by "many" and "cautious"). Both sides suppose history to speak logically, but they are like competing priests at Delphi, each carrying away his own report on what the oracle has said.

"The past as a standard for the present" is really the informing theme of Chailley's book, and that will account for its unusual format. "Part I: In Search of a Past" is a sort of history of music history, a review of past ages with regard to the interest they have shown in their own musical pasts. His thesis is that each age has held up some previous age as a model for its own sensibilities: "The Renaissance and the 17th Century in Search of Antiquity"; "The 18th and 19th Centuries in Search of the Middle Ages"; "The 19th Century in Search of the Renaissance"; but "The 20th Century in Search of ———?" The twentieth century, that is, has rejected all models. (This seems quite wrong. Those rather naïve imagined reminiscences are something like Mozart's Turkish music. It is my argument, in a sense, that the success of history in this century has shaped standards as never before.)

The second and third parts of the book, entitled, respectively, "In Search of Sacred Music" and "In Search of Secular Music," are historical sketches meant to articulate the standards that the twentieth century has rejected. Part 2 concerns the uses of music, and traces a progressive decline from the use of music for the domination of cosmic forces through its use for the accompaniment of prayer and praise to the deities, through a period when music was employed less for ritual and more to give pleasure and arouse passions, down to music's present "old-maidish . . . isolation from life." Chailley's second thesis about the present state of music is that we stand at the low point of this decline.

The sketch of the history of secular music in Part 3 is written from the point of view of a single issue: the changing resolution through history of the tension between the standards represented by "paper music" and those of the ear. There is the usual reference to Machaut's *Ma fin est mon commencement* and to the complexities of the music of the following generation (one wonders why Chailley did not write a chapter entitled "The Twentieth Century in Search of the Late Ars Nova"). But "posterity allowed this aesthetic system to die a natural death" and to be succeeded by a "return to simplicity" that produced "the extraordinary succession of masterpieces of the so-called Franco–Flemish Renaissance." That period was marked by occasional "prodigious feats of counterpoint," but "with the advent of humanism at the end of the sixteenth century people began to tire of all this virtuosity."

The next brief triumph of paper music came, of course, in J. S. Bach's two masterpieces of exemplary counterpoint. But we are reminded of their special purposes, and that their composer also produced *Erbarme dich*. And now we come to the main point (and the third thesis): in dodecaphonic music the standard provided by the ear is totally rejected. Anyone can see this just from the way in which a twelve-tone work is produced, but it is further substantiated by a report on experiments, "carried out with the strictest scientific objectivity," on the perceptibility of twelve-tone structures.

First the recipe for a twelve-tone composition: "Write down the twelve notes of the chromatic scale in any irregular order . . . Your inventive work is now finished. All we have to do now [after combining two forms of the row] is put in time values and space out the octaves in order to obtain the beginning of a piece in two parts which will continue along the same lines [an example is given]. The author of the example pledges his word that he has placed the figures strictly at random and that he has not touched up the result in any way." This method "is the only and exclusive criterion for 'serial music.'" (Normally there would be no point in reporting on such aggressively simplistic stuff. However, our other authors have something like it, too, and for good reason. This notion of what serial composition is plays an important part in a general theory of modern music.)

As for the experiments, they showed that "composers, pianists, even Conservatoire professors were incapable of distinguishing between two different series employed in the simplest fashion." From such evidence "the author arrived at the conclusion that serial music was based on the rejection of any criteria of a perceptual order in favour of a purely conceptual approach in which perception plays no part."

How did music get itself into such a fix in so short a time? The answer is given in a version of what I shall call the "crisis theory" of the history of twentieth-century music. (I shall report on the versions of our other authors in due time.) "At the beginning of the 20th century the musical *evolution* of Germany and Central Europe was in a *desperately static* situation. Through Brahms, Mahler, and Strauss it had followed for half a century without essential modifications the impulse given by Beethoven and Schumann" (italics mine). "The desire for new sonorities, the logical outcome of a static condition which had gone on too long, was universal. It was normal and legitimate." The italicized words represent familiar themes: evolution becalmed, the implications of a single style too long followed out.

Two paths opened out of the crisis. The French solution, which Chailley embraces, was the expansion of the concept of consonance by Fauré, Debussy, and Ravel. This meant the stabilizing and individualizing of sonorities produced by new chords from tones that were at first alien to one another (e.g., chords of the eleventh). Thence developed the principle of bitonality and, eventually, of polytonality. But through all this the consonance-dissonance polarity was maintained.

The other solution was the central European one, owing to Schoenberg. This began with the abandonment of the consonance-dissonance concept and, with that, of the "ultimate criterion of the ear" (note the presupposition about the natural status of that polarity). With the consonance-dissonance principle gone there was no longer any sense of the *relations* between tones. The new line substituted the *succession* of tones as the central principle. The twelve-tone method was simply a systematic way of putting that principle to work.

But Schoenberg, and especially Berg, still "endeavoured to obtain through the series (or in spite of it) a means of expression to which traditional reflexes were still able to respond." Webern "carried Schoenberg's postulates to their extreme logical conclusion," relying "entirely on the numerical sequences in his series to replace any other melodic or harmonic conceptions." Still, he left the determination of "rhythm and line to instinct." This gap was plugged, in turn, by the total serialists. But their music, totally determined on the compositional side, was still put in the hands of performers for interpretation. That final gap was filled in by electronic music using definite pitch.

Two tributaries branch off from this main stream, but continue in the same direction. One is the introduction of random procedures into composition. If the sense of the modern movement is away from the composition of "music having its origin in an instinct which has been evolving for thousands of years," then the production of music *without any intention or impulse at all* on the part of the composer is entirely within that movement. The other tributary is a logical consequence of serialism. Because serialism has done away with all relationships between tones, there is no longer any reason to insist upon the use of tones at all. Composers of concrete and electronic music without pitches, and before them futurist composers who utilized "live" noise, have therefore merely followed out the implications of Schoenberg's invention of the twelve-tone system. Experiments with microtones belong essentially in the same category.

This story will be found, in one form or another, in most historical expositions on music in the twentieth century. I shall want to study its variants in our other authors. But for the present I want only to make five brief observations about it. First, it assumes, as in the quotation from Babbitt's essay, that a becalmed evolution is unacceptable and creates a pressure for change. Second, it is based upon a single critical event, moment, or style that has implications for the future. Third, the following out of those implications is a logical process. (Chailley's dislike for the process is beside the point. Schoenberg committed the original sin, and his followers were swept along by the necessity of its implications.) By spelling out the process, Chailley has created an order for a large number of the general phenomena of twentieth-century composition. Fourth, in one of its dimensions the story traces a gradual transformation in the relationship between music and people (both composers and audience): from the subjective to the objective. Fifth, in following this course composers have opposed nature.

"Universal history" is one name given to Chailley's sort of thing—from the very beginning to the present, taking in everything that the eye can see in all directions. Historians did it in the eighteenth century, and we have come to regard that fact as an aspect of their spirit of enlightenment: perched atop their pinnacle, they surveyed the whole past as a development leading to their present. *40,000 Years of Music* and Walter Wiora's *The Four Ages of Music* belong to a new round of universal histories, once again breaking out of a recent and still current parochialism that does not flinch at the title *A History of Musical Style* for a book about Western music since the Carolingian age. Wiora states the purpose: "To prevent generalizing from the limits of some particular time-bound European style as though they were the limits set for all music, a prerequisite is to survey the subject from the point of view of universal history." In order to find within the present multiplicity of tastes "the essential coherences of our time" we are obliged to trace the "development and progress" that have brought music to its present condition, to pick out from the "many currents" of the "river of history" the "main water-courses."

In this round the scope can be far wider, for the art history and archaeology that were just getting started in the eighteenth century have been going for two hundred years, and we have already had a half-century of ethnomusicology. But there is a far more important difference. The earlier universal histories saw humanity floating up to an eternal heaven; the current ones see us sinking into an eternal hell. Whatever their claims, now, as then, universal histories are written in order to prove something about the present: then, that the present was the beneficiary of a long progress; now, that the tradition rejected by the avant-garde has the weight of universality. Wiora writes, "Its spread throughout the world rests upon the imminent universality of Western music and its systems." "Universal history" turns out after all to be a kind of super-parochialism, and the familiar historicist apparatus serves an ultimately propagandistic purpose.

The commanding idea in Wiora's estimation of the musical present is not new: a march to the limits of music, and, by some composers, a crossing over to the other side. Three questions clamor for immediate attention: how we define limits (the old question about what is and is not music); how the limits are approached; and what lies on the other side. The answer to the third question is obvious, but not very interesting: speech and noise. The answers to the first two questions are to be found, of course, intertwined in the study of universal history.

Wiora describes music's lemming-like drive to the brink in terms of two opposite processes. The first is a process of stripping away the "layers that constitute a fully musical work of art." This ecdysiastical review will recall Chailley's tracing of the stepwise removal of the aspects of human participation in music. First, "the more music lost of its share in general connections like religion, home, style of living, the more of its corresponding properties vanished: aura, ethos, perspective, and so forth." ("Character" and "meaning" may be added from elsewhere.) Second, "As the background and content of the musical work of art have been weakened or eliminated, so also have the strands of its fabric: the theme negated, harmonic logic, modulation, architectonics renounced." What is left is a music that is "atonal, athematic, anhedonistic, culturally ascetic." (counterpart to Chailley's "old-maidish isolation from life"). Elsewhere the process is described in terms of increasing "dehumanization," and of course that brings the parallel with Chailley's exposition more sharply into focus. "To begin with, there is replacement of the performer by apparatus . . . Even the listener in this technical Age plays a far from fully human role . . . Carried to extremes, the radio needs no listener at all; the music is broadcast at the stated time, even if there is no one to take it in . . . At the same time those musical structures that correspond directly to man's psychophysical organism, like pulsating rhythm, plastic melodic forms, and the periodic alternation of systole and diastole are eliminated." (These are identified as "natural orders"; their position in Wiora's theory will be discussed shortly.) Further, "music is dehumanized by the suppression of the chief subject of most earlier music—man, a psycho-physical whole—as well as by the loss of all former sense of music as something possessed and inherited."

"Expansion," on the other hand, is the "conquest of new territory" (new techniques, new realms of expression). Now if territory is to be conquered it must have been there to begin with. With this Wiora opens the floodgates to that old torrent of concepts: "Music is not a purely imaginary region that genius produces out of nothing, but by and large a realm of actual potentialities [sic!] that are discovered and realized." The expansion of music is the "gradual conquering of inherent and objective problems through prolonged common effort. In accord with this dynamic and with historical logic continuous developments take place. The historical significance of masters like Josquin, Monteverdi, Bach, or Haydn consisted not only in their having given expression to their own character and that of their time and country . . . but in their having mastered the objective tasks set them by the state of development at which music had arrived in their times. They actually and objectively labored at the shaping of genres . . . and at solving problems of form . . . Like research men concerned with the solution of scientific problems, composers went after problems that arose from their material itself, consistently unfolding whatever possibilities its varied content offered."

It is surely significant that Wiora can regard as normal this objective role of the composer vis-à-vis history for the past, while at the same time he reads slogans expressing the same attitudes as signs of the demise of music when they appear, somewhat sharpened, on the banners of the avant-garde: "The most advanced stage at which technical procedures have arrived sets problems against which traditional harmonies show up as impotent clichés" (Adorno). "The new situation places the artist with no possibility of escape before the obligation to say what has never been said" (Stuckenschmidt). It seems a central fact about our time that in their slogans the composers of the avant-garde and their spokesmen-ventriloquists have merely fallen in with old historicist-objectivist attitudes about how things happen in music history. Wiora seems on the verge of recognizing that connection when he associates these slogans with the progressivism and futurism of the early nineteenth century. What he does not observe is the common origin between his own historical apparatus and those same currents.

If historians see composers as objective workers at history's tasks, why should they raise such a fuss when composers begin to see themselves in the same role (for that is in a sense what the "dehumanization" or "objectification" of the musical transaction is about)? If "dehumanization" is the word for what is happening to music, then it is also the word for the ideal that historians have been pursuing for a long time.

The ideal of objectivity represents a philosophy about the relation between human beings as cognitive creatures and the world they come to know. There is no ultimately reliable defense to be made for the case that it should regulate the transactions called history but not those called art.

To pick up Wiora's thread again: If expansion is the conquest of territory (the realization of potential), and territory, to be conquered, must have a prior existence, sooner or later the territory must be exhausted, the potential used up. The process of expansion runs its course and ends in the same region as does the process of contraction: in the "border zones of music." And that tidily defines the condition of the musical present. There remains the third question: How shall we determine what constitutes "a fully musical work of art," in order that we can know what is meant by the assertion that we have reached, and crossed, the borders of music? Once more the answer to the question "What is music?" can lie only in music's history.

We must enter into the total scheme of Wiora's book. Here is the key: "The *exodus from the realm of music* corresponds in reverse direction to the historic transition from *pre-musical* and *part-musical* forms into the *realm of music*" (italics mine). The four ages of music are represented by the italicized phrases, and one sees that they are related in a cycle of growth and decline—Spengler's scheme, more or less. Premusical forms are those of the "prehistoric and early period," the First Age. It goes back some sixty thousand years before Christ, but extends, in primitive societies, to the present. It is a *pre*-musical age because "primitive music was interwoven with supramusical activity" such as cult, dance, and shamanism. But its study constitutes a necessary part of a history of music, for it stands to music's total history as the first act to a play or the first movement to a symphony, and "one cannot understand a drama without the first act, or a symphony without its first movement."

Part-musical forms are those of the high civilizations of antiquity and the Orient, and they comprise the music of the Second Age. (The notion of cultural survivals from earlier ages in peripheral [that is, non-Western] civilizations is a central aspect of Wiora's system. Western culture pushes on while other cultures remain fixed in an earlier age, until the Fourth Age, when Western culture becomes universal.) It is distinguished from primitive music first by virtue of its position in *high* cultures, which are characterized by the development of writing, the building of cities, the organization of states, and so forth. As for the *intrinsic* distinguishing marks of Second Age music, these are mentioned: music can be divorced from cult; it becomes elevated and prominent; special varieties of instruments are developed that are no longer directly associated with practical implements through magic; music philosophy and music theory are developed; notations are devised; and the structure of music begins to be based upon what are referred to as the "natural orders."

This last notion occupies a most crucial position in Wiora's system. The natural orders, or gestalten, are the harmonic overtone series, with fourth, fifth, and octave as the basic elements of musical harmony, regular metric pulse organized in four-measure periods, and the principle of tonality (broadly conceived, to be sure). Now we begin to sense what is meant by "fully musical." The expression "part-musical," which Wiora never clarifies directly, must be understood to refer to the still tentative way in which the natural orders are grasped in the Second Age. And the process of history is now to be seen as the gradual *discovery* of the natural orders, and the eventual exploitation or realization of their potentialities. This is the objective task at which musicians through the ages have worked collectively. Whatever their immediate and narrow concerns, history, writes Wiora in the words of Hegel, has kept them at the larger task "through a trick of reason."

The Third Age, the age of Western music, is the one most substantially responsible for the accomplishment of that task. It is the age of musical notation, polyphony, fixed composition, and architectonics on the basis of the natural orders.

In the most literal sense Wiora has written a more ethnocentric history than those who, like Crocker, simply take no interest in any music other than that of the Third Age. For the configuration of *all* the world's music is formed about that age as a zenith; the rest is preparation and decline. I have summarized the details of the decline in its last stages (the Fourth Age); its beginning is told, once again, in what I have called the "crisis theory" of the history of twentieth-century music. Here is Wiora's version.

Over-rich in tone-colors and chord-formations, chromatics and modulations, dynamic shading and variety of expression, works like Strauss' *Don Juan* or *Salome* appear to be peaks and end-points of a development. At the same time, however, signs of stagnation and atrophy gave indication of a process that, often interpreted as decadence, was just as much transition to the Fourth Age as decline of the Third. The possibility of finding new chords and modulations within the framework of the major-minor system came to an end. Rapid passage into remote tonalities had become easy and smooth, losing its value as it lost the genuine character of modulation . . . The more radical tendencies of the "New" music [in the Fourth Age] followed upon evolutions and crises in the period preceding . . . Thus Schoenberg went beyond certain elements in the *Tristan* style and freed them from the diatonic counterweights that in Wagner provide contrast and help the play of equilibrium.

And so began that process of peeling off the layers "that constitute a fully musical work of art." Just as in Chailley's exposition, this little episode occupies the position of life-trauma in the Freudian sense. With it the story is more or less complete; but we might well wonder whether it is really a story about music—what we experience at concerts, even those of avant-garde music.

Almost at the end of his book there is a hint that Wiora, too, has had enough of all this narrative apparatus and historicist jargon. He writes, "However much the will to progress grows and stiffens, a number of facts indicate that it no longer altogether corresponds to the present stage of evolution." And then he suggests a "second mode of historical becoming." It is a process not of movement toward the future but of a "deepening in another direction." New works are "not to be understood as inspired primarily by the idea of continuation along a single-track line of progress . . . The history of composition may go from one high point to another but make no actual progress." This becomes the central idea of Meyer's book, but the thought that it might be inspired by "a weariness of progress, a weariness of history" (Wiora's expression, not Meyer's), and not by an analysis of what is happening, is interesting.

Perhaps this weariness on the part of the historian is an ironic consequence of the composer's acceptance of the scenario that the historian has been writing for so long. There is a hint of that, too, in Wiora's discussion of the place of ideology in the Fourth Age. "In the new age music is conditioned as never before by ideological cogitations. Programmatic writings, reviews, criticisms, commentaries, and school courses are not extras one could do without; they are necessary to make possible the secondary system [music] they sustain." This condition of the modern musical situation has already been discussed in the second section, but not with the same sense of exhaustion. Stanley Cavell has given it a better expression: "Whether what [present compositional procedures] produced is music or not, they certainly produced philosophy . . . Perhaps it would be nicer if composers could not think, and felt no need to open their mouths except to sing."[18]

From all such concerns Crocker stands at some distance in his very unruffled book. It is perhaps the most ideologically consistent—and certainly the most ideologically bound-up—book of music history yet written. If there were some belief that textbooks are for presenting facts as against opinions or theories, then Crocker's book would fall quite as wide of that category as Chailley's and Wiora's books, despite its avoidance of open controversy. But if textbooks are regarded as paradigms that embody the assumptions and beliefs of a field, then this is the most representative textbook we have.

The presence of historical ideology is felt almost everywhere in this book. (The outstanding exception is the section on medieval music from 700 to 1150, a field in which Crocker has himself done distinguished original work. This is easily the best general treatment of the subject now in print. That this section, with whose subject Crocker has had the most intense direct engagement, should be relatively free of the formal apparatus of the rest of the book, shows in reverse that the forms of historical narrative have dominated their substance.)

Here is how Crocker cuts through the multiplicity of today's musical world, in Part 5, "Beyond the Triad: 1900–1964." The narrative "must limit itself to the serious, progressive repertory, primarily because this is the only one that carries out the thrust of development traced so far." And how do we identify that repertory? "Only the long line of history can help us sort out the development of style in our time." There is the essential self-deceiving tautology of our logical systems of history.

How the story begins is revealing of several important aspects of Crocker's system. Styles grow out of the initial thrust of a single work or group of works. These set the course for the future both because they constitute repositories of potentials and because they pose problems upon which succeeding composers are at work. In both senses the beginning of a style carries implications for its subsequent development. Styles end when their implications are realized, exploited, used up. At such a time styles break up into fragments (that is the aspect of the system that is uniquely Crocker's), and history awaits the arrival of some person who will put the fragments together in new ways, perhaps adding new elements.

The story of the twentieth century begins in the overlap of an end and a beginning—the brief period in which is located the crisis in other versions of the story. Strauss had lived "hopelessly beyond" the end of a style. "Only his early symphonic poems are stylistically significant." (This is a special concept which does not necessarily depend upon intrinsic value; Haydn's London symphonies are stylistically insignificant in Crocker's narrative.) With *Salome* and *Elektra* Strauss "cut away the foundations of his own further development." "Musical sensationalism," "wasteful extremes," "expressive dissonance" and "distorted modulation" are aspects of the decadence. Mahler made his symphonies "larger and larger until their shape no longer bore any real musical relationship either to the expressive fragments with which they were filled or to the shapes of Haydn and Beethoven from which they were descended." These were contradictions of style to which Mahler reacted with a "musical expression that tended [to] become convulsive . . . The extraordinary intense, hypertense language so produced became one of the starting points of a whole new style, but only in the hands of . . . Arnold Schoenberg, who saw that this intense language had to be dealt with *objectively*" (italics mine). Mahler's symphonies, thus, also marked the end of an era.

Debussy found a way out of the practice that meant the end of Strauss's progress, excessive modulation. He minimized the functions of chords, playing instead on their sonorous quality. With "the sense of key and the force of modulation virtually eliminated" his music became static, and as he got older his music "tended to become bright and hard" and "less dreamy." The Violin Sonata "seems at first prophetic of the new style of the 1900's—harsh, discontinuous, largely without a sense of key." (This is one of a number of descriptions of pieces that seem more to be designed to fit the story than the work described.) But Debussy was not the messiah of modern music. The Violin Sonata "only shows how Debussy was breaking up traditional style into its smallest fragments without finding a way to combine them into a new style." Nevertheless he seems to have found those qualities—"static" and "discontinuous"—that came to dominate the modern.

At this point there is a fork in the road. "The choices confronting composers right after 1900 can be conveniently polarized around Wagner and Debussy. On one side lay developmental forms, based on chromatic modulation and leading to extremes of expression [the "radical post-Wagnerian," Viennese line] . . . on the other side lay the discontinuous forms, based upon static sonorities or interrupted progressions [the "radical post-Debussyite," Parisian line]." The Parisian line was more prominent right after 1900, the Viennese line more obscure.

Stravinsky and other young composers around Diaghilev picked up Debussy's static and disjunct qualities, depending upon the narrative of the ballet as "substitute for the tonal line previously sustained by harmonic function." (The contemporary experiments of Henry Cowell, Charles Ives, and Luigi Russolo are mentioned next, but are immediately dismissed as novelties which "did not of themselves result in new shapes," but rather "belong to the disintegrating phase of the old style.")

Now if words like "static" and "disjunct" describe the basis for the continuity of the Parisian line, then it is clear that the story is no longer about style (as the preface insists) but about ideology—on the level of the greatest generality and in the terms that are the currency of the most slogan-ridden discussions of the modern situation. As Wiora observed, the prevalence and necessity of ideology is itself a condition of the modern musical situation, and as these reviews show, that is as much so for the critical and historical understanding of the music as for its composition.

Concepts of such generality are devoid of critical precision, of course, and it is perhaps for this reason that the long line of history begins now to meander and snarl, never again to recover its sharpness and sense of direction for the remainder of the book. In the second decade the Parisian avant-garde led a reaction against Debussy's "dampness" (Cocteau's term), producing a "music-hall style" that is "bright, hard, brassy, commonplace, and objective." The foremost exemplar of that style was *L'histoire du soldat,* which became a model for the 1920s.

The Bartók quartets are in the opposite position; they continue the "stylistic curve traced by Beethoven's late works" that was left hanging in the 1800s, but they have no implications for the future. So much attention given over to a line that ends abruptly is a fault in the execution of the author's design, an ideological lapse that seems to betray a personal proclivity to the music itself.

Now the attention shifts to Vienna, and the central figure is Schoenberg. "When asked on one occasion if he was *the* Arnold Schoenberg, he said 'Someone had to be; no one wanted to be; so I volunteered.'" This quintessential anecdote falls into place in Crocker's narrative with greater ease than coincidence will explain. It is worth asking how much responsibility Schoenberg bears for the historical style of the modern century, as well as for its musical style. The answer will surely be that, as has happened before, historians have accepted with insufficient reflection and then perpetuated a self-image that has the authority of documentation. What Crocker reports of Schoenberg's historical beliefs are no more or less than the essentials of his own system. "Schoenberg had a strong (almost obsessive) sense of stylistic history and its continuity. He *knew* that music had to spring from its *immediate* past . . . He was convinced of the necessity of developing, in *logical continuity,* from familiar musical ideas to new ones . . . What set his work apart was the *speed* with which he *traversed the development* from *past* to *future;* even he, it seems, could not *fully comprehend* the *implications* of what he did" (italics mine).

Schoenberg's stylistic progress to 1912 is marked off mainly by four pieces. *Verklärte Nacht* was "not an end but a beginning," with "developmental shapes, chromatic modulation, and progressive transformation of themes," which "remained the framework of Schoenberg's art for the rest of his life." In the Five Pieces for Orchestra "Schoenberg spoke a violently ejaculative, *disjunct* language in the loud movements, an abnormally *static* tone in the soft one" (italics mine). *Erwartung* "is one of the pieces that *had* to be written: it is the extreme form of music-drama, as conceived and developed by Wagner. It is also a logical endpoint, the end of all purely musical means of expression. An attempt to pursue this line of development could only result in a scream of terror, the next piece sounding just the same." The way out of that blind alley led to *Pierrot lunaire,* which "set a standard for intensity" but was "not more convulsive than its predecessors." Beyond that expressive significance, *Pierrot*'s place in history is earned most of all for its thrust toward the twelve-tone system.

The background of this episode is the chromatic modulation practiced since Haydn and Mozart. Composers of the 1800s searched for keys that would sound fresh and unexpected, but still logical. This ultimately created a tonal diffusion, through tonal concentration in individual triads. Schoenberg (in *Pierrot*) extended this principle to individual notes, which "acquire individual significance instead of being merged into conventional groups (triads or their derivatives)." As for the chords that *are* used, "they are ad hoc constructions," and "as chords they have to satisfy two negative conditions. They must not sound like traditional harmonies" and "they must not sound too simple (octaves, say, or fifths) . . . Chords, like notes, must now be chosen to avoid any kind of tonal confirmation."

Pierrot was written "almost automatically." Schoenberg did not consciously recognize the solutions that it embodied until the Serenade op. 24 and the Suite op. 25. The twelve-tone method was a systematization of those solutions. Crocker's exposition of the method is to be compared with Chailley's, bearing in mind that a difference in language is made inevitable by Chailley's polemical purpose. "First a suitable series of twelve tones has to be preselected. If such a series is to realize its basic purpose, it must avoid outlining a triad or triadic derivative; it must avoid suggesting a triadic progression; it must avoid in even more subtle ways any feeling of tonal focus. Such a series, once preselected, can be used repeatedly, taking the notes in order for as long as the piece needed to go on . . . twelve-tone technique made it possible to select the next note without going laboriously through all twelve [as Schoenberg had to do in composing *Pierrot*]. The composer had only to reach into the series for the next note, and then drop it into place." His attention was now largely freed from tonal considerations, and he could concentrate on "melodic character, choice of figure, texture, timbre, overall shape," which dimensions were "as yet subject only to the composer's intuition." (Note the dichotomy here as well as the implication that these latter dimensions, too, will eventually fall into the automatic category.)

That the student is offered no hint of how the row might be "preselected" for the "melodic character," "overall shape," and even harmonic organization that it would lend to the piece will be objectionable to anyone who knows this music well. But Crocker means it that way, for later he writes, "The negative function of the series is a more important formal element than whatever positive function the series might have." What "important" means in this context I shall come to in a moment. But first, this idea is false. It is false to suggest that the relationships among pitches in *Pierrot* are to be understood entirely in terms of what they do *not* produce (see, for example, David Lewin's discussion of pitch-structure in *Die Kreuze*).[19] It is false to imply that the interval content and order of a row are of little import, so long as no triadic structures are implied (a rule not very well heeded in any case). And it is, above all, false to offer students the simplistic view of composition in which the first consideration is systematic avoidance, and the rest is a matter of intuition.

This discussion of music in terms of what it is not—this tracing of the stepwise departure from a point of origin—is in basic form like the history of twentieth-century music as striptease offered by Chailley and Wiora. That is the only context, after all, in which the approach has any worth at all. It is like "atonal" and "nonrepresentational." These anti-critical concepts do not open ways into works of art. Their only value is for the gross comparison of works of art with earlier works of art, in order to show their location on the long line of history. All this is confirmed with candor in Crocker's remark that "the importance of Schoenberg's *Serenade* and *Suite* for twelve-tone technique has sometimes overshadowed their integrity as pieces of music." It is necessary to offer just one corrective, in the spirit of my introduction: It is historians who do the overshadowing, but the material does not require them to do so.

We come eventually to a fork in the Viennese line, that is, the radical post-Wagnerian line. One road continues with Schoenberg, the other follows the way of Webern. Actually Webern "began in Brahms rather than in Wagner," hence his "course was not identical to Schoenberg's but ran parallel to it . . . Like Schoenberg, Webern moved logically from old to new; but here the move was so swift that even now the developmental curve is hard to trace." The first problem is that of the Five Pieces for String Quartet, op. 5: written at the time of Schoenberg's Chamber Symphony and Five Pieces for Orchestra, and before *Petrouchka* and Mahler's Eighth Symphony, but already showing the progressive disjunct character. Op. 10 "has old pieces alongside new ones. The long, static, central piece is frankly coloristic [hence, presumably, old, although 'static' has already been identified as a progressive quality]. The last piece, however, is *properly* disjunct" (italics mine).

Webern's adaptation of the twelve-tone technique emphasized its "static" rather than "dynamic" aspects. "The sense of *being in* a segment of a twelve-tone field . . . was stronger than the sense of *moving through* that field" (italics mine). Crocker has here (unwittingly?) picked up one of the slogans of the avant-garde: "The new music aspires to Being and not to Becoming." Despite that difference, however, the basic negative function of the row is preserved, while (speaking of op. 21) "the inner logic, as in Schoenberg, is provided by whatever intuitive direction the composer gives to the twelve-tone material."

Berg was the only composer of the group who found a compromise between this negativism and tradition, represented through its expressive shapes. *Wozzeck* is "on one hand a stream of relentlessly emotional music, and on the other hand a succession of serial constructions." (Again description that is more faithful to the story than to life.)

For a brief interlude in the 1930s, the line of history becomes slack, taking on a tone of "stylistic nostalgia" especially in the composition of large numbers of symphonies (Milhaud, Honegger, Hindemith's *Mathis der Maler,* the Russians, Respighi, Malipiero, Bax, Vaughan Williams). Like the Viennese, Stravinsky kept the gains of the preceding decades. The *Symphony of Psalms* clearly displayed the static, disjunct, nondevelopmental features of the new music. And so did the Symphony in C, despite its symphonic form. But in this "Stravinsky was right; it was the symphony that was now wrong. The new music was simply not symphonic, any more than it was developmental."

Tiring of this intermezzo, and "picking up the threads of the twenties, music now seemed to press forward to do what it had to do." But by this time we are five pages from the end; the narrative begins to race and dissolve into the roll call that is almost invariably found in the last sections of general textbooks of music history; and despite the ringing tone, it is difficult to pick out of the narrative what music's destiny is supposed to be.

These, in any case, are some of the elements: a "stylistic compromise with the past," exemplified in Stravinsky's *Orpheus;* a move to establish Webern as "the model of really new music," especially for his "static, timeless quality"; a tendency to "control all aspects of a complex, detailed musical fabric" (in place, remember, of the reliance upon intuition). This leads to the serialization of the nonpitch elements of composition, and reaches back to the objectivity of the Parisian music-hall style of the twenties. In the fifties the negative function of the series finally gave way and the principle became one for organizing new patterns.

Electronic music is broken down into works that tend in the direction of noisemaking, which is a nonprogressive return to the historical position of Russolo, and those that work with pitch. Because electronic media can produce an unlimited gradation in pitch, they place pitch on a common basis with timbre and rhythm, and thereby they make more feasible the step of generalizing serialization to these other parameters. It is evidently for this reason that pitched electronic music is called "progressive." (Note that from the same historical system Chailley was able to regard Russolo and nonpitch electronic music as logical consequences of the abandonment of pitch *relationships*, that is—whether he approves or not—as *progressive.*)

Chance or random procedures are *not* progressive, however. For, "insofar as their results are totally unique and *irreproducible* they do not belong to the history of style" (italics mine). (Readers should note the utter consistency of this judgment within the historical scheme, but that it could not have been reached outside the scheme. This is the exact sense in which only the long line of history can enable us to make order out of today's multiplicity.)

At the last the outline of the whole process is quickly reviewed, and a "classic style" is tentatively defined. The basic direction: "Music must move beyond the triad into a twelve-tone space" (Boulez's "imperative of our time"). But Schoenberg and Webern "did not, and could not, destroy triadic tonal order—did not, *because it was deteriorating at its own rate* quite independently of their efforts; could not, because the same steady rate permitted functional harmonic references to survive both of them" (italics mine).

The "classic style" is devoid of the "explosive violence" and "incongruous extremes" of the early 1900s. It is "refined and well bred." Some of its exponents are Mel Powell, who writes serial and electronic music with "great charm and a smooth finish," music that is "least likely to sound too static" (is this a reversal?); Mario Davidovsky, whose electronic music is "convincing"; Luigi Nono, whose *Intolleranza* "fused a variety of techniques into a spectacle in the high Italian tradition"; and Lukas Foss, who has "worked out successful means of improvising twelve-tone music with an instrumental ensemble." Perhaps so, but what is "classic" about all this, and in what way has the long line of history yielded exactly this selection and these judgments? The final element of the "classic style" will round off our puzzlement: "The counterpoise of tradition is now represented by composers who have long been at ease in the twelve-tone field; they write serial music when they feel like it, but emphasize less disjunct, more rigorously developmental forms" (is it a synthesis?). Two representatives are Roger Sessions and Alexander Goehr.

In the end we are left with the impression of a line that moves in terms of three polarities very grossly defined: from the triad to the twelve-tone field, from a developmental style into one that is static and disjunct, and from a reliance on the composer's intuition to an ever-increasing objectivity. About the first of these there can hardly be questions. For the second, now very much in the air, the terms as Crocker gives them are far too imprecise to be of much use. They are handled with more subtlety by Meyer, as I shall suggest. But the greatest difficulties are over this pervading notion of objectivity. What integrity is left that word for measuring the history of style when it labels both the droll style of *L'histoire du soldat* and the nonintuitive deadpan of the total serialists?

In Crocker's book the notion of objectivity informs the entire historical process. The key lies in the recurrence of these themes: logical continuity, necessity, and right (or wrong) reading of the necessary next step. The historical process begins with a model that constitutes a repository of potentials. Each stage in the process constitutes a working out of the problems and potentials of the preceding stage and holds implications for the next stage. The process is logical, then, in the strict sense that each stage follows deductively from the preceding one. What does not follow or carry further implications (what is not anchored on both antecedent and consequent sides) is not a part of the process (the London symphonies, Ives and Russolo, Cage). What does follow, follows by necessity, and one can say that "it had to be." When it is said, either by Crocker or by avant-garde slogan-mongers, that it is for composers to see what is necessary to do next, it is in effect suggested that they make the deductions that carry them from one stage to the next. This is essentially an objective task (compare Wiora), but it requires ability; some composers get it right, others get it wrong; some do it speedily, others more slowly. The historian is a monitor picking out the premises and conclusions at each stage and identifying the composer who has made the correct deductions.

Crocker's achievement is to present an account of music history from 700 to 1964 entirely in the form of this model. His insupportable assumption is that in doing so he has given a true report of "what happened." And thus he has involved himself in an unresolvable paradox. For in the most literal sense, to be objective is to give a report that is determined exclusively by the characteristics of the object; whereas everything here has pointed to the exceptional degree in which the controlling aspect of this narrative is its *form*. The message is overwhelmed by the medium.

Stanley Kubrick's film *2001: A Space Odyssey* is a universal history of humanity, told through the allegory of a science-fiction fantasy. Our simian ancestors are shown in the first part, "The Dawn of Man," in their struggle for survival. They feed on the sparse vegetation and fight, one pack against the other, for possession of the small water hole. They succumb readily to stronger predators. They huddle together for self-protection and can do nothing but screech to defend themselves. One morning they awaken to find a huge black rectangular monolith set into the ground in their midst, toward which they show a reverent, fearful behavior. Immediately following, one of them, crouched near a pile of bones, studies them thoughtfully, rather like the chimpanzees of gestalt psychologists. All at once he picks up a long bone and begins to swing it against a parched skull, which shatters. Now he becomes a meat-eater, for he can kill other animals. His pack can drive away their enemies from the water hole, using bones as clubs. They have effected an enormous expansion of their powers.

The ape, in ecstatic celebration, throws his bone end over end into the air. There it remains, transformed by the camera into an elongated space ship sailing through the void with a lyric grace. By this simple trick of cinematography a continuity is suggested, from that first extension of bodily strength, through four million years of evolution, to the extensions of both body and mind—machines and the computers that tend them—in a civilization with whose garish technical advancement and modernity the film is now at pains to impress us. Furniture is in Day-Glo colors, pushing buttons is the most vigorous work performed, men no longer wear ties (but the Americans still do not trust the Russians, and Russian women still wear black stockings).

Another one of those monoliths has been discovered, on the moon this time, in the midst of a magnetic field of enormous energy. It sends a single ear-splitting radio signal in the direction of the planet Jupiter, and with only that clue and the inferred knowledge that the object was buried in its present site four million years ago, the earth people launch an expedition to Jupiter. A gigantic space vehicle is manned by a crew of two astronauts, a survey team of three men placed aboard in a state of suspended animation, and a computer named Hal, which is navigator, stoker, valet, nurse, and governess to the crew. Computer technology has advanced to the point where Hal can speak both idiomatically and with feeling, so that, as one of the crew explains, it will seem natural to talk to it.

During the course of the voyage Hal appears to commit a technical error, then performs destructive acts that are more and more obviously willful, and finally—and with this the illusion of Hal's sinister independence is complete—causes the destruction of four of the five men and very nearly the fifth. The latter outwits him, however, and manages to disconnect the terminals of his higher mental functions. Hal goes to pieces, and just as his taped performance of "A Bicycle Built for Two" is running down, the spaceship with its lone survivor enters the world of Jupiter. The title of the ensuing final portion of the film is "Jupiter, and beyond the Infinite."

Now all rules about the relatedness of events and about the sequential and progressive nature of time are suspended. Once inside Jupiter's world the surviving hero witnesses a gorgeous phantasmagoria of color whizzing, undulating, and oozing across the screen. After this long display the survivor's little landing craft *is in* (does not land in) a large and elaborate Louis XIV boudoir in cool whites and olive greens. Through the glass visor of his space helmet one can see that the astronaut's hair is white and his face wrinkled. It is the first sign of an accelerating but yet discontinuous progression of his life history. He is seated next at a table in a dressing gown, hair white and thin, skin quite wrinkled, dining in silence and elegance. His arm brushes against a wine glass; it falls to the floor and breaks. He stares at the pieces for some time, incredulously. It is as though the sequence of events had no natural connectedness for him: knocking-over, falling, breaking. Now suddenly he is in bed, enfeebled, no more than skin and bones. He raises his hand in a helpless gesture toward the foot of the bed, and the camera turns in that direction to show another of those black objects, plainly this time lording it over the earthling. In the end he is a transparent embryo in an egglike encasement, fixed in space forever.

The allegory unmasked: from primitive beginnings humans have been evolving continuously. (The black monolith is Kubrick's deus ex machina—the idealist force working behind the scenes.) The crude tools and weapons by means of which we first gained leverage on our immediate environment were the antecedents of all that is now at our fingertips for extending and controlling the universe. But the potential for our advance, for the growth of our power, is limited. There is a barrier, toward and through which the human will to progress impels us. At the boundary zone, cataclysmic disruptions of our own making launch humanity into the next (final?) stage of evolution.

It is a state of being without progress and without history, without any distinction between past and present; a state in which the sequence of things doesn't matter, in which causality is nonsense, in which whatever happens is no longer a consequence of human will or intention. For humanity it is an eternal and static state. And we have been advancing steadily toward it ever since that ecstatic moment when we first learned to reach beyond ourselves.

The film shows an interesting reversal in the ideas of progress and evolution. For us those ideas have filled the screen—we have known hardly anything else. But in this universal history the whole of human evolution is only a brief moment. The universe is little affected by our passage through it. It is as though the powers represented by the black monoliths had wound up a toy and allowed it to play itself out. The norm is the static state before and after. Progress, it turns out, is a game of relatively short duration. Kubrick's fantasy is representative of the transformation that has taken place in the idea of progress since the eighteenth century. It is the injection of the biblical and Faustian forecast that there is a disastrous price to pay when we push our knowledge beyond its natural limits; the joy in progress sobered by the fear of the unknown—the belief that progress exhausts itself in some sort of disintegration. Perhaps this doomsday fear is a scar from the disappointment of the eighteenth and nineteenth centuries' utopian hopes for progress. It is the basic form of the books by Chailley and Wiora, and even Crocker's book thrives on little doomsdays in which individual styles reach their limits and disintegrate.

———————

The film has picked up and reflected a gathering theme about what lies (or rather, what does not lie) on the other side of the barrier: no progress, no history, no past or present, no causality, no rationality, no intentionality. Here is the "objectivity" that our authors have wanted so much to talk about. Very like this myth is Leonard Meyer's vision of the past, present, and future of music. I want to discuss his book under four headings: beliefs about the nature of the historical process; the nature of the past—what Meyer calls "traditionalism"; the transition from past to present; and the nature of the present—what Meyer calls the "New Ideology."

Meyer is plainly not at ease with the simplistic traditional vision of orthogenic history that our other authors cheerfully perpetuate with their long lines, waterways, and Lamarckian evolutions. He tries a number of refinements, of which some constitute genuine improvements, other appear—but only appear—to be alternatives. In the latter category belongs the classification of historical changes as "developmental," "trended," and "mutational." The distinctions among these varieties have already been summarized and reasons given why the refinement is only apparent. Meyer's example of a nondevelopmental change showed, first, how very much a logicodeductive (i.e., orthogenic) system in Crocker's sense his notion of historical development is. It showed, second, that it is only because of this fact that the nondevelopmental concepts are at all necessary. (Darwinian evolution is a model for developmental change that accommodates mutation with ease. References to evolution in music-historical literature are in general non-Darwinian, and it should be a high priority in this field to consider the advantages that the Darwinian model offers. For art history this has been persuasively done by James Ackerman.)[20] And third, it showed how directly Meyer's classification was associated with certain traditional and misleading assumptions about causality and influence in the history of art.

But Meyer derives a very beneficial idea from the notion of implication, too. It is the suggestion that we think of historical relations in terms of hierarchies. Rather than the exclusive attention given over—because of the obsession with causality—to the connections of immediate succession, Meyer argues that we relate events on different levels, depending on the sense in which events have implications or meaning for later times. The chief benefit of this idea lies not in the notion of hierarchy itself, but, as I have already suggested, in the alternative it offers to the objectivist epistemology. For it says that the meaning or significance of an event is not fixed once it has happened by what it is, or what it causes, but that it may change according to what happens, perhaps much later, and according to the questions one is asking about it. (If Meyer uses this notion in his arguments about the present but turns out in effect to ignore it in his assumptions about the past, that does not rob it of its potential benefits.) For the eternal problem of periodization in history this approach offers a flexible alternative to the scheme of one progression, divided once and for all into so many successive segments. "Period" measures the length of time during which the implications of a style continue to be felt—its "reverberation time." This will vary, depending upon the level on which one looks, or on the questions that one asks. Different aspects of a style are "closed out" at different times, and any aspect may be reopened at any time. Hence the notion of an integrated period with fixed characteristics and fixed time boundaries is impossible.

Alas, this is flatly contradicted by the model that Meyer builds later on for explaining the history of styles. Meyer's ideas about the differences between the past and present musical situations depend on this model, so it will be necessary to give a brief description of it. Now the language in which it is given is that of information theory, and because I wish strictly to avoid the controversial question whether special insights accrue from the description of musical communication in that language, I shall translate into ordinary language. (Of course, my claim that I can do so without any loss of meaning has certain implications about that question.)

"Perceived information" (I shall say "musical understanding") is a function of "compositional redundancy" (I shall say "the explicitness of the musical structure," which in turn depends upon the range of implications of any given event, the directness with which implications are carried out, repetitiveness, and so on) and "internalized redundancy" (I shall say "the learning of the conventions of a style by some community"). A law is given about the history of styles that defines this function more closely. It has two parts that may be stated thus: (a) The explicitness of musical structures tends to vary inversely with the learning of style-conventions. At the beginning of a style period explicitness is maximal and learning is minimal. During the major portion of a style period the two factors achieve a balance and remain relatively constant. Toward the end of a period explicitness is minimal and learning maximal. The early phase is called "preclassic," the balanced phase "classic," and the latest phase "mannerist." (b) As the result of this inverse relationship, musical understanding tends to remain at a relatively constant level. (There is a diagram that accompanies all this, which I do not reproduce here because of its implication, supported by the language, that "perceived information" and "compositional" and "internalized redundancy" are quantifiable. Thus in the preclassic phase compositional redundancy is *greater than* internalized redundancy, while in the mannerist phase it is the other way around. I do not disagree with this; I simply do not understand what it means. Similarly I do not understand why "perceived information" should be maintained at a constant level. What the model seems to say is that at the beginnings of styles audiences have the fewest expectations and artists provide the most explicit structures, while at the ends audiences have the most expectations and artists provide the least explicit structures. That does not seem to be the same state of affairs at all, so far as musical understanding is concerned.)

Now certainly it seems sensible to suggest that, in a general way, artists and their audiences will tend to learn styles together, and that as artists broaden the range of possibilities audiences will learn something about the norms of the style. In later stages of this process artists may be expected to depart from norms with increasing confidence. This would seem to be a fair description of the changes in the Viennese Classical style. But it would be a very poor description of, say, the history of the so-called Notre-Dame style. That style is generally regarded as having an early and a late phase, associated with the names of Leonin and Perotin, respectively. It is also generally agreed that Perotin's music is far more concise, compact, directed, explicit, and repetitive—far more "redundant"—whereas Leonin's music is comparatively ornate, loose-jointed, free-flowing. It may be that we are mistaken in calling this the music of a single style. Perhaps Leonin represents a "disintegrating" style and Perotin a new style, newly put together.

This thought reminds us of something that Meyer has said, but does not ever seem to believe hard enough—that historical concepts such as "style," "early," and "late" are constructs. Meyer's model might serve as an operational measure for the beginnings and ends of styles, and I would offer as a serious suggestion to the author that close study of various "styles" on these lines and through detailed analyses of whole pieces might prove invaluable. The first step would be a responsible effort to quantify the referents of "information" and "redundancy" in music, at least sufficiently so that "greater" and "lesser" take on some meaning.

Meyer's book is certainly not history in any ordinary sense. But its main business is nevertheless the comparison between a present and a past. It is really, in effect, an elaboration upon his *Hudson Review* essay "The End of the Renaissance?" reprinted in Part 1 of the book ("As It Has Been").

The articulation of present and past follows consistently from the principle of history as hierarchy. The past is the era of the Western tradition, and its beliefs and values are explicated in all of the essays reprinted in Part 1. (The others are "Meaning in Music and Information

Theory," "Some Remarks on Value and Greatness in Music," "On Re-hearing Music," and "Forgery and the Anthropology of Art.") The present begins in the post–World War II era, when those tenets ceased any longer to dominate Western culture; and the future will be as the present, for it is one of the consequences (or aspects) of the radical break between past and present that history in the linear sense has come to a halt. All this is explicated in Part 2, "As It Is, and Perhaps Will Be." Part 3, "Formalism in Music: Queries and Reservations," is mainly an argument suggesting the inefficacy of certain aspects of contemporary compositional procedure. It has little to do with the large historical vision of the book, hence it does not fall in the purview of my subject.

The criteria by which Meyer marks off the Western tradition of the past from the "New Ideology" of the present are matters of a high order of generality, but they seep down into the details of style and into the transactions between men and art. They are "established esthetic values" which function as "deep-seated dispositional habits of mind and body and . . . constitute the fundamental framework within which we apprehend, interpret, and respond to [art]." These values may be discussed under two headings: Beliefs about the creation of artworks (presented in the essay on forgery) and characteristics of traditional music and musical communications (summarized in "The End of the Renaissance?").

In the Western tradition the act of artistic creation is the making of something new, and in this the artist is exercising a freedom of intention and choice. This defines originality, but originality comes at the risk of failure. Regarding the artist as entrepreneur in this sense favors an emphasis on individuality and on artistic creation as personal expression. This explains the great interest in our tradition not only in works of art but also in their makers. It is important to us that we know their names, the circumstances of their lives and of the creation of their works, and how those works relate to other works, including those by other artists—their implications for the future, what influences they show, and so on.

Thus our interest in history is traced to a conception of artistic creation. But note how sharply that view of creation is contradicted by what we have learned about the dominant vision of the historical process, even as it is presented in Meyer's model. In that vision creation follows from the conditions of the inherited past, not from the artist's will (perhaps in biography, but not in history; that Crocker's book abjures biographical information about composers is fully consistent with his embracing of that vision). And as I have been suggesting and shall suggest again, that same vision has been not rejected but reaffirmed by the "New Ideology."

The first principle among the characteristics of the Western musical tradition in Meyer's exposition is what we might call the principle of musical implicature. Musical events imply other musical events, and from this simple fact follow Western notions of musical structure and pattern, grammar and syntax. The learning by a musical community of the grammar and syntax of a style (compare the model for stylistic development) constitutes the basis for the work's communication to its audience. In listening we make predictions about where the piece is going and how it will get there. The relation between the expected and the actual constitutes the basis for the communication of meaning. By virtue of the property of implicature Western music is called "goal oriented" or "teleological."

Meyer's analysis of the aesthetics of antiteleological music is the real virtue of his book. It is the most thorough and thoughtful treatment of a subject that has lately been gathering a good deal of attention. The themes are those we encounter in the history books, but the analysis of their patterns is more enlightening here. The ultimate effect of the attitudes that he understands as the "New Ideology" is the halting, at least for the foreseeable future, of the process of historical development; that is the central—although I do not believe it is the most valuable—contention of the book. Because Meyer has, even if somewhat shakily, endorsed the conventional understanding of that process, one has to ask what can have happened to bring the machinery to a stop.

Reading "The End of the Renaissance?" one has the impression that this revolution, which has "left the world of traditionalism so badly shaken," has been the collective and willful enterprise of just about one generation of artists in all media who have recognized our old assumptions as just that and, finding them no longer persuasive, chucked them. On this impression the postmodern movement is a consequence of thought and will, an exercise of free choice according to the traditionalist conception of the artist. Consistent action according to a paradigm leads to its negation.

But given Meyer's endorsement of the view of history as process, there must be a historical account of the way in which that process led to its own negation. No doubt Meyer does not regard it as his business to give such an account, yet there is enough to hint at what its terms and its form would be. It comes in a single brief passage about the "origins of the twelve-tone method."

The musical practice of the nineteenth century was characterized by a markedly increased use of the ambiguous chords, the less probable harmonic progressions, and the more unusual melodic and rhythmic inflections possible within the style of tonal music. The distinction between the exceptional and the normal became more and more blurred; and, as a result, there was a concomitant loosening of the syntactical bonds through which tones and harmonies had been related to one another. The connections between harmonies were uncertain even on the lowest—the chord-to-chord—level. On higher levels, long-range harmonic relationships and implications became so tenuous that they hardly functioned at all. At best, the felt probabilities of the style system had become obscure; at worst, they were approaching a uniformity which provided few guides for either composition or listening. Schoenberg's conscious abandonment of tonality (in his non-serial atonal works) merely recognized the situation for what it was and carried the dissolution a bit further.

It is the crisis story again, in which, simply by following logically in the direction they had been taking all along, composers found themselves in a fully negative situation at the limits of a development. In that situation they had to solve two problems: first, to invent constraints that would circumvent the necessity of choosing every pitch purely on the basis of the composer's "own taste and as much of tradition as he cared to bring into play"; second, "to avoid implying functional relationships appropriate to the syntax of traditional tonality." Schoenberg's solution was the twelve-tone system, of which "almost all the basic rules follow" from Schoenberg's basic stipulation that "even a slight reminiscence of the former tonal harmony" was to be avoided (recall Crocker's formulation). And from this invention followed—by extensions with which Meyer quarrels—the wing of contemporary musical practice to which he refers as "Analytic Formalism" (let it suffice for now to identify it as the total serialist wing). No clues are offered as to the origin of the other major wing of contemporary practice, called "Transcendental Particularism" (for now, the chance wing).

––––––––––

Having now reviewed this story four times I should like to pause over it for a moment before continuing the summary of Meyer's case. It seems a matter of the greatest urgency for the history of twentieth-century music that it be reopened, and that this time it not be written to conform to the needs of the larger story. These are some of the questions that should be asked: Of which pieces is it said that higher-level harmonic relationships hardly functioned at all? (Are they by Strauss or Mahler? What would their music sound like if we did not hear it as a manifestation of crisis?) Of which pieces is it said that every pitch is chosen from scratch with only intuition and the avoidance of keys as guides? Why are motivic and other configurational relationships not taken into account, either in the "disintegrating" old or the groping new? How long will it be before the explication of twelve-tone practice in general discussions goes beyond such kindergarten-level exposition of things to be avoided?

History aside, the ideology of transcendental particularism proceeds philosophically from either one of two apparently opposed worldviews which, nevertheless, ultimately converge upon a single set of beliefs. In one view the world is seen as a complex network of relationships, in which everything is related to everything else. To single out any one relationship from all the others is to present an arbitrary and necessarily distorted image of reality. Therefore, any *re*presentation is a *mis*representation, and only the immediate experience of the world as directly *presented* is to be trusted.

In the other view the world is regarded as a collection of unique particulars. *Any* concepts that relate particulars necessarily distort them. So this view leads to the same conclusion as the first, that only the immediate experience of the world as directly presented is reliable. From this prescription follow all the tenets of transcendental particularism, as Meyer sees them.

Art, regarded now as a succession of direct experiences, expresses only itself. Any concepts that serve to organize the experience will distort it. Habits and predispositions that the audience may bring to art will interfere with the communication of art (whereas in Meyer's explication of tradition these are fundamental to communication). The reader will recognize at once that this is a version of the old objectivist dream that experience can be the exclusive function of the properties of objects. And so far as artists are concerned, their role is not to invent but to discover and present (again the old historical view).

From the disqualification of relatedness as the center of interest follows the suspension of sequences governed by order and causality, and the substitution of a random and timeless, hence static, present. With causality suspended prediction becomes impossible, and anything may happen. Hence explanation becomes irrelevant, to be replaced by observation.

The elimination of the distinction between past and present means the elimination of history, and the dominating ideas of impersonality and objectivity in art make it unlikely that art will take prevailing directions. Thus the ideology of transcendental particularism is itself one of the sources of Meyer's prediction about the stability of the future.

The manifestations of this ideology in all the arts are familiar enough: John Cage, Karlheinz Stockhausen (at times), Robert Rauschenberg, Claes Oldenburg, Nathalie Sarraute, Andy Warhol, and so on. But I believe there are paradoxical aspects of either their work or their utterances, given this exposition of their ideology. The most glaring one is recognized and rather too easily dismissed by Meyer: the denial of the distinction between past and present and of history in general, coupled with the obsession with novelty (see the remark of Cage quoted early on). It is of no help that Harold Rosenberg's easy resolution is cited, to the effect that new art must be new only to *someone*. (It seems not only that anything may happen, but that anything may be said!) One cannot both profess to be uninterested in the difference between what is past and what present and insist upon the necessity of doing only what has not been done in the past.

Still on the subject of history, the genesis of artworks is of no interest under this ideology. Yet there is so often emphasis upon the spontaneous *process* of art-making, and a deemphasis on its *products*. Indeed there is a well-represented position that under Western traditionalism the artwork is closed and objectified, whereas in the Orient and again recently in the West the experience of art is of its *making*.[21] This is one of the considerations that has led some critics to regard the art of the avant-garde as highly subjective.[22]

Some curious coincidences—if not full-blown paradoxes—arise from transcendental particularist ideas about the nature of artistic creation. It is discovery, not invention, and by this denial of the old Aristotelian dichotomy art is assimilated to nature. But this radical break has managed only to bring the avant-garde around to the view expressed by Wiora—but not first or alone by him—that art has to do with the discovery of natural orders. What is more, with the rejection of the idea that art has to do with the exercise of choice in favor of the idea that artists should accept and present what they find, the avant-garde has come around to Hegel's dictum: "das Aktuelle ist vernünftig."

Perhaps the answer to all this is that the idea of internal consistency is itself inconsistent with the ideology of transcendental particularism. But another answer is that this ideology is in some respects intensely historicist in orientation, and, as Wiora observed, very old-hat.

Between transcendental particularism and analytic formalism there is considerable overlap, and it is in this overlap that Meyer finds the new ideology of our time. Under the former artists discover; under the latter they construct. Under the former there cannot be any question of value; under the latter value inheres only in the construction or the design of the work itself. Because of this contextual emphasis, art is capable of expressing only itself under the latter as well as under the former. Because the value and meaning of an artwork inhere in its design alone, the history of its making is an irrelevant consideration. For making art is solving problems, and we are interested in the solutions, not in the way they are found. Then the circumstances of time and place of creation, and the person of the artist, are all irrelevant to the understanding of art. Art is objective and antihistorical. The distinction between art and nature is broken down under analytic formalism, but in the opposite direction. Because we come to know all things through constructs our knowledge of nature is like our knowledge of art. The posture of formalist art is said to be antiteleological, principally in connection with its nonfunctionalism or what Meyer calls "flat hierarchies" (relationships on the moment-to-moment level only). Again, formalism's antihistorical attitude is said to favor stasis.

The impersonal and objective bias of formalism encourages composition by means of precompositional systems. Therefore, music based upon the serial ordering of nonpitch as well as pitch elements, and that in the composition of which computers are employed, are the chief embodiments of this ideology. In addition, the antihistorical bias of formalism tends to equalize the music of the present and the past so far as their present relevance is concerned. As with transcendental particularism, all of history tends now to be simultaneously present. This encourages the use of music or styles of the past in new composition (the recent experiments of George Rochberg are cited).

Together with the values of traditionalism, these ideologies comprise the philosophical base of the modern situation in the arts. (It must surely be a matter of some puzzlement that a classification scheme which throws Carter and Varèse together and regards them both as belonging more with Kabalevsky than with Boulez can be thought to be very enlightening. But it must be remembered that the subject here is not composition or its products, but ideology.) Their coexistence is the mark of the pluralism of our time, and that they have achieved a sort of balance suggests that this will be a time of stability. On these grounds above all is based the contention about the coming stasis, and the denial that there is any crisis in the modern situation of the arts.

Here is where Meyer's vision departs from Kubrick's (and Wiora's) and becomes like Crocker's. It also begins to take on the appearance of a certain contemporary political position. Pluralism is not to be seen as harmful dissension but as a healthy, stabilizing condition. The activity on the extremes will work toward a consensus in the middle ("toward a common practice," in Crocker's language). The "center of gravity in the stasis predicted for the future" (Meyer's language again) will be analytic formalism, because it represents a "middle ground between the goalless world of extreme transcendentalism . . . and the severely shaken world of traditionalism."

But so far as music is concerned formalism is not yet ready to assume the leadership for which it is destined. Meyer gives over a third part of the book to the demonstration that formalist music has not been viable.

His argument is directed entirely against the theory and practice of total serialism, and it comes down to the thesis that the music has been complex beyond the limits of the human perceptive-cognitive process. It is Chailley's experimental evidence raised to a very much higher level of sophistication, but grounded on the same premise about the limits imposed by nature. The argument is concluded with this appeal: "If the method and theory [of serialism] are to transcend the private pleasures of ingenuity, the unheard order must be validated in the public arena—in the realm of aural experience. To present the complex simply and the convoluted plainly is to meet the most formidable challenge, to demonstrate the highest skill, to achieve the greatest elegance." And, one has to add, *to abandon the tenets of analytic formalism and embrace those of traditionalism.*

For here is something about the ideology of modernism that has not been said by any of our authors—indeed that has been violated by all of them: The open quest for the public arena is anathema to a true modernist. Perhaps the great unarticulated mob of traditionalists will take exception to the shadow under which the historian and critic leave them. But I should think that any true modernists among the avant-garde would be even more offended by the embrace of these two. (They would react, I imagine, like the students who were greeted by Lyndon Johnson on the White House lawn as "fellow revolutionaries.")

Modernism is by its very nature unfathomable and unpredictable; it is evasive and inconstant; it thrives by holding out. But it is not new. What our authors have ignored, and with them the sloganeers of the avant-garde, is the struggle of the present—*any* present—against history. One perceives that struggle not only in "difficult" music of today's present, but also in the hundredth hearing of a great work of two centuries ago. One feels that the composer has achieved not the probable or the necessary but the impossible. That is what stands one's hair on end.

What lies at the root of the paradoxes that we have encountered throughout this review is the insistence of our culture upon taking its temperature every few moments to see how things are going, and especially the insistence upon doing so with ancient preset thermometers. Perhaps Wiora and Meyer are right in their suggestion that the process of history has come to a halt. But if so, it is because of our incessant tinkering with it. If the prognostications of our authors are correct, history has achieved a fantastic success. For then history need no longer pause, as Crocker writes in his final sentence, "waiting for the present to become past." History will whistle the tune, and music will dance to it, and there will be no telling the dancer from the dance.

Systems of history, which are invented as useful and even necessary ways of lending coherence to the varieties of artistic expression, end by dictating how art shall be. Networks of concepts, born of the need for descriptive categories, come to claim a place in the objective world of things and eventually claim to determine the choices that artists make— or to leave them no choice at all. The highest refinement of the historian's technique is a narrative in which art is the shadow of ideology. If our authors are right, music is on the verge of a totalitarian situation.

But they can be right only in a tautological sense. What these books demonstrate is that systems of history, as they become more vainly ambitious to explain the currents of music, also become increasingly crude and inaccurate as morphologies. They create a discipline of their own, and their value is to be reckoned by their internal shrewdness and consistency—not by their correspondence with the experience of events in the concert hall, which are not governed by the ineluctable logic of things.

CHAPTER 6

What Kind of Story Is History?

In the summer of 1980 I received the most surprising news of my career as a musicologist. A paper of mine was being discussed in a seminar on legal history in the Harvard Law School.[1] Naturally I was flattered. But I needn't have been, as I learned when I met with the instructor. His interest was in attacking the paper, as symptom of a malaise that was incapacitating historical studies in virtually all fields of the humanities and social sciences, including his own. I had summarized a theory of historical knowledge—historicist and hermeneutic—that emphasized sympathetic understanding, analysis, and interpretation, reconstruction of intentions, and representation of the past as a present. I had written that "this viewpoint has the important implication that temporal order and the concept of change are not of the essence in historical judgment," and that in seeking "knowledge of the past in its individuality and its particularity [the historian] aims to stop the past in its tracks and hold it still." And I had implied strongly that this attitude was an appropriate one for music historians to hold. That was the issue over which the legal historian wished to criticize my point of view.

For he shared an opinion—now widely held, as I came to learn, among historians of more than one subject—that "history at present seems to be in the process of self-destruction" owing to its preoccupation with the sort of "motionless history" that I seemed to be advocating. Deep analysis and technical problem solving, presented in monographs whose readers "can sometimes be counted on their [author's] hands," have served "not to illuminate the central themes of Western history but to obscure them." "Modern historiography in general seems to be in a stage of enormous elaboration . . . Historiography grows ever broader—and, one would have thought, deeper and more meaningful. But depth of understanding is a function, at the least, of coherence, and the one thing above all else that this outpouring of historical writing lacks is coherence." "The results of all this for history have been little short of chaotic."[2]

It is not that my critic took me to be an advocate for a music-historical counterpart of the heaps of lifeless technical studies that had inspired this much deep concern. It was my implication, which he had correctly gauged, that the "tendencies to represent the past in continuous narratives, and to make *change* and *novelty* the principal subjects of history" did not serve our best interests as historians, that he found objectionable. Indeed I had gone on to state that belief quite explicitly, and to claim that a recent formulation of our goal as "understanding the music and musical cultures of the past . . . catches the spirit in which many musicologists are now working." Comparing that with the task of investigating the development of style, which had been assigned to musicology by Guido Adler in the early part of this century, I had claimed to recognize a changing epistemology in our field, "a shift from the genetic to the ontological . . . Like historians of literature and art, we are becoming more interested in contexts of meanings than in contexts of causes" (see Chapter 2).

But as an engaged *Musikliebhaber* my legal historian was less interested in my proposed explications of meaning than in questions that could be answered only by narrative accounts. How was it that Beethoven came to compose the Ninth Symphony—not in the biographical but in the historical sense? What is the historical process that connects Mahler's symphonies with Beethoven's? (Carl Schorske's account of Mahler's music would not have satisfied him, for it rests on a complex interpretation of a particular social-cultural milieu.)[3] What has brought the art of composition to its present state? Such are the questions that he expected musicologists to address, just as he maintains that legal historians should return to giving narrative accounts of the evolution of systems of belief about the nature and administration of justice. His attitude, as I have suggested, is widely shared, and in prestigious places.

Bernard Bailyn's paper, from which I have been quoting, was delivered as the Presidential Address to the American Historical Association meeting in 1981—delivered, as he put it, *ex cathedra*. "The great challenge of modern historical scholarship," he wrote, is "to write . . . essential narratives—dominated by a sense of movement through time, incorporating the technical studies, and devoted to showing how the present world was shaped by its emergence from a very different past and hence concentrated on critical transitions from the past toward the present." That was the burden of Bailyn's message to his profession as outgoing president. But it was delivered in such emphatic style, and with such deliberate redundancy, that I must quote more of his text in order to convey the sense of urgency that is in it.

The greatest challenge that will face historians in the years ahead . . . is not how to deepen and further sophisticate their technical probes of life in the past . . . but how to put the story together again . . . in readable accounts of major developments. These narratives will incorporate anecdote but they will not be essentially anecdotal; they will include static, "motionless" portrayals of the past, but they will be essentially dynamic; they will concentrate on change, transition, and the passage of time; and they will show how major aspects of the present world were shaped—acquired their character—in the process of their emergence . . . Historians must be, not analysts of isolated technical problems abstracted from the past, but narrators of worlds in motion . . . The historian must re-tell, with a new richness, the story of what some one of the worlds of the past was, how it ceased to be what it was, how it faded and blended into new configurations, how at every stage what was, was the product of what it had been, and developed into what no one could have anticipated—all of this to help us understand how we came to be the way we are, and to extend the poor reach of our own immediate experience.

The last clause provides a clue as to why this must now be the main work of historians; not only in order to reverse the trend toward the dissolution of the dicipline, but as a public duty. The call for the return to narrative historical writing is usually accompanied by the admonition to aim for "a wider reading public" (Bailyn). C. Vann Woodward, the general editor of the *Oxford History of the United States,* identifies as the aim of the work to "provide an interpretive synthesis of the findings of recent scholarship" in a readable narrative "that will be readily accessible to the general public."[4]

Bailyn writes that the "lack of general coherence" in modern historiography has its roots in the "absorption [of historians] in the fascinating technical problems of history"—"captivating and strangely satisfying . . . yet severely vision-limiting." The success of that detailed work has meant the "erosion" of "the most venerable structure of Anglo-American history known in its narrowest form as the 'whig' interpretation . . . which explained the present in terms of an inferior but improving past." (Gordon Wood writes that "the old political backbone of history has been broken, and nothing has been put in its place".)

The Whig interpretation which narrated English history as a gradual and inevitable development toward liberty, was but a version of a historiographical paradigm that had begun to inform historical writing on every subject in the late eighteenth century, and has continued to do so until very recently.[5] It was a way of reconciling continuity and change in stories of transformation that were immanent, gradual, unilinear, progressive, and teleological, and that were marked by steady improvement in the sense of the fulfillment of a purpose, the realization of a goal, or the approach to perfection. In the nineteenth century it assimilated the metaphor of history as organic growth, especially in the history of the arts; and, especially in social and cultural history in general, it assimilated the doctrine of evolution, with the peculiar consequence that conceptions about the evolution of the arts have never been very much influenced by Darwinian theory, which posits a very different process of change. I must return to that presently.

That kind of historical narrative structure could not sustain the weight of evidence that was produced by ever growing numbers of scholars working with increasingly sophisticated research methods in ever narrower areas. It is not so much that the evidence showed it up as false, but as too simple and superficial, too heavily reliant on the influence of great events and the decisions of great men, too little aware of "deeplying conditions," "collective mentalities," "demographic patterns," "economic circumstances," "aggregate products of human action but not of human intention"—all factors that are suppressed by narrative and revealed by "structural analysis."[6]

Bailyn's carefully chosen language is aimed at this dilemma. The new narrative must be "rich" and "complex"; it must have an "analytic dimension never envisioned before"; it must depict the "continuing interaction of different dimensions in an evolving story"; it will be the product of "an alternative dipping and soaring motion of the mind as it drops down to scrutinize puzzling, tangled details, then struggles, not always successfully, to rise again to view the landscape whole."

Gordon Wood, whose review is the other source of the remarks I have been quoting, is not so optimistic about the possibilities. He, too, regards the state of modern historiography as "little short of chaotic." But

the revival of narrative will not be easy, [for] the plots, coherence and significance of narrative are always retrospective . . . The ending has to be present in the historian's mind, transforming everything . . . The past is not a series of stories waiting to be told. Such teleological narrative history cannot be truly scientific, it is simply story telling, not essentially different from fiction . . . [Whereas] monographic history is scientific history, the present call for a revival of narrative is essentially a protest against the spread of science in history writing . . . While intellectuals everywhere are promoting "structuralist" and other forms of non-linear thought, most historians cling innocently to their Newtonian belief that one thing follows another in a coherent and causally related narrative pattern.

This belief persists despite the reordering of "our conception of the historical process" that has been achieved by social science. In conclusion, Wood writes that "Narrative form as a representation of past reality . . . may not bear much looking into." And to correspondents who have either accepted in one way or another the continuity of history into fiction, or despaired altogether of writing history, he replies that "When all is said and done, when all the concessions to subjectivity, 'imaginative reenactment' [Collingwood], and the use of 'regulative fictions' [Kermode], have been made, historians still remain necessarily tied to the view that the past 'out there' really exists and that they can through the ordering of evidence bring us closer to knowing the truth about the past 'as it really was.'" The historian will remain, one gathers, permanently impaled on the horns of the dilemma between this "old-fashioned epistemology" and old-fashioned narrative.

But there is news of a reconciliation in unexpected quarters, one of the spawning grounds of the "nonlinear thought" of structuralism. The anthropologist Marshall Sahlins wrote recently, "Structural Anthropology was founded in a binary opposition of the kind that would later become its trademark: a radical opposition to history . . . In a way parallel to the Saussurean distinction between language and speech, structural analysis seemed also to exclude individual action and worldly practice, except as they represented the projection or 'execution' of the system in place."[7]

The social anthropologist E. E. Evans-Pritchard long ago traced the roots and consequences of this attitude of "hostility, or at least indifference," as he put it, to history. The reason for it is familiar:

> The precursors and founders of our science had attempted, mistaking irreversibility for inevitability, to formulate laws of historical development by which all human societies pass through a determined succession of stages. Even those who did not do this . . . sought to explain any institution in terms of its origins, or at any rate of its antecedents, which is the characteristic feature of historicist methodology. The so-called functionalist critics of these (also socalled) evolutionary theories had no difficulty in exposing their inadequacies. [They] should have challenged them, not for writing history, but for writing bad history. As it was, they dropped the history and kept the pursuit of laws, which was often precisely what made the history bad.[8]

But now Sahlins writes that

> all these scruples are not really necessary; . . . one can determine structures in history—and vice versa . . . The great challenge to an historical anthropology is not merely to know how events are ordered by culture, but how, in that process, the culture is reordered. How does the reproduction of a structure become its transformation? . . . Structural transformation involves structural reproduction, if not also the other way around . . . The dialectics of history are structural throughout . . . The historical process unfolds as a continuous and reciprocal movement between the practice of the structure and the structure of the practice.

These discussions and swings of the pendulum have presented themselves to me in a firsthand and vivid way not only because of my unexpected encounter with legal history, but also because of a confrontation in my own mind between the attitudes that had provoked that encounter and the more recent experience of trying to write some part of a narrative history.[9] Its subject is the origin of music writing in medieval Europe, and the early history of its relation to musical performance, composing, and pedagogy. It is an inherently dynamic subject, concerning the rise of a technology and the history of its relation to a changing culture. It can be described and explained only in terms of change. Wood is wrong; some aspects of the past *are* stories waiting to be told. The discussion on both sides is misleading, insofar as it implies that we always have a choice about whether or not to write narratives.

All the same, the yarn must be spun, and there are choices all along the way about how to do it. It demands technical analysis over a wide range of domains—paleography, semiotics, diplomatics, ecclesiastical history, liturgy, the literature of music theory, music. But when those have been done, and even before, the story can be put in motion only through acts of the "a priori imagination."[10]

The paleographer Bernard Bischoff has charted the numbers and provenance of books surviving from the late eighth and early ninth centuries in Europe and has evinced a pattern of growth in book production and the establishment of active scriptoria.[11] The historian F. L. Ganshof has observed an increase in the number of administrative documents surviving from the reign of Charlemagne and concluded that the use of writing for administrative purposes had become a matter of policy during that period.[12] There is a well-known letter, sent from Charlemagne (but believed to have been composed by Alcuin) to the abbot of the royal monastery at Fulda about 795, in which the latter is charged with the responsibility not only of assuring for his monks "a regular and devout life" but also of "teaching those who have received from God the capacity to learn . . . Doubtless good works are better than great knowledge, but without knowledge it is impossible to do good."[13] The oldest books written entirely in a finished Caroline minuscule hand are dated to the 770s. The oldest books whose texts are marked in the differentiated punctuation system that is still in use are dated to the 780s. From such evidence has emerged a story of a deliberate—and successful—drive to establish a script culture in the Carolingian era and kingdom.

The concept "script culture," the intentions implied by "deliberate," the verb "establish," the judgment entailed in "successful"—all these are supplied by the imaginative and critical faculties of the historian, and they are as true as it is plausible that such evidence fits together in that way, according to one's experience and a priori ideas about how the world is.

The oldest surviving book about Gregorian chant (*Musica disciplina,* by Aurelian of Réôme) was written about 850. The author's primary purpose was to provide a guide to the differentiation and proper execution of the chants of solo and choir singers according to modal-melodic-liturgical categories. At the time that he wrote, those chants circulated through oral channels; only the texts were written down. The features according to which he characterized the melodies are matters both of melodic pattern and of the manner of their performance (voice production, speed or duration of notes, mode of attack, perhaps pitch shading). By the end of the ninth century the practice had begun of writing neumes above those texts, many of which were derived from the signs of the punctuation system that had been introduced a century earlier.

Each of the statements in the preceding paragraph has been gained through the primary analysis and interpretation of some bit or bits of evidence. They merge in a continuation of the story begun in the paragraph before: as an aspect of the growing tendency to precipitate whatever was important to know into writing, a system of musical notation was invented during the ninth century, partly through adaptation of the system of punctuation that belonged to the writing system for language. Like that system in its original usage, the neumes were signs that indicate differentiation in the performance of language. They were written above the texts of the solo and choral chants as mnemonic signals that were to trigger the melodic patterns and performance features that the singers had learned through the oral tradition. Their primary task initially was to guide the singer in the proper fitting together of the patterns and performance features that were in his mind, with the text that was before him. They were not primarily signs for pitches that the singer deciphered in working out a melody. That notation eventually came to function in that way was the result of long evolution.

This narrative need not be retrospective, to transform its content from the point of view of the outcome, as Wood fears (although the *selection* of contents is necessarily determined by our present-day interests). But it has not been easy to avoid that in the history of this subject. It has been difficult for scholars in this field to write from the point of view of the present without treating the outcome as a goal or norm inherent in the process of change. It has been difficult to think concretely about the dynamics of a musical culture that functioned entirely without any writing system at all, in concepts appropriate to such a culture.

And then it has been difficult to think of a system of music writing as something other than an imperfect but improving system of pitch designation. It is the general problem that Walter Ong focused when he spoke of the concept of "oral literature" as akin to referring to a horse as a wheel-less automobile.[14]

In fact the most persistent obstacles throughout this investigation have been thrown up by something like the Whig interpretation. I can best exemplify that with a passage from a book that has been one of the most paradigmatic for the study of this subject: Peter Wagner's *Einführung in die Gregorianischen Melodien*.[15] In the course of an exposition on the evolution of precise intervallic notation, Wagner reproduced a page from a manuscript of the tenth century in which psalm verses are notated so as to show clearly only the contours of beginnings of cadences in their recitation.

This diastematy is of a primitive sort; it limits itself to showing occasionally through the individual signs whether the melody is rising or falling. But what is striking is that . . . one did not proceed further in this direction once the way was opened; that just in St. Gallen, where so many talented artists performed the musical service of the Abbey, no one drew from that the conclusions that, regarded at least from our standpoint, lay so near at hand . . . Unfortunately the circumstances drew the energies of the St. Gall artists in a different direction, which certainly put interesting and new tasks, but thereby removed the goal of neumatic writing from before their eyes.

In other words, the function to which neumes eventually evolved— the designation of pitch patterns—was inherent in the process of evolution as its goal, and accordingly progress toward that goal depends on the recognition of it by the actors in the story. This brand of evolutionism—it is essentially Lamarckian—had been superseded by Darwin's theory, but that has never really made a significant impression in the realm of the humane disciplines. Perhaps it is because the Lamarckian version could be readily assimilated into the general conception of gradual transformation, whereas Darwin's theory was actually quite dissonant with it. The difference is currently much under discussion among biologists in a new outpouring of writing about evolution, partly in observation of the hundredth anniversary year of Darwin's death in 1882, partly in connection with the current attack on evolutionism from the political right in this country.

Darwin's revolution consisted not in establishing that species evolved through transformation of other species, or even that they did so through the action of natural selection:

[His] real revolution consisted in the epistemological reorientation that had to occur before the variational mechanism could even be formulated. It was a change in the object of study from the average or modal properties of groups to the variation between individuals within them . . . Darwin revolutionized our study of nature by taking the actual variation among actual things as central to the reality. That revolution is not yet completed.[16]

That is, descriptions of change, even in biology, still miss that essential point.

Change in a species is not a matter of the uniform transformation of each of its members—the Harvard class of 1950 growing grayer as the years pass, the legs of the flamingo growing longer as the waters in which such fowl feed get deeper, the upper voices of organa growing more mobile as . . . Change is a result of individual variation. That means it need not occur at uniform rates. Such a view of human practices accommodates creative invention, accident, and collective behavior as sources of variation. From such a view the outcome of variation is neither inevitable nor foreseeable. It requires analysis of the particular circumstances under which particular changes occur.

The narrative structure through which the early history of music writing has been presented—it is a matter of descent, either from the prosodic accents of ancient language, or from Byzantine neumes—presents neumes as if they were really the microorganisms they resemble, languishing in a laboratory culture, each one gradually undergoing the same preprogrammed transformation independently of anything that any one of them does or experiences.

But neumes did not evolve in that way. They were invented, under particular circumstances, by persons with certain intentions. They were used, adapted, modified, imitated. But there is no place for any of that in the notion of evolution that has shaped narratives about this subject.

The history of style, which had once been the preeminent subject of music history, came to be told in similar narratives. It is an irony that, in the mode of historical writing that came to dominate music history, there was no place for individual creation as a factor in history. "Evolution" and "creation" are antonyms on the political front these days. But it is a weak notion of evolution in the arts that does not regard individual creation as the central factor of historical continuity and change. Perhaps it was the desire to make political history scientific that brought on monographic history, and perhaps the call for narrative represents protest against science in history (as Wood writes). But in musicology the ambition toward scientific status produced style history, and if there is a protest against science in our field, it has manifested itself in a "loss of interest in history."[17]

The general idea of gradual transformation does not have the appeal in the second half of the twentieth century that it had as of the late eighteenth century. The world outlook and aspirations with which it concorded—the Enlightenment ideas about the perfection of man, progress toward freedom or toward humanity, the political-historical program entailed in the Whig interpretation (progress without evolution), the need to accommodate a growing awareness that the physical and biological world could not have been what it was at the creation, the idea of the organism as a model for continuity with orderly change—all these coincided to define a place into which the idea of gradual transformation fits exactly, and made a strong commitment to that idea inevitable. None of those conditions really obtains now. The habit of construing history as a process of gradual transformation does not survive recognition of the weakness of that idea as an explanatory theory—both for explanation of particular things or events and for the explanation of real historical processes. And the idea of history as a sort of gradual improvement is simply not believed.

But the interest in narrative has survived the loss of faith in gradual transformation, and not only because the diachronic spread of a subject can sometimes suggest it. There is a satisfaction in narrative, a sheer narrative pleasure. Narrative is not restricted to the representation of movement through time. To narrate is to depict, and to evoke a sense of what happened—telling what all was going on at a certain moment, or telling about a sequence of events, but usually some mix of the two.

In my engagement with the early history of notation, I found myself striving for an account that could show those separate and distant items to be connected, and in a way that placed them plausibly in the context that eventually comes into focus. Nothing is more satisfying than the formation of a pattern in one's mind through which once disjunct items from the distant past become recognizably connected. The present call for narrative reflects a wish to restore that particular kind of definiteness to historical accounts, a wish for sharp images. This is what happened: "In 795 Charlemagne wrote to Baugulf, the abbot of Fulda . . ." Real people, intending and doing. Such a phrase reflects a desire to see history as a piece of life. This has to do not with the methods but with the satisfactions of history. To be sure, they have something in common with the satisfactions of fiction. But an important component of the satisfaction of history is the belief that one is depicting some real world of the past as it was, and that one has understood something about how some aspect of the present world is connected with it. Man is "fundamentally an historian," wrote Erwin Panofsky.[18]

Some years ago, at the end of a long evening's conversation with Michel Huglo about the origins of European notation, Huglo told me about an encounter with a Greek musicologist who asked him why "you Westerners" were always investigating the origins of things. Carl Dahlhaus, in the book already cited, writes "In the nineteenth and early twentieth centuries it was taken for granted that we had to know the origins of a thing in order to know its essence. By now, however, this basic tenet has forfeited much of its credibility." Indeed, it has lost power along with the faith in the scientific authority of diachronic narrative history. But the interest in origins has not gone with it—only the illusion that it reveals essences. People still visit the Washington Monument and the Green in Lexington, Massachusetts. The preoccupation with a question like that about the origins of our notational practice can become obsessive. As a matter of fact, however, the epistemology that Dahlhaus cites is in practice exactly backward. In order to understand the origins of notation, we have to get a better understanding of what kind of thing it was, but for that we must first have a better understanding of what kind of thing it is in the present. I interpret the current rumblings about narrative history as a maneuvering about its status, a new coming to terms with what it can accomplish. It is being called back not only with better research but also under more realistic terms.

———————

Considering the differences of discipline, intellectual tradition, and historical situation in which they wrote, between Dahlhaus—a German musicologist writing in Berlin after the experience of the 1960s, and "building upon the philosophical tradition of idealism"[19]—and Bailyn and Wood, North American historians writing North American history in the academically peaceful 1980s from the standpoint of the Anglo-American analytic tradition blended with American pragmatism; considering those differences, the correspondences in their diagnoses of the situation of historical studies and its background, and in their beliefs about the challenges to and possibilities for history, is interesting, to say the least.

Dahlhaus's book was first published as *Grundlagen der Musikgeschichte* in 1977. It was intended as a propaedeutic, on the model of Johann Gustav Droysen's *Historik* (originally lectures delivered in 1857). The tone—sometimes ferociously polemical or ironic, always dialectical—is not quite that of a *Lehrbuch,* something that must have to do with the atmosphere in which it was written (although regardless of circumstance Dahlhaus is perhaps the most dialectical writer in our profession). The attack in those days came from the political left and from sociology, but, while it certainly had an especially sharp edge then, it was a démarche on historical musicology of basically the same sort that leveled history in general and anthropology: a "loss of interest in history," Dahlhaus writes, an "aversion" to it, a "suspicion and nervous uneasiness toward the idea of music history as the principal concern of musicology," and a wish to supplant history with monograph studies focusing on sociological structure, system, and process. (History, for Dahlhaus, is history told, and in narratives: *Geschichte*—"worlds in motion," in Bailyn's words.) The book is newly relevant today, and its appearance in English in 1983 is an important publishing event in our field.

The possibility of writing narrative history depends on the positing of an "ideal object" whose continuity is followed in the narrative. In political history such ideal objects were the idea of "humanity," or of "national spirit." (In the Whig interpretation it was "liberty.") In music history that role was taken by the aesthetic concept of the "autonomy of art," as basis of a narrative of the "evolution of music presented as an account of the origin of autonomous works, born of themselves and existing entirely for their own sakes." The correlate is a history of compositional technique, or of musical logic. That meant music history as a narrative of change, with the emphasis on novelty. What "belongs to history" is what is new. The framework of continuity in such narrative was the biographical or organismal model.

What is thus described is "style history," designed as the alternative to writing history as "mountains of unassimilated facts," and to the "explanation of works by the biographies of their composers." But the "ideal object theory has largely fallen into disrepute," the organismal model "cannot be salvaged," and style history "has fallen by the wayside without argument." Historians write monographs, leaving narrative history to journalists. (In the United States the division of labor is internal: musicologists write narratives for undergraduate students and monographs for graduate students and for one another. Storytelling is reserved for the young, evidently.)

Style history began as an effort to "mediate between aesthetics and history," to write history without "doing violence to the aesthetic autonomy of works," to the "strong concept of art." But it ended by defeating its purpose, by "reducing works to illustrations of ideas and techniques." The other side of the crisis in history is a crisis in art theory: "The authority of the art work has atrophied in an age imprinted with the thought processes of ideology critique" (something like revisionism).

But "the concept 'work' is the central category of music, and hence of music historiography as well." That is the extra complicating factor for music history in comparison with history in general; music history is sui generis because of it. Dahlhaus leaves no doubt about what he means. It is the conception of an "abstract text, an *a priori* body of material content," with a "real" and "precise meaning," an "aesthetic object contemplated in isolation." The "waning of interest in history" is coupled to the loss of authority of the "work" concept. Without it there can be no music history. The alternative is the conception of music as "process," as basis of a sociological, anthropological, or functional study of music systems. Dahlhaus is not opposed to such studies in principle: he even offers a sketch of how one might be done. But they cannot supplant music history, and those who think they can are taunted for having done better at criticizing music history than at establishing a body of alternative theory and analysis.

This strong defense of the reification of the musical work as principal premise for music history is just that: a defensive move, against strong attacks. In content and context it is like Gordon Wood's recourse in the end to the view that "the past 'out there' really exists." But considered apart from that context it is a bad move. (I say this only about Dahlhaus's stance.) There are many reasons, but I shall state only the one from my provincial stance as a medievalist: the "work" concept has a history that is at least a thread in one of the central plot-lines of Western music history; it cannot sensibly be taken as a premise for that history. As Dahlhaus recognizes quite explicitly, that plot-line reaches its *kairos* only in the nineteenth century (but, as he does not acknowledge, even then the "work" concept in his sense represents "only one face of a notoriously two-faced century"[20]). But as it turns out when Dahlhaus begins to reconstruct the possibilities of writing music history, he does not depend only on the epistemology embodied in the "work" concept in the strong form in which he has formulated it.

Like Wood, Dahlhaus appears at one point to throw in the towel: "It would seem that attempts to reconcile history and aesthetics and to settle on a level of abstraction that would allow the writing of lucid history without violating the aesthetic nature of works . . . are all doomed to failure by their very nature." Yet "It must be possible to reconcile the autonomy aesthetic with a sense of history, to do justice at one stroke to both the historical and the aesthetic dimensions of musical works without sacrificing either coherence of presentation or the strong concept of art"—to obey the dictates of both "aesthetic autonomy and the concept of continuity." That is the challenge to modern music historiography.

The old narrative history having failed in its principal task of narrating the history of works, one cannot just start over again with improved analytical methods. The failure is immanent; it lies in the narrative model itself. Here, too, the return to narrative is undertaken with sights set differently. Dahlhaus's program is based on what amounts to the compromise of two principles: the large-scale orthogenic narrative and the epistemology entailed in the work concept.

Dahlhaus develops a conception of what is really entailed in narrative, beginning with an idea for which he acknowledges his indebtedness to Droysen, but whose pedigree really goes clear back to Vico. It is the distinction between historical data and historical facts: data (Latin, singular *datum:* "something that is given"); facts (Latin, singular *factum:* "something that is made"). Data are the items of primary evidence, more or less directly given. They are the products of intentional acts by persons in history. They become facts through the efforts of the historian to reconstruct those intentions. Thus the facts of history are interpretations made by historians. "An historical fact is nothing more than an hypothesis." But "Facts from the past do not become historical facts until they are made part of an historical narrative, or a description of an historical structure." Droysen wrote that no one before the mid-nineteenth century thought to speak of a history of music. (Dalhaus comments that the idea is right but the date is too late, in view of Charles Burney and John Hawkins. But in a way Droysen was not so far off; see Kerman's paper cited in note 20). "Historical facts have no other reason for being than to substantiate historical narrative or the description of historical systems." That means that historical narrative is a first principle. So Dahlhaus has reasoned and argued his way to an attitude that Bailyn displays intuitively, and that Wood fears: "The material of history can be said to be determined by its form [and] mode of presentation." The facts of a narrative are colored by the mode of their presentation. In beginning my narrative of the origins of European notation "About the year 795 Charlemagne wrote to Baugulf, abbot of Fulda . . ." I aimed to convey more than the raw facts about that letter.

Ranke wrote his history on the narrative model of Sir Walter Scott, but the historian of today is not bound by such nineteenth-century models. Dahlhaus proposes the narratives of Proust and Joyce as more appropriate ones. That means abandoning the position of the omniscient observer and presenting different perspectives, allowing contradiction, eschewing fixed beginnings and ends, giving up the illusion of seamless continuity, writing narratives of fragments of the past. "It makes eminently good sense to talk about a history of the nineteenth-century tone poem," but "'Music' writ large does not lend itself as a subject to narrative history." Thus "there arises a tendency to view history, not so much as the preliminary buildup to the present . . . but rather as a broad panorama to be gazed upon in aesthetic contemplation"; unmistakably like Bailyn's image of the "alternating dipping and soaring motion of the mind as it drops down to scrutinize puzzling, tangled details, then struggles . . . to rise again to view the landscape whole." The decisive difference is that phrase "aesthetic contemplation," always, for Dahlhaus, the point of departure and the center of the historian's constructions. (The language in this passage can be misleading: "aesthetic contemplation" is the contemplation of aesthetic objects, which entails analytical work. It is not meant in the sense of "gaze in rapture," but then again it seems clear that something of what first comes to mind on reading the phrase "aesthetic contemplation" is intended. That is, after all, the heart of the difference between music or art history and history in general.)

All this has to do with narrative form. After reading these discussions no one can possibly take the old "gradual transformation" model seriously. Dahlhaus has brought home for music history what Hayden White has been showing for history in general, the crucial importance of attention to *how* we write history for *what* we wish to say.[21] But what is music history *about*? What is the actual consequence for history—regarded as narrative in the broad sense that has emerged from all viewpoints that have been presented here—of the central position of the work?

Music history is possible only insofar as the historian is able to show the place of individual works in history by revealing the history contained within the works themselves, that is, by reading the historical nature of works from their internal constitution. To develop this assertion we must unpack the concept of "reading the historical nature of works from their internal constitution." What can come out is not a formulation of a methodology, but an impression of a counterpoint of narrative registers and dimensions with the text as cantus firmus.

A. The work is read through an analysis in terms of the history of forms and genres—in a way like reading the positions on a chess board at any moment in terms of the history of the game to that moment. This idea makes sense of a remark that Dahlhaus throws out at the very beginning but leaves unexplained: the phrase "memory made scientific" as a short definition for history. Memory is just such an ordering of cognitions about past impressions, reordered with each new impression. "The historical consciousness," wrote Dilthey, "has enabled modern man to hold the entire past of humanity present within himself."

Analysis in terms of the history of forms and genres became the basis of a mode of historical narrative for literature in the theory of the Russian Formalists, on which Dahlhaus reports with sympathy—at least in principle. It is a narrative of the dynamic between the stereotyping of aesthetic perception and the generation of new stylistic and generic norms with the aesthetic attrition of older ones.[22] In the field of art history, it seems to me that E. H. Gombrich's theory of the coupled evolution of the reading and making of visual images produces a narrative on similar principles.[23] Both theories entail very concrete ways of "reading the historical nature of works from their internal constitution."

B. In another sense the historical nature of the work lies in the composer's intention, "which the historian, in his faltering way, seeks to reconstruct." This is helpfully broadened to terms less likely to fire off stereotyped skepticism on this side of the ocean: it is in "the poetics that underlie the composer's work," and in the "consciousness of the original public for whom the work became an event," as far as these can be reconstructed by the historian.

But however successful the historian may be at that task, the "inner truths" about works—especially major works—may "remain largely latent at first and only gradually come to life." The identity of the work may then be thought to reside in the continuity of its subsequent history (what Walter Benjamin called the "afterlife" of artworks), rather than in its immutable text alone. This recognition becomes the basis for a different sort of narrative, a narrative of the "evolution of the inner truths of art works."

C. "History not only depicts a fragment of the past, but documents the present time of writing." The past is changeable in the sense that it is "always the past relative to a particular present, and hence is prey to the open-endedness of the future . . . Past and present form an indissoluble alloy." One of the dimensions of historical narrative will be a narration of the changing relationship of the present to the past, generated by the historian's engagement with past engagements with the subject. Despite Dahlhaus's unremitting irony about "ideology critique" he cannot and does not escape it, given the matrix he has set up for history.

This is a long way to have come from the strong defense of the "work" concept early in Dahlhaus's book. But that is the nature of the dialectic, as is made plain in the following: "History written in full knowledge of the nature of history strikes a precarious balance between two false extremes: naive objectivism and destructive radical scepticism."

In this summary, which is perhaps more accurately called an impression, I have left out refinements, qualifications, the caveats of antitheses that almost invariably follow statements on one side of a question. Dahlhaus believes very much in the specialness of the problems of music history. But reading him alongside thoughtful historians of other subjects one gets one general image, not several, about the motives for writing history, and the possibilities for doing so. It does not have sharp outlines, but it is strong.

And if my critic the legal historian is still up to his extracurricular reading, and wonders whether he persuaded me of anything, the answer is "yes, but . . ."

CHAPTER 7

Mozart and the Idea of Absolute Music

In 1814 E. T. A. Hoffman, the foremost music critic of his time, proclaimed the music of Haydn, Mozart, and Beethoven a "new art, whose
origins first appear in the middle of the eighteenth century." He called
those composers "Romantic," a characterization that has been lost to
tradition through its replacement by "Classic," with its very different
purport and emphasis.[1]

In identifying a new art Hoffman himself displayed new ways of
thinking about art altogether, replacing the idea that art is primarily
mimetic, that it represents something outside of itself—the outer world
of nature, or the inner world of affections. (The Doctrine of Affect
would be a case of that general view.) The formulation of an alternative
is something in which he participated together with some of the most
important literary figures of the time: Friedrich Schiller, Ludwig Tieck,
Wilhelm Wackenroder, Friedrich Schlegel, Novalis. The insight of Carl
Dahlhaus allowed us to grasp in the writings of those critics a coherent
new aesthetic of "absolute music" that was the dominant aesthetic of
the nineteenth century.[2] The more recent work of John Neubauer has
illuminated the background of this fundamental shift in ideas of beauty
in the arts.[3]

The slogan "absolute music" was originally Wagner's, coined in reference to Beethoven's Ninth Symphony.[4] In one of those ironic head-
stands on which historical tradition likes to build, it became primarily
associated with the anti-Wagnerite critic Eduard Hanslick, after the
middle of the nineteenth century. What is more, the idea of absolute
music that developed after the turn of the century does not seem to re-

semble very closely the representation of Hanslick's aesthetic that is in general circulation. But that representation is itself skewed toward views that came into fashion after he wrote. All told, the slogan "absolute music" took on its own power, like a political banner that is seized by persons of quite divergent persuasions—a fact that can sow substantial confusion for anyone reviewing the subject today.

Yet there is a core of belief that the slogan signified throughout. At the center is the conception of an autonomous instrumental music that is essentially musical because it is not determined by any ideas, contents, or purposes that are not musical. Freed from its ties with language, music is capable of a pure expression that is absolute because it is not conditional upon the associations—cultural and personal—that language necessarily carries as its historical baggage. To speak of absolute music is to refer both to music in its autonomy and to the absoluteness of its expression in that state. Its quintessence is the symphony, with its "beautiful entanglement of musical character."[5] (The paradox that Wagner should have coined the slogan "absolute music" for a work with text becomes understandable in the light of his conception of opera, discussed below.)

Pure and absolute expression on the model of music came, at about the same time, to be an ideal for poetry as well—a poetry that would depend on the sonorous beauty of words, but that would evade the concreteness of their conventional meaning. The difference is that the theory of absolute music could refer to an established body of works; the ideal of a pure poetry on the model of music was spun out in the air, so to speak. An open claim for its realization was made first in the age of the symbolist poets—for example, by Mallarmé in this remark about his poem *L'après-midi d'un faune:* "I was trying actually to make a sort of . . . musical accompaniment which the poet himself composes."[6] Still, something of that intention can be read in the poetry of Wordsworth, particularly in his portrayal of nature "diffused with feeling" and viewed from a distance that "freed the senses from the distortions of a particular moment." The distant visions of the painter Caspar David Friedrich likewise tended toward the "evasion of conventional symbolism" and the "elimination of the picturesque."

Poet and painter alike sought through distance to fight free of the ordinary concreteness of subject matter, the specificity of time and place, in order to gain a "universally intelligible expression" in a language "evocative of asceticism."[7] That pursuit reflects an aesthetic ideal parallel to that of the critics who set out the foundations of the aesthetic of absolute music. (Later, poets and painters would turn to abstraction as means to the same sort of end, and it is striking that abstraction has often grown out of the opposite of distance, an involvement with the object so close and intense that it universalizes and loosens the object from its concreteness.)[8]

An idea was born during this time that was powerful throughout the nineteenth century and that survived struggles with equally powerful opposing ideas to prevail in our own era. Roman Jakobson conveyed it in a famous essay, quoting the philosopher Edward Sapir: "Does not the very potency of music reside in its precision and delicacy of expression of a range of mental life that is otherwise most difficult, most elusive of expression?"[9] T. S. Eliot gave it a particularly eloquent formulation in his essay on *Poetry and Drama:*

It seems to me that beyond the nameable, classifiable emotions and motives of our life when directed toward action . . . there is a fringe of indefinite extent, of feeling which we can only detect so to speak out of the corner of the eye and can never completely focus; of feeling of which we are aware in a kind of secondary detachment from action . . . This peculiar range of sensibility is reachable by dramatic poetry at its moments of greatest intensity. At such moments we touch the border of those feelings which only music can express. We can never emulate music, because to arrive at the condition of music would be the annihilation of poetry . . . Nevertheless, I have before my eyes a kind of mirage of the perfection of verse drama, which would be a design of human action and of words, such as to present at once the two aspects of dramatic and of musical order.[10]

We recognize it again in another comment of Mallarmé, in language that is specifically evocative of what was said around 1800: "Either by the musician's will or unknown to him, the modern one among the meteors, the Symphony, approaches thought that no longer claims kinship with everyday expression only."[11]

These references are but fragmentary reminders of an important fact, that we have inherited our consciousness of Haydn, Mozart, and Beethoven as paragons of a new music from critics who were stirred by a far-reaching and radical new aesthetic movement that by its very nature touched all the arts, and whose ideals have been carried into our own era. We have forgotten that, and now we are used to thinking of the newness of this music as a matter of stylistic language (the *locus classicus* of that conception is Charles Rosen's *The Classical Style*).[12] It is good to be reminded that it was once understood—particularly by members of the culture in which the music was produced—in terms of its effect on the listener.

My project here will be to try a reading of the new aesthetic as a theory of the new music, with detailed reference to a single work by Mozart. I want to ask whether, in the encomium with which the critics surrounded the music that was from the first the model for their theory of art, we can read a direct and sensitive response to the music itself, and whether there is a chance for us to find resonance with their response in our own.[13]

It is *not* my purpose to identify a kind of music, to be called "absolute music," that I would differentiate categorically from other kinds of music. It would not surprise me if the reader were to wonder, "Why could one not characterize some fantasy or fugue of Bach, or some movement of Handel, in such terms?" One could. Nor would I be surprised if the reader were to wonder, "Did the Doctrine of Affects disappear from the field of active aesthetic ideas at the end of the eighteenth century?" Surely not. We find it manifested still in the ideas of composers about key-character, for example (see my discussion of Beethoven's beliefs on that subject in Chapter 2). Neither musical styles nor aesthetic beliefs are switched off with the suddenness and thoroughness of television channels.

I shall take the display of a new mode of thinking about art that is evident in the writings of critics around 1800, and the focus on the symphonies of Haydn, Mozart, and Beethoven, as historical givens; and I shall address myself to the question of how far those critics' ideas can resonate with my own apprehension of a work chosen from that repertory. It seems to me that we can really understand what they had in mind only to the extent that we can find such resonance. And to that extent we will have gained in the effort to locate the horizon between our vantage point on the music of Mozart and that of a sensibility that is contemporaneous with it. In that sense this is an exercise in hermeneutics, or, I may say, in historical criticism. Questions about continuity and change from the music of Bach and Handel and the aesthetics of their time will not be addressed further here. But surely there will not be substantial disagreement with those critics that a fundamentally new aesthetic is at play in the music of their contemporaries.

As I proceed I shall engage in a sort of dialogue with the most interesting book on Mozart that has appeared in recent years, Wolfgang Hildesheimer's *Mozart*.[14] Hildesheimer presents Mozart as a hero of the aesthetic of absolute music, but without any recognition that he is doing so. That so forceful and contemporary an interpretation of the composer reverberates with that aesthetic is itself testimony to its enduring influence. Once, writing about Mozart at the piano, he drops a palpable clue, probably to an unconscious connection: "These must have been moments . . . when he reveled himself [*sic*] in blissful self-forgetfulness, when he severed his connection with the outside world; here was the unadorned Mozart, who needed no intermediary in order to communicate . . . Here, and perhaps only here, he achieved pure pleasure in his own genius; here he transcended himself, becoming the absolute Mozart."[15]

This is Hildesheimer's Mozart figure in its essential purity, like the name Mozart standing alone as the title of the book. There is a paradox in the title, for it suggests by the isolation of the name the isolation of the figure as well, and that is surely intended. But it suggests, too, that Mozart is the book's subject; yet if he were, the whole point of the book would have been realized with the author stepping forward and confessing to his readers, "I regret, ladies and gentlemen, that my subject has eluded me."

It is not Mozart who is the book's subject, but the case of Mozart. And the presentation of the case as an enigma really depends on the author's tearing down of a popular romantic portrayal of the genial, Apollonian Mozart. In the course of the discussion about *Don Giovanni* Hildesheimer writes, "Mozart's dramatic music does not indicate motives for the characters' behavior or merely underline it; it does not follow the text but directs or leads it to that plane of expression where music is the parable of life itself . . . Mozart conceived his characters intuitively and preconsciously . . . He universalized their motives and psychic impulses in music . . . It was not life but music that moved him . . . His tone language, music, is fed from sources unknown to us . . . Mozart sublimated life in its universality without knowing it."[16]

The first sentence of this passage embodies a view of the relation of words and music in opera that grows out of the idea of absolute music. What Hildesheimer's understanding is of the subtle psychoanalytical concept of sublimation, he does not say. But we can take it in the plain chemical sense: Iodine sublimates from the crystal to the vapor state without passing through the liquid state, that is, without leaving any visible sign of an intermediate state. Earlier in the book Hildesheimer sets out as a thematic image the record of Mozart's life as a score, in which the upper voice represents the works and the lower voice the outer life. The inner voices, representing the inner life, are missing. This idea of the missing inner voices is repeated in the image of the sublimation of life. For it is not for lack of evidence that the inner voices are missing. They are gone, absorbed into the upper voice, that is, the works themselves: "Whatever part of Mozart's human understanding might have emerged and been applied to daily life had already been drained by this process of sublimation . . . In his music he freed himself from himself."[17]

But the inner life—the mental life—even though not recognizable as such in the works, makes its mark on them. To express that and to explicate it was the very difficult task that the writers around 1800 set themselves.

The problem of the relation of the inner life to the works is posed again by Edward T. Cone, writing about Schubert's *Moment musicale* in A-flat, op. 94, no. 6. Cone characterizes the piece as a "psychic pattern."

As I apprehend the work, it dramatizes the injection of a strange, unsettling element into an otherwise peaceful situation. At first ignored or suppressed, that element persistently returns. It not only makes itself at home but even takes over the direction of events in order to reveal unsuspected possibilities. When the normal state of affairs eventually returns, the originally foreign element seems to have been completely assimilated. But that appearance is deceptive. The element has not been tamed; it bursts out with even greater force, revealing itself as basically inimical to its surroundings, which it proceeds to demolish . . . The Trio . . . tries to forget the catastrophe just as one might try to comfort oneself in the enjoyment of friends . . . No matter; the Trio is doomed to failure. The memory of the original course of events is bound to recur, and the *Da capo* leads inevitably to the same tragic conclusion.[18]

In the surprise conclusion to his essay, Cone suggests that the psychic pattern displayed in the work models Schubert's mental reaction to learning that he had contracted syphilis the year before the composition of op. 94. To put it in Hildesheimer language, he claims to reconstruct the inner voices of Schubert's life from the evidence of the outer voices. If he had been writing about a work of Mozart's in this way, Hildesheimer would have protested it can't be done. The writers around 1800 would have sided with him, and more forcefully: They would have said it can't be done and shouldn't be attempted—but with reference to Romantic music in general, not just Mozart's music. It is a flaw of Hildesheimer's book that he presents this subtle relationship between the inner life and the works—one of his main themes, really—as though it were unique to the case of Mozart.

The "psychic pattern" of Schubert's piece is just the sort of musical narrative that writers around 1800 prized in symphonies. Cone has gained here a valuable link with the sensibilities of those writers. But he has lost it again in suggesting a concrete correlate in Schubert's life. For that suggestion undermines the recognition that for composers since the late eighteenth century the involvement of musical ideas in such dramatic scenarios was pursued for its own sake, in realization of an idea about what music should be and do. Language like "the interjection of a strange, unsettling element into an otherwise peaceful situation" and "the element has not been tamed; it bursts out with even greater force" could as well describe an aspect of the Mozart work we are soon to consider closely, but there the outcome is more positive.[19]

The mapping of musical narrative onto concrete subject matter would have been thought an act of trivialization in the eighteenth and early nineteenth centuries. The temptation to make such connections has its source in the tendency of music around 1800 to display characteristics in the way it progresses through time that resemble the patterns of mental life. But the temptation is always misleading. The narrative dimension of the music is not an invitation to invent programs for it, and likewise in my effort to display the narrative dimension of my example, I will not be outlining a program for it.

The symphony appealed to Tieck most among instrumental genres because of the beautiful entanglement (*Verworrenheit*) of musical characters that it entails. It has that in common with opera, but without the burden of plot and flesh-and-blood characters.[20] So Hoffman called the symphony "the opera of instruments."[21] In the word *Verworrenheit* there is the suggestion of a value for the chaotic. That is reinforced by Novalis, writing that "the ideal narrative is the tale whose wondrous, inexplicable and chaotic events constitute a completely musical texture."[22] Schiller's friend Christian Gottfried Körner wrote, "If the composer follows the emotional flux he will produce a cacophony, but if he represents a single affect he will depart from realism, for the soul experiences nothing but variety and constant change."[23] The tensions of different strains pulling against each other are a fact of mental life; they keep the possibility of chaos always in view, and they interfere with the possibility of a consistent texture to mental life, and of a smoothly linear progression through time.

Wackenroder wrote that symphonies present dramas such as no playwright can make. For they represent the enigmatic (*das Rätselhafte*) in an enigmatic language. They are not bound by any obligation to have the appearance of truth (*Wahrscheinlichkeit*); they are not tied to any specific plot or characters; they remain in their own purely poetic—as distinct from prosaic—world.[24] Under this conception opera is prosaic. Instrumental music is a higher, prior form. I believe it was in a sense prior for Mozart, as I shall try to show.

That the world of the symphony was characterized as poetic has a special significance. It is not that symphonic music has the attributes of poetry but rather the contrary, that it achieves that to which poetry aspires—purity of feeling and expression, without any evocation of conventional language or the ordinary world to which language refers. Because this condition is poetry's highest goal, it is regarded as the quintessence of poetry, that quality that can be called the poetic.

The paradoxical claim that music could be the highest embodiment of the poetic has its counterpart in the equally paradoxical claim from a much earlier era that poetry could be the highest embodiment of the lyric. That recognition brings into focus a different sort of historical context for this subject that we should keep in mind. It is the long story of the relationship between music and language, a story that I would liken to the history of a relationship between lovers—so close in the beginning as to be each a reflection of the other, followed by shifting relationships of dominance, moves toward independence and trial separation, now by one, now by the other, each emulating the other at different moments in their history, yearning for one another just when they appear to have achieved a measure of independence.

The idea of absolute music proclaims the "emancipation of music from language," as Neubauer puts it in his title. The paradox is that instantly upon its emancipation from poetry, music should have been held up as the ideal of poetry. Four centuries earlier it was poetry that was declared emancipated from music. Poetry withdrew from its cohabitation with music in the human voice as the only medium of its self-expression and took up an independent life in books. It was the first such separation in the history of our culture, and it had a great deal to do with the evolution of literacy. Until the fourteenth century the relationship had been so intimate that Latin and French hardly bothered to differentiate between speaking and singing. How utterly radical a change it was, then, that poetry no longer existed only with music in the ephemeral, corporeal act of song, but could be set apart, objectified, made permanent, collected. Just as the newly emancipated music around 1800 was held to be the model of the poetic, so the newly emancipated poetry around 1400 was held to be the model of "natural music" (what we would call music was identified, in that context, as "artificial music").[25] Like separated lovers each, in its time, pretended in its autonomy to embody what they both were only when they were together.

Wackenroder wrote that in music "one thinks thoughts without any painstaking detour through words; feeling, fantasy, and power of thought are one."[26] Novalis, sketching an idea of poetry in a pointedly fragmentary way, wrote, "Narratives, without connectedness, but with association, like dreams; poems, just sounding well and full of beautiful words, but also without any sense or connectedness. At most a single strophe that is understandable . . . like so many fragments of the most different kinds of things. True poetry can, at most, have an overall allegorical sense, and make an indirect effect, like music."[27] For Friedrich Schlegel the mental process reflected in music is like philosophical thought: "Must pure instrumental music not create a text for itself? And is the theme in it not developed, stated, varied, and contrasted, like the subject of a meditation in a sequence of philosophical ideas?"[28] We shall see that this is an important point of continuity with the aesthetic of Hanslick.

"Narrative," "emotional flux," "fantasy," "thought," "discourse," and "meditation"—all are terms in the vocabulary of the writers around 1800 for characterizing the mental processes that are modeled by instrumental music. They represent the efforts of those writers to describe the sense of the experience of mental life with which music leaves the listener. A difficulty is that, although they differentiate qualities of mental process rather clearly, they do not differentiate so clearly qualities of mental process embodied in musical flow. Can we differentiate musical narrative, discourse, meditation, and fantasy? Certainly not in any way that would elicit widespread agreement. In the following I shall generally refer to music's narrativity, recognizing that I could as well say discursiveness. In respect to language we know the difference between a narrative about an adventure and a discourse on weaving. We can draw no such clear distinction with reference to music.

In speaking of narrativity I refer to the palpable trace of that process of sublimation of which Hildesheimer writes—the residue of mental process in musical works. It answers to the experiential character of music that critics described around 1800. That was a foot in the door for the entry of the composer's life into the compositional process.

Hildesheimer does see this historical dimension, even if he presents it in somewhat paradoxical fashion. It is his central idea that we do not—and cannot—really know Mozart. On one side he presents that as an aspect of Mozart's peculiar genius: this wonder who thinks directly in music, a music completely divorced from life, which he precipitates in pristine scores that do not show the least sign of labor. "In the score of Mozart's life the voice of assimilated experience and elaboration on it is lacking."[29] On the other side we are to see something historically typical in it.

Thinking [the personality of the genius] can be a key to his work, [history] makes it into a doll which it clothes in the garments of that work. And lo! The clothes fit! Biographers have made them all to measure; the further removed in time, the finer their designs and decorations . . . [But the clothes] will not fit the true genius from eras before the French Revolution, before psychological discoveries were made, or were even possible. Neither Haydn nor Mozart can be constructed satisfactorily . . . Classicism and Romanticism introduced subjective feeling into music as a conscious element of expression . . .[30]

Hildesheimer seems to exclude Mozart from the categories of Classicism and Romanticism. But his real effort is to exclude him from history altogether, through language that could have been written around 1800: "In Mozart's rather deliberate objectivity we see that unique element, the absolutely puzzling [the German is Wackenroder's word *Rätselhafte*]. We don't know how it arises, or how it achieves its effect . . . Mozart's music reproduces the depth of experience for us without the experience; as the expression of the absolute it does not reach the experience itself, nor does it want to."[31]

Narrativity is a quality of awareness that arises out of the order in which we mentally experience our lives. The widely held and deeply rooted belief that events are realistically represented when they are given the formal coherence of a story indicates the strong need to bind events in a narrative context. Narrativity entails an engagement with time. It is the dimension of the life of consciousness moving in time and organizing constellations of experience as it does so. The phrase "moving in time" is carefully chosen, for the time of narrative is not restricted to the serial succession of instants. It seems to have extension, like space, for when we begin to recount, everything is already spread out in time. The narration is a movement over the plane of extension, but it may be a spiral movement, or any other kind of movement as well as rectilinear.

Musical narrativity models consciousness of thought and experience, and that corresponds to the special idea of musical drama under the aesthetic of absolute music. This claim seems more or less like Wackenroder's claim that "music reveals all the thousandfold transitional motions of our soul." And it corresponds to Hildesheimer's conception of "that plane of expression where music is a parable of life itself."

Central to the functioning of narrativity is the interplay between two intersecting patterns: the chronological sequence of the events' occurrence, and the order of their unfolding in the telling. The chronological sequence is commonly reordered in the telling to achieve particular effects. The interplay of the two is functional in the apprehension of the narrative, as we can tell in the following four reports about a horse race.

Excalibur broke last from the gate, took the lead by the far turn, then dropped back to fourth coming into the stretch, but rallied to win by a nose.

Excalibur won by a nose, though he was fourth coming into the stretch after leading at the far turn despite having broken last from the gate.

Excalibur, though he broke last from the gate, won by a nose after having dropped back to fourth, coming into the stretch, from the lead he had taken by the far turn.

Excalibur won by a nose although, after breaking last from the gate and taking the lead at the far turn, he had dropped back to fourth coming into the stretch.[32]

The first version reports the events in chronological sequence, and is therefore the shortest. The second and fourth begin at the end. They might be directed to someone who had bet on Excalibur and wanted to know how he had come out. But the decision to tell the end first has consequences for the form of the narrative. As we listen to the four versions there is an increase in the distance from the events. Because of the directness of the first version it sounds like a representation of the events themselves, as in a newspaper account or a radio broadcast from the racetrack. In the other versions we sense a tampering with the order of events. That alone promotes a sense of distance. We are no longer moving along *with* the events; we learn their total array, as though they were laid out on a table, and watch as they are shuffled and reshuffled. The difference between the first version and the third and fourth is the difference between telling and telling about. But it is not one thing or the other that is at work in the apprehension of the story, it is the inter-action of the two.

We recognize a gradient from direct to indirect presentation in musical narrativity, as well. An instance that leaps to mind is the qualitative difference in the first and last presentations of the first *allegro* theme of Mozart's G-minor Symphony (Ex. 7.1a, b). The last presentation is like a reflection or conversation about the theme in the upper strings, above a lingering inflection of the tonic in the bass. It has the quality of a meditation on a remembered past, after the turmoil and before the silence. The presentation is indirect—more a telling about than a telling. Our word "exposition" carries the sense of direct presentation, but we

EX. 7.1A

EX. 7.1B

should be explicit about recognizing the implication of the opposite, in-direct presentation, in "recapitulation"—not only telling again, but also telling about.

There would be general agreement about interpreting the last presentation of the theme as coda. But coda, as a convention of the genre, speaks to a consideration for balance in the form and extended resolution and closure in the harmony. The quality of recollection or reflection is not generally identified as a constituent attribute of coda. But it is a quality that the composer may wish to vest there or in other elements of a sonata form. It is the interaction of the order of such rhetorical gestures with the paradigmatic order of events peculiar to the genre that is the focus here. Narrative movement is driven by such interaction.

The sense that the total array of events in the horse race story is laid out before us once we begin to narrate it is confirmed by the possibility of telling it in so many versions. If we call that array in its fixed chronological sequence "the story," then we may say that the story serves as a guiding paradigm for each telling of the story, and for the listener's organization of it in hearing or reading. The story is implicit in every telling, and interacts with the order that is explicit in the particular unfolding. It is as though the story were laid out below, and the narrative were hovering above it, swooping down to make contact at important junctures.

In the theory of narrative the distinction here is sometimes generalized as a distinction between story and discourse. As Frank Kermode puts it, "We may think of narrative as the product of two intertwined processes: the presentation of a fable and its progressive interpretation. [The interpretation] distorts the sequential propriety of [the fable]."[33]

The apprehension of a musical work depends, in quite similar ways, on two intertwined processes: on the one hand the underlying patterns of conventional genres and implicit constraints arising from the grammar of style (harmony, voice-leading, and so on), and on the other the progressive interpretation of these determinants through the unfolding of the work in time. The first dimension is not exactly like the chronological sequence of the events of a story, but it is the counterpart in being the dimension of determinants that are more or less fixed prior to the unfolding. The first dimension constrains the second, the second interprets the first.

A famous illustrative case concerns the interpretation of the first movement of Beethoven's Ninth Symphony. The tones A and E are presented enigmatically at first, with no clues about their tonal and metrical orientation. In the harmonic "structure" of the movement as a whole they belong to the dominant harmony. But they cannot be identified as dominant at the outset; they *become* that as the piece progresses, just as the identity of an enigmatic character in a play and her relationship to the other characters might be clarified in the unfolding.

The evasiveness of the opening sounds in the Ninth Symphony is a source of that sense of the infinite that has long been a topos in talk about the work, and that lies at the heart of the "absolute music" concept. Their emerging identity is a main process in the unfolding of the work. Tovey quipped, "Half the musical miseducation in the world comes from people who know that the Ninth Symphony begins in the dominant of D-minor."[34] To be sure. Still, someone might protest, "But the opening *is* on the dominant." And in some sense, grounded in the grammar of harmonic tonality, that is so. That is why we must take our perspective from the interaction of the two dimensions.

I shall try now to take such a perspective on my example, the *Andante* movement of Mozart's Symphony no. 39 in E-flat, K.543, composed in 1788 (Ex. 7.2). The aim, once again, is to give an account that will make plausible the sorts of things that were written around 1800 about the experience of this music. It will be an effort to catch something of what those writers responded to, what made them say the sorts of things that they said.

The movement's action is touched off by the merest melodic transformation: The elaboration of a subdominant chord in the second half of the first measure—just the in-breath of the opening phrase—separates itself off as an answering phrase and pushes its way alone up the scale, isolating and thereby identifying the treble register as an element in the colloquy that is being set in motion (Ex. 7.2, A). The answering phrase takes off, stretching upward and outward to make the first of a series of unsupported treble excursions that mark the movement. In a third phrase it falls back into a subordinate role (B). This initiates a second exchange

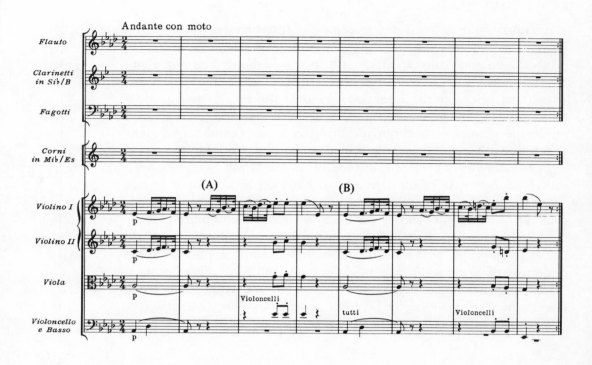

EX. 7.2 Mozart, Symphony no. 39

(*continued*)

MOZART AND THE IDEA OF ABSOLUTE MUSIC

EX. 7.2 (continued)

(continued)

EX. 7.2 *(continued)*

(continued)

EX. 7.2 *(continued)*

(continued)

EX. 7.2 (continued)

(continued)

EX. 7.2 (continued)

(continued)

EX. 7.2 *(continued)*

in what is now recognizable as a dialogue between the two elements of the principal theme. As often in such movements by Mozart, much of the energy of the narrative movement is created by dialogue.

In the second exchange the answering phrase accelerates its upward reach substantially through the leap of a fifth, and in cadencing the violins fall only to the level that they had reached at the height of their first response. The D-natural just before the leap opens a gate that the first time was closed so that the line rebounded back to the point of departure. Now the D-natural tonicizes the E-flat as its leading tone, enabling a close on the dominant. Together the two exchanges constitute something like a rhymed couplet, balanced, yet oriented toward the double bar.

These initial eight measures of rather straightforward business set the mode and subject and players of the action. The complications begin instantly with the continuation. The second violins initiate a new exchange in their darkest tones, reinforced in their darkness by the cellos and double basses and by a pulsating E-flat pedal tone in the violas (C). The first violins respond, alone in the treble. The exchanges are compressed into one-measure utterances. The first violins strain to break away from their E-flat mooring. The dialogue has taken on an air of urgency and anxiety. On their third try the first violins succeed in breaking away (D) and immediately become frisky in their new freedom. The lower strings abandon their seriousness (had they meant it?) and join in the spirit of the first violins, contributing staccato punctuation while the first violins replace the dots with rests to lighten their iambic rhythm (E).

Playfulness turns to teasing when the first violins (F) put off for two measures their descent for the return to the orderly exchange of the beginning (G). The descent is a kind of reining in, taking control of the first violins and literally lending gravity to their frivolity—they are joined by the seconds (G), then replaced by the cellos and basses (H). The coming reprise is signaled already by the stalling at the dominant (F), and the sense of its approach is reinforced successfully at (G) and (H). We know from these signals not only that a reprise is coming but that it will be the reprise of a rounded binary form:

$$\text{\textbardbl:}\quad A \quad \text{:\textbardbl:} \quad BA \quad \text{:\textbardbl}$$
$$\quad\;\; \text{i–v} \qquad \text{v–i}$$

Here is a moment when the unfolding narrative links up closely and recognizably to a conventional course for the genre.

The reprise, when it comes, begins as though it would be an exact repetition. But in the first response the C-flat in the second violins (J) is another minimal signal of a coming complication, or perhaps it is better understood as a provocation—the injection without warning of an element, however small, that is uncongenial to the prevailing atmosphere and inevitably provokes trouble. The C-flat gives the return the aspect of a reconsideration—going back over that first response and shading it darker, casting a shadow over the future. It is a rather cinematic gesture, like a sudden close-up on a face thought to be benign, that sounds alarms in the viewer's mind. In instant reaction the opening phrase comes back in the minor altogether (K), whereas the responding phrase, which had injected the disturbing element, comes back as though nothing had happened (L). But only momentarily. The innocent cadential figure (M) leaps over the double bar into the relative minor (N), its repeated eighth-notes drawn out to a full measure, with the shrill coloration of woodwinds (especially so when played by eighteenth-century instruments!). Again there is a sudden seriousness in the air. It is the sort of moment in Mozart's instrumental music when we are given to thinking, "How operatic!"

An actual operatic parallel does come to mind—not by Mozart but by Verdi. It is the turn of the screw between the first two scenes of *Otello*. At the end of the first scene Iago sends Cassio into a deadly trap, to ask Desdemona to intercede on his behalf with Otello, an appeal Iago knows will inflame Otello's jealousy. He sings, sweetly, "*vane*" (go), and the orchestra punctuates with innocent concluding figuration. Once Cassio is out of earshot the orchestra, knowing Iago's real intention, jacks up that figuration a half-step and, with added winds, transforms it to mocking scorn. Iago repeats his "*vane*" in the new key and through clenched teeth, and so begins his *Credo*. Objectively described, the two passages have in common the repetition of a closing figure in an unexpected new tonality as the start of a new section with contrasting character. It is a device used often by Mozart, for example in mm. 12–13 of the Andante movement of the "Linz" Symphony (Ex. 7.3).

In the Andante of K.543 this device unleashes an outburst: a wide

EX. 7.3

melodic range traversed back and forth in angry pacing, a heavily dissonant sonority, strong thrusts in the harmonic motion, a highly agitated
rhythmic surface, shrillness of orchestral color. The passage has the
character of desperate thinking, looking for a way out, first in one direction, then in another. The escape is to the secondary dominant key,
B-flat (O). Instantly upon its firm establishment the energy level drops,
and in the hush of the moment, against the ominous background created by the sustained horns and pulsating violins on B-flat, another sequence of exchanges of the principal motives begins (P), as at (C). But
in these exchanges the portent is heavier, with the added horns and
the reversal of roles—the initiating gesture in the treble, the reply in the
bass. One senses, especially because of this register reversal, that the
outcome cannot be the same as at (D). The whole sequence passes like
something relived in a dream: familiar, inverted, outcome unknown,

then an explosion (Q) into something wholly unexpected, an outburst of still greater fury than the one after (N).

The passage at (Q) draws on the same kinds of resources as that after (N), but in escalation: dashing back and forth, this time with leaps of a seventh as well as triadic spans; the woodwinds playing their dissonances in sixteenth-note repetitions rather than sustaining them, the lower strings playing an agitated counterpoint. But this passage is directed in a steady, sequential drive that signals the approach to another main juncture in the movement, the attainment of the dominant at (S). This outburst, though wilder, yet imposes control. As the last step to the point of arrival at (S), however, Mozart has contrived to let the first violins have their giddy little high-wire act after all (R). He hadn't really wanted to forgo the crazy juxtaposition of that with the high seriousness of the passage at (P); he just put it off until the contrast would be even more eccentric. It is a characteristic piece of Mozartean trickery, and it is just on this side of chaotic, that quality of which Novalis and Körner spoke.

On a larger scale these events can be interpreted in terms of the grammar of sonata form. The passage from (N) to (S) would be a kind of transition, in the exposition, and what begins at (S) would be a second subject in the dominant key. But with the character that Mozart has given those materials, it is hard to apprehend them that way. What would be transition seems like the main action, and what would be second subject seems stable and meditative, after the tensions of the transition. Students tend generally to call it a "closing section" because of that quality. Indeed it has a similar quality to the coda of the G-minor Symphony: Above a pedal in the bass the upper voices pass about a principal melodic figure from earlier action, as though in recollection of and reflection on its associations. We should not lose sight of the irony of the associations in this case. The melodic figure at (S) is a transformation of the extended cadential figure at (N) that had set off the whole stormy passage that is just now being assuaged; appropriate enough that it should be the vehicle for reflection. (The transformation of a motive to effect irony is another of Mozart's characteristic devices. An instance in the Andante of the "Linz" Symphony is the transformation of the sixteenth-note violin figure in mm. 20–21—all innocence—to a stealthy tiptoeing bass figure in m. 45 [Ex. 7.4].)

EX. 7.4A

EX. 7.4B

If we say that Mozart has, to this point, followed the model of sonata form, then we must say it is a sonata without development. And so it is put in some rather authoritative literature: the *New Grove* article on Mozart, and even Tovey, in his essay on this symphony in *Essays in Musical Analysis*.[35] That is all right if our interest is in locating the piece in some kind of classification scheme, but hardly so if the characterization is addressed to our apprehension of the work. For it would suggest that the *absence* of a development is a salient point in the work's unfolding. But it is not. The qualities of development and subsequent resolution are not missing from the rhetoric of the work, they are vested in passages that would not count as development and reprise in the sonata genre.

Yet I hear again the protestor to Tovey's wry remark about the Ninth Symphony: "But it *is* a sonata without development" (this time in agreement with Tovey). And again the answer is that it is not one thing or the other. The conventionalized tonal, thematic, dynamic procedures, and the character profiles—not the "form"—of the sonata genre are active as leading elements in the unfolding of the work's narrative. Mozart assumes them into his own idiosyncratic repertory of moves and devices, by which he fashions a unique work. We apprehend the direction and shape of its narrativity in the interaction between those leading, in a sense fixed, elements and the actual unfolding.

Consider again the passage beginning at (P). If we have been attentive to the tonal-formal dynamics through (M) we recognize at that point closure in the tonic key of a largely expository section based on a single thematic idea. And we recognize that what follows is tonally transitory, although highly active and demanding of attention. The passage at (P) utilizes material from the one at (C), a perfectly normal relationship between transition and exposition. But the particular way in which it does that is neither prescribed nor proscribed by the grammar of sonata procedure; it proceeds not by a motivic shredding through a succession of keys, but by the very special manipulation of register to reverse the roles between the participants in the dialogue and thereby to place the whole passage under a shadow. Such manipulation is not normally in the vocabulary of prevailing analytical modes, but here it is rich with meaning. It is a highly characteristic device for Mozart. An account of the passage is inadequate if it does not recognize the interaction of the two kinds of factors.

The passage at (S) plays into three short measures of re-transition (T), and the reprise begins at (U). It is given real swing by the conversion of the strings to an *obbligato* voice after four measures, as the winds take over the thematic work. And there is a similar effect when the winds come cascading down as *obbligato* voices at (V). The activity of these crossing roles, something like a contra dance, enlivens the reprise, and diffuses the tension that had attended the business of (C). Altogether the reprise seems to have gotten some trouble out of its system. That is signaled, too, by the absence of the sudden flash of the minor at (W).

But it turns out to be a false signal, just as the opposite was a false signal the first time around. Suddenly (X) the *obbligato* voices vanish, the theme comes in the minor, in the next measure the winds whisk the harmony chromatically from E-flat to B, for three measures there is a royal procession toward B major. Wrong again. The B attained (Y) is in the minor, an outcry by the full orchestra that initiates another display of passion, parallel to that following (N). Yes, of course this is the reprise and it had to come. But that grammatical fact alone does not account for this emotional roller coaster. Again there is a quest for an exit key, now longer and more desperate, turning in one direction after another until, led by the winds at (Z), the band homes into the dominant at (AA). The greater length and complication of this passage is an instance, of course, of a favorite device of classical composers: the flim-flam of a more complicated transition between first and second subjects in the recapitulation, hiding the fact that it is a movement to the same key. Mozart's idea of unfolding these episodes in ever rising peaks of fury is again made to coordinate with a conventional strategem of classical sonata procedure.

The whole passage, from the moment when the reprise is no longer exact (W), is unpredictable and psychologically complex. It seems again very operatic. But does that not really put things backward? Is it not, rather, that when Mozart composed opera he gave concrete content to musical narratives of the sort he was inclined to compose in any case? He could do so because the narrativity of his music so much modeled the experience of mental life. That characteristic of his music allowed him to be the composer of opera of such supreme psychological accuracy. That his symphonic music creates an impression of the experience of action and that it models thought and feeling corresponds to the idea of absolute music. This idea survives or is reborn in Hildesheimer's conception that Mozart led his operatic texts to "that plane of expression where music is a parable of life itself."

There is yet another way of putting the relationship between symphony and opera in Mozart's production: his operas are symphonies with singers. That is the reverse side of the same coin. Its special interest is that it brings to mind Wagner's concept of opera, the idea that the musical expression constitutes the substance, the innermost essence of the drama that is made visible and concretized by the words and stage action. (Is that not the sense of Hildesheimer's claim, cited earlier, that "Mozart's dramatic music . . . does not follow the text but directs it or leads it"?) It reduces the paradoxical aspect of the claim that opera could be the highest form of absolute music, and it allows us to see that the association of the absolute music concept with Hanslick does not stand that concept on its head as much as it might seem to do.

The conception for which Hanslick is mainly known is that the essence of music is sound in motion—"forms moved in sounding." [36] As he develops his idea of form, it becomes a concept of architectonic form, and that has tended to support a formalist idea of music, an idea that the beautiful in music lies in its abstract forms. To many today the phrase "absolute music" calls up just such a formalist view. [37] This can seem especially sustained by Hanslick's continuing polemic against the same mimetic theory of music that the writers around 1800 had already rejected. The subtitle of his book is "A Contribution to the *Revisal* of Musical Aesthetics" (italics mine). The core of what he characterized as the prevailing view, still in his day, is the idea that music can express or represent feelings or actions, and that is just the idea on which he focused his attack. But with a close reading of his book, especially against the background of the aesthetic of the writers around 1800, we are bound to see that the alternatives are not reduced to formalism or the view that music represents feeling and action.

Hanslick's music conception flows from music's dynamic aspect. Form, in his conception, is a consequence of movement. The coherence of music is a matter of its logical succession. Music is therefore a language, a discourse, a kind of thinking. It has meaning, but that is intrinsic and strictly musical. It has character; it may be diffused with feeling, although it does not *represent* feeling. This conception is essentially continuous with that of the writers around 1800.

Come back to the Andante of K.543. From (AA) onward the narrative is guided by the track that had been laid down the first time through. The two departures that are forced by the tonal constraints for a recapitulation take those formal constraints as occasions for new psychological nuances. First, there is the more attenuated treble excursion at (BB), compared to the counterpart at (R). The later version becomes stuck on its highest note in the fourth measure, which instantly wipes out the frivolous character that the figure had earlier on. The diminished intervals that dominate its descent give it a new seriousness. The departure at (DD) from the corresponding moment (U) is understandable in view of the rather subtle psychological effect of the rest of the movement. The two measures beginning at (CC) make a gesture as though to close the movement (it would require just one more repetition of that figure—indeed that is how the movement does ultimately close). But the harmony is dominant; the clarinets gently lead back to what seems like yet another presentation of the first episode. It continues to seem that way until (EE), in the second presentation of the theme, where, instead of the answering phrase that heads into all the quarrelling, there begins a warm, lyrical extension of the melody that is reaffirmed (FF) with everyone singing. That affirmation seems to be what was needed to let the melody close in peace, really for the first time (GG), and the movement ends with the four-measure cadence that it began at (CC) but did not, could not finish.

A note on performance. This *Andante con moto* (the tempo designation in the *Neue Mozart Ausgabe*) can be heard in an astonishing range of tempi: from a metronome marking of 76 for the eighth note (Bruno Walter conducting the Columbia Symphony Orchestra) to one of 114 (Jaap Schroeder and Christopher Hogwood, with the Academy of Ancient Music).[38] Walter's tempo represents the main performance tradition of this century (the outstanding exception is Toscanini's performance, at 112).[39] The lively *andante* of the Academy of Ancient Music, characteristic of their Mozart performances in general, is an aspect of their efforts to follow eighteenth-century performance practices. Evidence for the historical authenticity of such a tempo has been published by Neal Zaslaw, who was a consultant for the recordings.[40] The interpretation that is offered here constitutes evidence of another sort, but to the same effect. At Walter's tempo the frivolity and eccentricity, the contrasts and deceptions and shifts of character and playfulness and high seriousness, and manipulations of harmonic and instrumental color, and the play of register and roles, and the thematic transformations and ironies—all that fades into a uniformly benign "expressivity," a realization of the Apollonian Mozart image that Hildesheimer was concerned to pull down. It requires a livelier tempo to bring out the immense range and fluency of expression in the movement, and to give us a glimpse of what the writers around 1800 might have heard in this music, to write as they did.

CHAPTER 8

Dufay the Progressive

In 1933, when Brahms would have been one hundred years old, Schoenberg delivered a lecture honoring his music. In 1947, fifty years after Brahms's death, Schoenberg recast his lecture as an essay under the title "Brahms the Progressive" for publication in his collection *Style and Idea*.[1] When I was asked to contribute to a celebration of Guillaume Dufay in the five hundredth anniversary of his death I could think of nothing more appropriate than to call attention to strivings and achievements of the Cambrai Master that—so it seems to me—bring him into contact with the Viennese ones.

Schoenberg had something very special in mind when he said "Progressive," and not simply the hackneyed historiographic concept. Art, he said, is a matter of the presentation of characteristic facts. The role of the formal element in music is to "bring about comprehensibility through memorability . . . to make the presentation of the musical idea intelligible."

The focus of Schoenberg's essay is on Brahms's method of motivic elaboration, not only as a basis of unity but even more as a source of Brahms's distinct and characteristic expression. It is a matter of the pursuit of musical ideas to their most distant implications, and thereby of extending the versatility of the musical language. That was what he regarded as Brahms's contribution to the creation of an "unrestricted musical language"—that is, a language restricted only by the musical idea—and therein lay Brahms's "progressiveness."[2]

The expression of such thoughts appears to have taken on a growing importance in Schoenberg's artistic life, as a counter to the increasing focus of his attention as a composer on the working of musical materials from the standpoint of their abstract relationships. He always insisted that for him the invention of a tone series began not with precompositional notions about the manipulations to which it was open, but with some characteristic idea which he then transformed into a workable material that would enable him to infuse the composition with that idea. His insistence on this was not a point of ideology, as it sometimes seems, but the expression of a serious aesthetic notion: that to be intelligible music must be memorable, it must make an *impression* on the mind of the listener, in the most literal sense of that word. In order to do that it must be characteristic and distinct. In the service of this ideal, motivic elaboration is not simply a matter of imposing a thematic unity over the composition. In a way "unity" is but an aspect of distinctness. Schoenberg was oddly defensive about his motivic analyses. He anticipated the doubts of skeptics who would claim that the motives he identified—simple seconds and thirds—"are present in every theme without constituting the thematic material."

The problem is fundamental: the paradox of idiomatic material given individual character. For the analysis of fifteenth-century music the matter is especially vexing, for principles of modal polyphonic composition go a long way toward shaping norms that operate from piece to piece, producing similarities of melody, sonority, and form everywhere. The music shows signs, if not of an awareness of the problem, then at least of a deliberate striving to create characteristic and individual expressions.

As was so often the case, Schoenberg gave his explanation of the phenomenon of motivic elaboration a psychological and, indeed, a personal turn: "The mind of a composer is dominated by every detail of his idea, the consequences of which accordingly will show up involuntarily and unexpectedly." He took it as the mark of divine gifts when composers manifested a capacity to persist in the pursuit of ideas to their furthest consequences and to create works of great unity and distinctness. When he wrote "It seems that [our Lord] likes helping in their spiritual problems those he has selected—though not enough in their more material ones," it is hard to escape the impression that he was thinking as much of himself as of Brahms.

I shall construe the problem this way: How has Dufay focused the idiomatic melodic language of his style as the characteristic language of a single piece, and how does that process interact with principles of polyphonic composition that were normative for him? An approach to the first question is offered by the study of a cantus firmus Mass: the musical idiom is concretized through the cantus firmus, with which the composition has constantly to reckon. I choose the *Missa L'homme armé,* whose cantus firmus is a model of the melodic style in ways that I shall shortly suggest. But the choice of this approach only transforms the question: How is the cantus firmus assimilated into the substance of the Mass? What are its distinct features, and how are these taken into account in the composition of such an extraordinarily extended four-voiced piece? It comes down to a question about the nature of the cantus firmus technique in the composition of the individual movements, and of the sense of "cycle" for the Mass as a whole; and it seems to me the question might have interested Schoenberg greatly. What follows is an effort to give expression to a perception about this piece that I have had for some time.

I should like to look at a number of passages in the *Missa L'homme armé* from the point of view of the interaction among the following: (1) reflections of the cantus firmus in melodic and harmonic aspects of the composition; (2) modal principles of melodic organization; (3) voice disposition, the roles of the individual voices, and the control of register, all in relation to the cantus firmus melody; and (4) cadence formation and pattern.

The focus will always be on motivic associations in relation to these factors, and I shall try to confine my attention to passages where such associations are made explicit by some aspect of the context. That is, it will not be a matter simply of picking out cantus firmus–like motives in the texture, but of showing how Dufay has explicitly identified melodic and harmonic details and procedures with those suggested by the cantus firmus, hence of showing how the distinctness of the Mass is owing to its use of the cantus firmus as a source. The musical examples are reproduced from Heinrich Besseler's edition.[3] The phrases of the cantus firmus are labeled in Example 8.1.

The first Kyrie (Ex. 8.2) shows some norms for the piece as a whole that arise both from principles that are general to the style and from the peculiarities of the cantus firmus. All four voices follow consistent modal procedure, articulating and elaborating a pentachord on G and a tetrachord on D. The dispositions are plagal for the superius and con-

EX. 8.1 The *L'homme armé* melody

EX. 8.2 "Kyrie I," mm. 1–24

EX. 8.3 Disposition of pentachords-tetrachords

trabassus, authentic for the contra and tenor (see Ex. 8.3). As a direct consequence of this disposition the principal tones of collateral modes— the final and cofinal—come together in the cadential sonority on G that is by far the most common in the piece, accounting for about 75 percent of all cadences. About 20 percent of the cadences are on the cofinal, D, establishing A as a temporary cofinal, and three cadences go to A itself. There are consistencies about the occurrence of cadences with respect to the progress of cantus firmus phrases: almost always a cadence on G at the end of the A1 phrase, often a cadence on D coinciding with the beginning of A2, almost always a cadence on D at the end of B3. There is often a cadence on G at the end of A4 or coinciding with the beginning of B1. But in addition to, or instead of that cadence, in every tenor exposition but one there is imitation of A4 between the tenor and contrabassus. As I shall suggest in another context, those imitations serve the articulation of the form, just as the cadences do.

All of this is in accordance with principles that I have shown to be operative in Dufay's secular music, and that Leeman Perkins has demonstrated with respect to the Masses of Josquin.[4] One of my purposes here is to observe the consequences of these principles of voice disposition in the composition of a single piece.

Every voice but the superius has a B-flat signature, so that the pentachord and tetrachord species on both G and D are identical. (I shall return later to the absence of a signature from the superius, and to the consequences of species identity in the other voices.)

The overall voice disposition is articulated in special ways, based on the roles of the individual voices and on the peculiarities of the cantus firmus. The four-voice texture can be understood analytically in terms of the contrapuntal relationship of two fundamental voices, tenor and superius, with two adjuncts of the tenor, the high and low contra voices. Of the two, the contrabassus has the more distinct role, for with its tetrachord it defines the lowest stratum or register of the sound space, particularly in phrases preparing cadences on both G (for example, mm. 7 and 22) and D (mm. 14–15). The activity of the contrabassus in its tetrachordal register comes to be motivically characterized later in the piece and it is that sort of association between register and motive that constitutes one of my main subjects.

In general the register in which each of the contra voices sounds at any moment depends on the locus of the tenor at that moment. As it is the special feature of the cantus firmus that it proceeds in discrete phrases that are marked by rests or sustained notes and are registrally differentiated, so register in the contra voices is a function of register in the tenor, depending on the kind of articulation or support that is wanted of the contra voices.

The superius is not tied to the tenor in this way. Its role is to set the upper stratum and melodic surface of the sound space as its pentachord. It is guided by principles of modal procedure, and is related to the tenor through principles of counterpoint. Compared with the other voices it is not much identified with motivic material derived from the cantus firmus. It has its own characteristic melodic material, consistent with its role in the texture. The most obvious is the head motive, which is paradigmatic for the superius throughout: upward movement through the pentachord to the cofinal, descent by step to the final, sometimes continuing through the tetrachord, as in the first Kyrie, and in that case returning by skip to the final (see Ex. 8.2, mm. 1–5).

The high contra articulates the tetrachord, and the contrabassus balances supportively on G. (All subsequent movements open with two voices, and then the role of the contrabassus in the Kyrie is carried by the contra in the other movements.) The space left by this initial setting of the registers (the pentachord G–D′) is filled with the entrance of the A motives of the tenor, beginning in m. 5. With that entrance the contrabassus moves down into the tetrachord, setting up a disposition that is one of the norms for the piece: tenor in the pentachord, flanked by tetrachords above and below. (By corollary, when the tenor is in the tetrachord it is normally supported by at least one of the contras in the pentachord below.)

When the tenor rests (m. 9) the contrabassus moves up into the pentachord, then contrabassus and high contra move down together for the cadence on D in m. 15, which prepares the tenor entrance with A2 (m. 16). The leap to G in the tenor reestablishes G as tone center, and the imitation by the contrabassus reinforces that. There is a good deal of this sort of dovetailing imitative traffic with cantus firmus motives in the same register between the tenor and contrabassus and very little between the tenor and the other voices. The function is always the same: to sustain or reinforce the sonority. In that sense the sonority has its foundation in the lower extreme of the sound space. The imitation is of an older sort, more like voice exchange than like the imitation of the later fifteenth and sixteenth centuries. Like voice exchanges, these imitations of short motives simply achieve the effect of sustaining a sonority through the reiteration of melodic material in a fixed register.

Returning to the beginning of the Kyrie, we might interpret the first two tetrachordal phrases of the high contra, mm. 1–3 and 3–5, in the light of the B1 and B2 phrases of *L'homme armé,* and that of the superius, m. 9, and its approximate imitation by the contra in m. 10, in the light of the phrase B3. But at this point in the piece there is little reason for the ear to make that sort of association, as there will be later on. I believe it is one of the processes of the piece as it unfolds that motivic associations are made explicit, and once established they join the compositional resources. In that way an associative syntax specific to the piece is developed through the process of its composition, manifested as a growing motivic density. This need not be interpreted as the mark of a precompositional design; it is the consequence of a cumulative way of composing. I shall depart from the order of presentation in the Mass in order to show a single passage near the end that exemplifies this fact.

The second Agnus (Ex. 8.4) begins in a manner that is common to the several extended tenor-less interludes of the piece: free imitation in extended phrases, rhythmically flexible, melodically fluent, breaking down the role distinctions between voices—a contrast to and relief from the dominant four-voice sections of the Mass. The imitation is of a truly contrapuntal sort, unlike the strict motivic imitation exemplified by the Kyrie passage, and it serves an altogether different purpose.

EX. 8.4 "Agnus II," mm. 40–74

(continued)

EX. 8.4 (continued)

Things change after the cadence on G at m. 50. From that point to the end the contra voice presents itself as an abstraction of the full *L'homme armé* tune: A1, mm. 51–53; A2, mm. 53–54; A3, mm. 54–56, bringing about a cadence on G. At m. 57 this voice moves into the tetrachord as expected, but the passage from m. 57 to m. 61, with cadence on D, turns out to be a diversion, to which I shall return presently. B1 is presented in mm. 62–64, B2 in mm. 65–66, B3 in mm. 67–69; C1 in mm. 70–71, C2 in m. 72, C3 in mm. 72–74.

When I say abstraction I mean that the pitch order—the exact melodic contour—of the tune is preserved, but not pitch repetitions, nor necessarily the original rhythmic configurations. (A motive may be further reduced down to its pitch *repertory,* without its pitch *order,* and still retain its motivic association. The consequence is that in certain contexts it requires nothing more than a register and characteristic intervals to suggest a motive, and that is a corollary to the interpretation of motives as registers or intervals given concrete melodic expression. It begins to suggest the paraphrase technique of a later generation—I think, for example, of the abstraction of the half-step from the *Pange lingua* hymn in Josquin's Mass based on that melody.)

In this instance the motivic identity of the material presented in the contra voice is confirmed by its presentation according to the phrase order of the *L'homme armé* tune. In the case of the motivic material in the contrabassus of the Kyrie, the strongest confirmation is in the imitative relationship with the tenor. Those are the principal ways in which motivic associations are reinforced.

The contrabassus in m. 57 through the first half-note of m. 61 presents an abstraction of motives A1 through A3, transposed to the tetrachord and pentachord on D. Now consider the high contra in this passage. It is parallel to the contrabassus, and thereby it suggests a diminution of the transposed A motives, especially A1 and A3. The two voices together, descending through the pentachord in staggered fashion, produce a typical cadential passage in descending sixths. But the high contra in this passage associates, too, with the B motives, for the context of the tune has called for an upward move by that voice into the tetrachord. And this association is confirmed in mm. 62ff.

The contrabassus in mm. 61–63 has the same double association: with the transposed A motives, in whose register it remains, and which it seems to abstract even further, and with the B motives that it produces in anticipation of the high contra in mm. 61–66. The latter voice finishes with B3 in mm. 67–68, and at m. 69 the superius joins the game. It proceeds through A1 in the transposition on D, and then dissolves into its tetrachord before moving up in preparation for the cadence. The contra voice imitates in the untransposed register (mm. 70ff), and in presenting motives C1–C3 it brings about a return to the tonality of G. Then one of the consequences of these motivic manipulations has been the laying out of the passage in a tonal arch: from G (through m. 56) to D (through m. 69) and again to G (through m. 74.) I shall return later on to the other sections of the Agnus, which seems altogether something of a climax with respect to these manipulations.

Some of the observations that I have made about the Agnus passage reflect important things about the construction of the *L'homme armé* tune itself, and I should like to turn to that directly now (Ex. 8.1). The tune exemplifies normative modal progression for the authentic disposition of pentachord and tetrachord. The A and C phrases are in the pentachord, and they feature a prominent downward leap of a fifth. The contrasting B phrases are in the tetrachord above, with its upper neighbor, and they feature a prominent downward leap of a fourth. (I cannot help associating the isolation of the B phrases in the high register with the words at that point: "Everywhere they call, 'Arm yourselves, all!'") But beyond this overall disposition it is important to take note of the fact that both A and B open with tetrachordal motives and expand to a pentachord, and that both then descend through the pentachord by step. In the process of motivic abstraction of which I have spoken these parallels are directly exposed. And they illuminate the choice that Dufay has made for the modality of the tune, G, with B-flat. For that modality produces identical species of the tetrachord and pentachord on G and D, making possible the transposition of both the A and B motives into one another's register, as well as the association of both groups of motives with one another in the same register. In imitative passages the leap of the fifth in the A and C phrases may be answered strictly at the unison, or at the fifth below by the leap of a fourth in the B phrase. These relations in the tune may offer at least internal grounds for its popularity as a cantus firmus.

That there is no B-flat signature for the superius reflects the fact that this voice is in the main not involved with the tenor in relation to the cantus firmus motives.[5] (In the one such case that we saw in the Agnus passage, mm. 69–71, it is the A1 motive in the D tetrachord. That motive never appears in the superius on G.) On the other hand the head motive, which belongs alone to the superius, characteristically involves a fourth-species pentachord on G, that is, with B-natural.

One more general interpretation, and then I shall move on to the next passage. The second Agnus exemplifies a relationship that seems to me to be fundamental to the compositional process of the piece. I can try to bring it into focus by referring to two theoretical concepts that were formulated at a somewhat later time, but that seem entirely appropriate to this context: "procedure"—the progression of a melody through the characteristic interval species and toward the characteristic cadential tones of a mode; and "subject"—the melodic idea that is the basis for the musical invention. Principles of modal procedure will normally produce certain kinds of typical passages that are not necessarily thematic, but that can be made so by the context in which they occur. Measures 61–63 of the contrabassus in the Agnus passage (Ex. 8.4) present a normal tetrachordal formation, but in their context the motivic associations are clear. Comparing the first phase of the contra voice in the Kyrie (Ex. 8.2) with its phrase in mm. 57–58 of the second Agnus (Ex. 8.4), we note that there is a similarity of pitch content and contour; but the latter passage is motivically identified—recognizable as a subject—whereas the former is not. Throughout the piece concrete, distinct cantus firmus motives are crystallized out of, and dissolve into, the background of modal-melodic activity. The more distinct their profiles, the more explicit their associations, the more they are recognized

EX. 8.5 "Christe," superius, mm. 25–28

as subjects—or to put it the other way, the more the articulated registers of the sound space come into focus as cantus firmus–related motives.

Of course the coincidence of the organization of the *L'homme armé* melody with the principles of octave-species modality places the Masses based upon it in a special position. But in a way that coincidence placed a special burden on a composer who wished to create motivic concreteness through context, over and above melodic similarity. It is idiomatic to write pentachordal phrases; it is a special thing to give them the ring of the B motives.

At the beginning of the Christe (Ex. 8.5) the superius introduces a melody in D that, in this instance, covers the full octave. Here it plays a role similar to that of the head motive, providing a stable, tonally solid opening. Its stability and tonality-defining character are exploited throughout the Mass, especially through imitation, to confirm cadences and to open new sections within movements. The second Kyrie, for example, begins with this motive in imitation in three voices, this time in G (see Ex. 8.6). Of course in G the superius is limited to the pentachordal segment of the melody, hence that is its most characteristic aspect. I shall refer to it as the triadic motive.

In the Gloria (Ex. 8.7a) the triadic motive is associated for the first time with the motivic material of the cantus firmus. At m. 39 the tenor has arrived at phrase A4 of the cantus firmus. For the first time it presents this motive in a variant that is subsequently much used (see Ex. 8.7b). Of course this variant can be used also as A2 and C2. In this passage it is imitated by the contrabassus in m. 40, and in retrospect that clarifies m. 37 of the contrabassus. In mm. 39–40 the high contra gives out the triadic motive, but beginning with the B-flat it is in imitation of the tenor. And following the high contra, the superius picks up the B-flat–C–D of the triadic motive in mm. 40–41. Now these associations are used to march the A phrases through the texture while the tenor is presenting the B phrases. At m. 43 the contrabassus abstracts A1, the

EX. 8.6 "Kyrie II," mm. 55–59

EX. 8.7A "Gloria," mm. 31–54

(*continued*)

EX. 8.7A (*continued*)

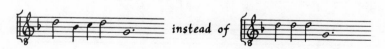 *instead of*

EX. 8.7B "Gloria," tenor, mm. 39–40

high contra follows in m. 45 with the A2 variant, the superius imitates from the B-flat at m. 46, suggesting the triadic motive, and the contrabassus follows with A3. This brings about a cadence on G (m. 53), whereupon the high contra gives out the full octave version of the triadic motive, hooking onto the B2 variant just preceding it in the tenor.

Now I should like to pause and take notice of the potency of such an invention: to transform a motive of the cantus firmus and then to establish a synapse between it and a much-used articulative motive that, taken by itself, is a melodic formation to be found very often in the style. It exemplifies what I am trying to suggest about the idiomatic and the characteristic.

A two-voice interlude in the Credo (see Ex. 8.8) closes at m. 81 with a cadence on G that coincides with the beginning of C1 in the tenor. The contrabassus is in the pentachord, expressed at once as the A2 (or C2) variant. That is imitated at mm. 83–84 by the high contra and at m. 84 by the superius, both identified rhythmically as the triadic motive. At m. 90 the contrabassus punctuates the end of the tenor's C1 with the triadic motive. As the tenor begins C2, the contrabassus moves to the tetrachord, inverting the tenor's leap of a fifth, but suggesting through its rhythm the A1 motive (m. 92). As the tenor leaps down through the fifth, the contrabassus characteristically leaps up through the octave and imitates the tenor. The high contra accompanies with the triadic motive through the octave. As the tenor begins C3 at mm. 99, the contrabassus is again in the tetrachord, suggesting both the A

EX. 8.8 "Credo," mm. 73–109

(continued)

EX. 8.8 (*continued*)

and B tetrachordal motives. When the tenor descends through C3 it is imitated by everyone: tenor at m. 103, contrabassus at m. 104, superius at m. 105, and then again tenor in augmentation in mm. 107–109. Such through-imitation is reserved exclusively for major points of articulation, and we must recognize a formal role for imitation already at this point in the history of large-scale polyphonic composition.

Later on in the Credo (see Ex. 8.9) there occurs a tenorless imitative interlude that, although it incorporates no cantus firmus material, nevertheless depends on relationships established motivically by the cantus firmus melody. The subject of the imitation proceeds in two parallel tetrachords a fifth apart, and recalls the parallel that has been established between the tetrachordal A and B motives. The imitation at the fifth by the superius brings about tetrachordal identity between the second phrase of the contra voice (mm. 207–209) and the first phrase of the superius (mm. 205–207). This D–G tetrachord serves as a pivot from the D to the G tonality, as the second phrase of the superius places its A–D tetrachord above the contra's D–G (mm. 208–209). The D tonality is confirmed by a cadence at m. 213. (I note parenthetically that the superius departs here from its normal modal procedure in articulating its upper register as a tetrachord. That exemplifies the tendency of these interludes to break down the functional distinctions among voices. The fifth relationship with the contra voice is associated, again, with the absence of a B-flat signature in the superius.)

The subject of the next imitative passage, beginning at m. 214 between the superius and contrabassus, is also based on parallel first species tetrachords, but somewhat more loosely. The D tonality is maintained, and the passage closes with a cadence on D at m. 222. At this point the tenor enters with C2, and the voices resume their normal relations. The tenor's leap to G in m. 225 constitutes a strong tonal shift after the prolonged passage in D, and the shift is confirmed all through the texture: by the variant of C2 in the contrabassus (mm. 225–227), picked up as the triadic motive in the superius (mm. 225–226) and contra (m. 226–227). The passage constitutes another tonal arch, again managed through motivic associations.

I show the following passage, the conclusion of the Sanctus (Ex. 8.10), in order to point briefly to the way in which the characteristic registers of the two contra voices may become motivically identified. In

EX. 8.9   "Credo," mm. 205–27

EX. 8.10 "Sanctus," mm. 168–96

(*continued*)

EX. 8.10 (continued)

m. 170 the contrabassus anticipates the tenor's A4. In the next measure
the high contra moves into its tetrachord and anticipates the tenor's B1.
Again the general task is setting the register, but it is motivically concretized. The contrabassus continues in m. 173 with another variant of
A4 as a reiteration of the previous two measures in the contrabassus and
tenor. Then it descends as in A3, but adapting the rhythm of B1 from
the tenor. After the tenor has presented B2 (mm. 179–182), mm.
182–184 of the contrabassus suggest both a reiteration of B2 and an
abstraction of A1. Measures 192–193 in the contrabassus suggest especially the latter (A1), as the passage follows immediately the C1 motive
in the tenor, of which it seems a transposition. But of course its tetrachord complements the leap of a fifth of C2 which the tenor executes
simultaneously with it.

I turn now to Agnus I (Ex. 8.11). With the entrance of the tenor the
high contra moves into its tetrachord, in accordance with the normal
procedure. The contrabassus again enters into an imitative motivic exchange with the tenor (mm. 8–9), then descends to its tetrachord to
give the accustomed support to the tenor's A3, with a suggestion of the
A and B tetrachordal motives. At m. 13 the contrabassus anticipates the
tenor. The high contra moves down to the pentachord, vacating the
tetrachord for the tenor's B motives, beginning at m. 17. For the tenor's
B2 (m. 22) the contrabassus moves up to the pentachord, expressed as
abstractions of A1 and A4. At m. 25 the high contra, in diminution,
anticipates the tenor's B3. At m. 31 the tenor presents C1 and the high
contra presents the same motive transposed to the tetrachord on D. At

EX. 8.11   "Agnus I," mm. 1–39

(continued)

EX. 8.11 (continued)

m. 33 the contrabassus abstracts B2 in the D tetrachord. So in immediate succession the D–G tetrachord has been concretized, first as an A motive, then as a B motive.

At m. 31 the superius presents the triadic motive, which is picked up at m. 35 by the high contra and again broadcast through the texture: in the contrabassus at m. 35, in the superius at m. 36.

What is of special interest in the third Agnus (Ex. 8.12) is of course that the first of its tenor expositions presents the cantus firmus in retrograde order. What does that stir up in the composition of the movement? The distinctness of the tenor fades: cadence points are wiped out, rhythmic contours disappear. But there are places where, because little

EX. 8.12   "Agnus III," mm. 75–131

(*continued*)

EX. 8.12 (*continued*)

palindromes can be isolated, one can catch a trace of the cantus firmus. And there the other voices respond according to the habits that they have formed by this time. The first such place is the presentation of B2 and B1, mm. 91–98. The contrabassus moves down to the tetrachord in mm. 94 and 95 and makes the B1 motive explicit. At m. 101, A4 becomes distinct in the tenor, and at once the contrabassus gives out a forward version of A3 (mm. 102–103) in anticipation of the retrograde A3 in the tenor at mm. 103–104, which is imitated by the high contra, both backward and forward, in mm. 105–106. The high contra goes right on in m. 107, imitating the backward A2 of the tenor's preceding measure and then continuing in mm. 107–108 with the familiar variant of A2 in the forward direction. That is picked up in mm. 111 and 112 by the superius and the contrabassus. In the meantime the high contra

busies itself in mm. 110–115 with the motives B1, B2, and B3, and it is
during that series that the crab surreptitiously shifts into reverse gear
and moves, with the cantus firmus, in a forward direction.

I trust that enough has been shown here about the influence of the
cantus firmus on the composition of the *Missa L'homme armé* through
motivic elaboration to warrant the conclusion that motivic elaboration
is in fact an essential aspect of cantus firmus technique. It is in the service of something like the principle of distinctness and individualization
of which Schoenberg wrote, and that principle played an important role
in fifteenth-century composition. As for Dufay, his inventiveness is
manifested not only in his ability to muster a systematic and fluent musical language, but also in the fact that he could give it characteristic
expression.

CHAPTER 9

Wozzeck *and the Apocalypse*

Among the central meanings in Georg Büchner's *Woyzeck,* there is one that comes clear only when we read the play in the context of the history of ideas—specifically in the light of certain currents of thought about human history and eschatology. Aspects of the play's expression are thereby elucidated which are forcefully brought forward through the organization and compositional procedures of Alban Berg's *Wozzeck.*

Near the end of the long third scene of the opera, Wozzeck appears suddenly at Marie's window and alludes cryptically to the mysterious signs that had come to him in the field the scene before, confiding to her that he is "on the track of something big" (the accompanying table summarizes the scenes of Berg's libretto). As those signs had first been presented through Wozzeck's eyes, they seemed like the imaginings and fears of a simple man about Freemasons and who knows what other objects of superstition. But now in the third scene he gives them a scriptural context, as though through a sudden insight: "Isn't it written, 'And behold, the smoke went up from the land, as the smoke from a furnace?'"

What Wozzeck has recalled here is a passage in the Book of Genesis, chapter 19: "Then the Lord rained upon Sodom brimstone and fire from the Lord out of heaven . . . and, behold, the smoke went up from the Land as the smoke from a furnace." The image is repeated in the New Testament Book of Revelation (the Apocalypse), chapter 9: "And the fifth angel sounded, and I saw a star fall from heaven unto the earth: and to him was given the key of the bottomless pit; and there arose a

Summary of Scenes

Act/Scene	Setting	Persons
I.I	Captain's rooms, morning	Wozzeck, the Captain
1.2	Open field outside of town, late afternoon	Wozzeck, Andres
1.3	Marie's room, evening	Marie, the Child, Wozzeck
1.4	Doctor's study, sunny afternoon	Wozzeck, the Doctor
1.5	Street in front of Marie's door, twilight	Marie, Drum Major
2.1	Marie's room, sunny morning	Marie, the Child, Wozzeck
2.2	A street in town, daylight	The Captain, the Doctor, Wozzeck
2.3	Street in front of Marie's door, overcast day	Marie, Wozzeck
2.4	Tavern courtyard, late evening	Crowd, Apprentices, Marie, Drum Major, Wozzeck, Andres
2.5	Barracks, night	Soldiers, Wozzeck, Andres, Drum Major
3.1	Marie's room, night, candlelight	Marie, the Child
3.2	Forest path near a pond, darkening	Marie, Wozzeck
3.3	A bar, night, weak light	Crowd, Margret, Wozzeck
3.4	The same forest path, moonlight as before	Wozzeck, the Captain, the Doctor
3.5	In front of Marie's door, bright morning, sunshine	Children, Marie's Boy

smoke out of the pit, as the smoke of the great furnace; and the sun and the air were darkened by reason of the smoke of the pit."

Both passages are about a holocaust visited by a wrathful God upon a corrupt and debauched people, and that is the idea that begins to form in Wozzeck's mind as he stands for the first time on the stage before his mistress. And he asks, "What will it all come to?" The answer to this thematic question lies in the strange unfolding of the drama, pressed forward by forces that lie, as Büchner had once put it, "outside of ourselves,"[1] and by Wozzeck, who guarantees the outcome as he imagines himself becoming aware of what it must be.

The Book of Revelation comes to command Wozzeck's perception of his situation. But its imagery and atmosphere—and most of all its portentousness—are not confined to Wozzeck's mind. Attention to that fact provides the focus for an interpretation of Berg's drama. (The opera is the principal subject of this essay, but in presenting my interpretation I shall sometimes refer to Büchner's play and to its philosophical context.)

––––––––

The point of departure is a reading of the libretto in the light of the Apocalypse. The following citations from the latter are most directly relevant.

6:12: And I beheld when the angel had opened the sixth seal, and lo, there was a great earthquake; and the sun became black as sack cloth of hair, and the moon became as blood.

16:1: And I heard a fearful voice saying to the seven angels, Go your ways, and pour out the vials of the wrath of God upon the Earth.

16:3: And the second angel poured out his vial upon the sea; and it became as the blood of a dead man; and every living soul died in the sea.

16:4: And the third angel poured out his vial upon the rivers and fountains of waters; and they became blood.

16:18: And . . . there were voices and thunders, and lightnings, and there was a great earthquake.

17:1: And there came one of the seven angels . . . and talked with me, saying unto me, Come hither: I will show thee the judgment of the great Whore with whom the kings of the earth have committed fornication, and the inhabitants of the earth have been made drunk with the wine of her fornication.

17:16: And [she shall be made] desolate and naked and burned with fire.

In the opera these images begin to be displayed in the second scene. (In Büchner's fair copy that scene opens the play, and that rather substantiates the impression one has of it as a source.)[2] As Wozzeck moves through the field cutting brush, he believes that the earth is hollow and quaking beneath him. He perceives the brilliant twilight as a fire on the horizon, and that impression is still vivid in his mind in the third and fourth scenes of Act 1 as he describes his visions to Marie and the Doctor, respectively. This, to him, tumultuous eruption of the second scene is followed by darkness and by deathly silence: "Still, Alles still, als wäre die Welt tot." In the third scene, as he relives it all for Marie, he says, "Und jetzt Alles finster, finster . . ." In the fourth scene of Act 3, as Wozzeck returns to the scene of the murder, it is no longer "as though the world were dead"; it is "Still, Alles still und tot." And at the end of the scene, as Wozzeck's drowning noises subside, the Doctor, taking the air with the Captain, says, "Stiller . . . jetzt ganz still." In the fourth scene of Act 1, the darkness is on Wozzeck's mind as he tries to bring the Doctor to understand what he has been experiencing. And in the tavern scene of Act 2, he expresses his agony at seeing the Drum Major paw Marie, pleading with God to bring down the darkness: "Warum löscht Gott nicht die Sonne aus?" To Marie, standing alone after Wozzeck's departure at the end of the third scene, the darkness is unnatural, and she is terrified by it ("Es schaudert mich").

Berg provided the most explicit lighting instructions for the staging of the opera. After the second scene of Act 2, the scene in which Wozzeck's suspicions are crystallized, every scene is played in darkness of one sort or another: overcast day, night, candlelight, red moonlight. In particular the death scenes of Marie and Wozzeck are both illuminated by the appearance of a red moon. Marie describes it as red, Wozzeck sees it as bloody in his own death scene, and Berg confirms this, again in his lighting directions ("Der Mond bricht blutrot hinter den Wolken hervor"). And as Wozzeck descends into the water that will drown him he cries, "Das Wasser ist Blut." Only in the very last scene does the morning sun that shone on the first scene illuminate the pathetic figure of the lone survivor. Darkness is one of the means whereby a sense of foreboding is projected. The descent of silence and darkness on Wozzeck's world is a central process of the drama.

The tavern scene in Act 2 forces upon Wozzeck the palpable evidence of what it had amused the Doctor and the Captain to insinuate in the second scene of Act 2. The sight of Marie dancing lewdly with the Drum Major launches him permanently into a morose and fanatic state of mind. It is not an ordinary act of infidelity that he sees, but a symbolic act of depravity. It is, he says, as though the whole world were waltzing about in fornication, and it is the whole world he wants punished at that moment, crying for God to extinguish the sun. From the moment that the idea of Marie's adultery had first entered Wozzeck's mind, he had assimilated it in his symbolic way; in Act 2, Scene 3, he speaks to her of "a sin so great and foul that it might drive the angels from heaven." In Berg's text for the murder scene, Wozzeck kisses Marie and expresses the wish that he might often kiss her thus. "But I may not," he says—"Ich darf nicht."

In Wozzeck's tormented mind the killing of Marie is an act that he has been called upon to carry out. There seems to be a premonition of this even as early as the interview with the Doctor in the fourth scene of Act 1, when Wozzeck speaks of a terrible voice calling to him. The murder is more an obligatory act of execution than a passionate act of vengeance. And just as inevitable is the mysterious course of Wozzeck's death. It never seems quite to the point to call it suicide, but it seems even further off to call it an accident. It just happens, and, like Marie's death, it is something to which events and circumstances seem to move ineluctably. Again, Wozzeck senses it coming. After the second scene of Act 2 he alludes repeatedly to his own death. At the same time, however, we cannot but see Wozzeck's hand, and behind it his perverse will, as active in both deaths.

This suggests a view of the complexities in the determination of events in the drama. First, there is a perfectly natural explanation based on circumstances and motives. Marie is weary of a bleak existence with Wozzeck. He works long hours, sleeps away from home, and when he turns up he can do no more than rave about his hallucinations; never mind that he does it all for her sake and that of their child. She betrays him with a man who offers her some diversion, and when Wozzeck learns the truth he kills her. It is a common enough story, but a tragic irony emerges from the tension between that surface view of things and Wozzeck's perceptions. Although Marie, as an adulteress, and Wozzeck, as a murderer, have violated the moral order of their world, they are nevertheless presented to us as the only sympathetic inhabitants of that world, driven to their acts by the cruelty of circumstances and of their fellow men. There would be pathos enough in seeing Wozzeck under these circumstances strike out against all that he has in the world. But the pathos is far more intense than that. Wozzeck imagines that he follows a divine calling in acting as Marie's righteous executioner, and the world that he thereby destroys is not the inhuman world represented to us by the Captain and the Doctor—it is the essentially innocent and worthy world of his little family. He acts, fulfilling a prophecy that he himself has spun out of hallucinations and superstitions and messianic religious ideas. In his mind what happens must happen, and so he causes it to happen in reality. He has no possibility of understanding Marie's actions on a human scale. She hopes for forgiveness, after the example of Mary Magdalene;[3] but he sees her as marked for destruction, after the example of the Whore of Babylon. He has assimilated her act, from the moment of its first glimmering in his mind, into a grotesquely paranoid mental construction in which there are no acts of will, no choices, only the inevitable, and in which individual events are understood always as signifying something larger. Marie too, but without any fanaticism, has resigned herself to the abandonment of choice. For when she yields to the Drum Major, she yields in utter despair: it makes no difference to her what she does.

Beyond any causal analysis of the action, and quite outside the minds of any of the characters, there is an atmosphere of foreboding and doom that hangs like a pall over the drama as it unfolds to its seemingly inevitable conclusion. The apocalyptic imagery is only the most concrete manifestation of that atmosphere; all of the main characters respond to it: Marie, standing in the darkness, terrified; the hysterical Captain, hiding his fear of the future behind his flippancy and callousness; the Doctor, desperately keeping himself under control through his compulsive rationalism. And Wozzeck.

The sense of doom—the sense that the things that happen were bound from the first to happen—is not only in Wozzeck's mind; it is an essential aspect of the drama's expression. We feel that most acutely of all in contemplating the fate of Marie's child, which is the ultimate fulfillment in the piece. He is left at the end, riding off into the world like the little child of whom Marie had told at the beginning of Act 3 (in Büchner's version, the tale of the Grandmother): "Once there was a poor child that had no father and no mother, for everyone was dead, and there was no one in the world, and he starved and cried day and night."[4] That is the answer to the question of meaning that the drama poses: there is no larger meaning; things move irresistibly forward, but to no greater purpose.

That idea belongs to the thematics and to the tone of the drama, and the impact of the tragedy depends on it. We can bring it more sharply into view if we enter into the philosophical context of Büchner's play.

In the tavern scene, just as Wozzeck has blurted out his apocalyptic curse, "Warum löscht Gott nicht die Sonne aus?" the drunken apprentice begins to preach a different view of things: "Wherefore is man? Verily, beloved listeners, I say unto you, everything is for the best. For how else could the farmer, the caskmaker, and the doctor earn their living if God had not created man? How could the tailor live if God had not implanted in man a sense of shame? How could the soldier and the innkeeper live, if He had not equipped man with the need to shoot people and to quench parched thirsts? Therefore most beloved, doubt not, since everything is lovely and fine . . ." This burlesque of a theodicy is reminiscent of the prattling of Pangloss in Voltaire's *Candide:* "Observe how noses were made to carry spectacles, and spectacles we have, accordingly . . . Our legs are clearly intended for shoes and stockings, so we have them . . . Pigs were made to be eaten, and we eat pork all the year 'round." It is the teleological view of the world that is being ridiculed here. Everthing is valued in terms of the purpose it serves or the goal toward which it moves, and since world history is seen as moving toward some higher good, everything is, in the long run, for the best.

Just a few years before *Woyzeck,* Hegel had lectured thus:

Our intellectual striving aims at recognizing that what eternal wisdom *intended* it has actually *accomplished* . . . Our method is a theodicy, a justification of God . . . [The reconciliation of the thinking mind with evil] can only be attained through the recognition of the positive elements in which that negative element disappears as something subordinate and vanquished. This is possible through the consciousness, on the one hand, of the true ultimate purpose of the world and, on the other hand, of the fact that this purpose has been actualized in the world and that evil cannot ultimately prevail beside it.[5]

But *Woyzeck* and *Wozzeck* embody a refusal to be reconciled to the evil they portray, a rejection of the idea that everything is for the best. There is no higher good that justifies this tragedy. Wozzeck's struggles to find wider meanings in small things merely show him victimized by a way of thinking that has somehow filtered down to him. It is another of Büchner's jabs of bitter irony to show his antihero fingering the crumbs of a philosophy that would dismiss him as one of the "innocent flowers" that must be trampled down by the juggernaut of history.

In 1836 Büchner was appointed to the Faculty of Medicine of the University of Zürich. He began his inaugural lecture on the cranial nerves by speaking directly to this very issue. "In the domain of the physiological and anatomical sciences we encounter two mutually opposed views . . . The first regards all manifestations of organic life from the teleological viewpoint: it finds the solution to the riddle in the purpose of an organ. It knows the individual only as something that is to fulfill a purpose outside of itself." This attitude Büchner identified as the "dogmatism of the Enlightenment philosophers," and he opposed to it his own insistence that "Everything that exists, exists for its own purposes."[6]

Büchner had said elsewhere that in writing plays he regarded himself as a kind of historian, and in the domain of history the teleological viewpoint was completely at odds with his attitudes.[7] Hegel had proclaimed that "Universal Law is not designed for individuals . . . In affirming that the Universal Reason *does* actualize itself, we have nothing to do with the individual empirically regarded."[8] Kant had written that the older generations must "pursue their weary toil for the sake of those who come after them . . . It is to be the happy fate of only the latest generations to dwell in the building upon which the long series of their forefathers have labored . . ."[9] The Turkish philosopher in *Candide* asks, "What does it signify whether there be good or evil? When his Highness sends a ship to Egypt, does he concern himself whether the mice on board are comfortable or not?"

The historiography of the Enlightenment arose out of reflection over the same perplexity that plagued Wozzeck. The difference is only in the grandeur of the formulation: How can sense be made out of the history of human existence when history daily displays so much of senseless barbarism and suffering? How could so much misery be reconciled with the idea of a rational and provident order? It could only be that the meaning of history is to be found in humanity's future. The question came to be formulated as a question about ultimate purposes; and the answer was a doctrine of progress, a secular copy of the doctrine of salvation, which decreed that the misery in individual lives must be suffered for the sake of what was to come.[10] No one had put it more eloquently than Hegel:

When we consider the spectacle of the passions; . . . when we behold individuals, with the deepest sympathy for their indescribable misery—then we can only end up with sadness over this transitoriness and, insofar as this destruction is not only a work of nature but of the will of men, even more with moral sadness, with the indignation of the good spirit over such a spectacle . . . But even as we contemplate history as this slaughter bench on which the happiness of peoples . . . and the virtue of individuals have been sacrificed, our thoughts cannot avoid the question, for whom, for what final aim these monstrous sacrifices have been made.[11]

The answer was formulated in systems of history that were complacent about the inevitability of progress and ultimately callous about the quality of individual human lives.

Büchner was one of the growing number to whom that answer was no longer acceptable, and *Woyzeck* is a powerful statement of opposition.[12] It answers exactly to Hegel's sneering characterization of the "litany of lamentation that the good and pious often, or for the most part, fare ill in the world, while the evil and wicked prosper."[13] It reverses the historical view of the Enlightenment philosophers. Where they saw the inevitable progress of humanity in the ascendancy of reason, *Woyzeck* enlarges upon injustice and suffering as a continuing condition. Where they read meaning out of history on the grand scale, *Woyzeck* insists upon the contemplation of meaninglessness. And as for the idea that reason and progress characterize the human condition, Büchner took that only as the object of grotesque parodies.

There is a scene in the play that Berg did not incorporate in his libretto but that shares the tone of the sermon of the drunken apprentice. A barker, speaking with a French accent, stands in front of a carnival booth:

Ladies and Gentlemen, step right up and see the astronomical horse and little canary birds—they're the darlings of all the potentates of Europe, members of all learned societies. They'll tell you everything: how old you are, how many children you have, what diseases you carry. [Pointing to the monkey.] He shoots a pistol, stands on one leg. It's all a matter of training; all he has is beastly reason, or rather a quite reasonable beastliness. He's no beastly-dumb individual like lots of people, present honored company excluded. Step right in. The commencement of the commencement will take its beginning at once.

See the progress of civilization. Everything moves forward, a horse, a monkey, a canary bird. The monkey is already a soldier—that's not much, the lowest level of the human race. Start the representation. Make the beginning of the beginning. The commencement of the commencement will take place at once.[14]

The issues over reason and progress are reflected again in the distorting mirror of the scene between Wozzeck and the Doctor: the Doctor, raving that the *musculus constrictor vesicae* is subject to the will, that in humans alone individuality is exalted to freedom; Wozzeck, paying no attention, confiding to the Doctor his secrets about nature; the Doctor, losing himself in raptures over the progress of science and about his own immortality, then remembering that he musn't lose his own self-control, assuring himself that it isn't worth aggravating oneself over another person—if it had been a lizard, that would have been something else again. In the opera that callousness reaches its depth in the fourth scene of Act 3 when the Doctor and the Captain hasten away from the sounds of Wozzeck drowning.

The provocation of these issues was already at hand in the celebrated case of the real Woyzeck, which Büchner took as substance for his play. Woyzeck was condemned to death by the Leipzig tribunal for the murder of his mistress. On the petition of his public defender the case was reviewed by the privy councillor Clarus, with respect to the question whether Woyzeck, given the miserable conditions of his existence, could be held fully responsible for his act. In a long and thoughtful analysis Clarus argued that, inasmuch as Woyzeck was fundamentally in possession of his senses (he was embittered but not mentally ill) he must be held accountable for the exercise of his freedom of choice. It would be an unacceptable precedent and an intolerable example for the young if Woyzeck were granted his life after having followed his passions and not his reason. Woyzeck was beheaded, and Büchner, to put it in the words of Berg's *Wozzeck* lecture, appealed the case to the public.[15]

Berg achieved an extraordinary operatic portrayal of the relentless progress of Wozzeck's entrapment between a murderous world and his own psychic disintegration. I wish to pursue in the remainder of this essay the most intense of the means by which he did so, the association and development of motivic ideas, which weave an ever more constraining and ever more clearly portentous network about Wozzeck and his family.[16]

The source is in the second scene. The scene-changing music following the first scene falls away quickly, leaving a sonority that develops in the first five measures as a motive based upon three chords. I call it mo-

EX. 9.1 1.2.201–206. Examples sound as written. They have been reduced to show the motives discussed in the text.

tive A (Ex. 9.1). It is recalled naturally enough in the third and fourth scenes, as Wozzeck tells Marie and the Doctor of his visions. But that it should be brought back in the barracks scene (Act 2, Scene 5) is a special idea. Wozzeck, plagued by nightmare recollections of the preceding scene in the tavern, is unable to sleep. To be sure, music from that scene returns to him eventually, but at the outset the atmosphere is set by those chords, moaned by the chorus of sleeping soldiers. In this way the music leads us to refer the tavern scene—which is in Wozzeck's consciousness— back to the scene in the field and suggests that the contents of the second scene are transformed from Wozzeck's unconscious, concretized as the episode on the dance floor, realized as the working out of what was portended. This interpretation will be substantially reinforced when I return to this scene near the conclusion of the discussion, and the role that the music here plays in projecting the penetration of the implicit or unconscious meaning of events in Wozzeck's mind onto their explicit, surface meaning will be exemplified in other connections.

Throughout the course of the opera the chords of motive A are unpacked, and their upper strand is transformed in stages into a number of distinct motivic identities. The moments in the action which these accompany are then always marked with the affect of their source in the second scene. More than that, those moments thereby fall together as the chain of consequents from that beginning.

In the initial presentation of the A motive, the upper voice of the chords turns on an augmented second, A-flat–B–A-flat (see the bracket in Ex. 9.1).[17] In the second and third presentations, that interval is distinctly isolated. With just those pitches, it will constitute a kind of fixed tonal reference throughout.

EX. 9.2 I.2.227

EX. 9.3 I.4.554–55

EX. 9.4 2.5.752–53

Two new motives evolve from the augmented second: I shall refer to them as B1 and B2. B1 follows immediately upon the reiteration of the augmented second in the third presentation of motive A. It accompanies Wozzeck as he points to the mysterious sign above the toadstools (Ex. 9.2); in the fourth scene it accompanies him as he asks the Doctor whether he has ever seen the toadstool rings (Ex. 9.3); and it is recalled to Wozzeck by the cello as he lies sleepless and afraid in the barracks scene (Ex. 9.4). After the introduction of B1 in the second scene, the motive is picked up by the French horn, then by the English horn (Ex. 9.5). The last phrase in the English horn is imitated in canon by the trombone, the harp, and the oboe. This is the moment in which motive B2 evolves from B1, with Wozzeck singing about the mysterious disembodied head.

Motive B2 is recalled at pitch and in canon in the third scene as Wozzeck cites Genesis (Ex. 9.6). It is recalled again in the barracks scene as the melody to which Wozzeck begins his recitation from the Lord's Prayer, "and lead us not into temptation" (Ex. 9.7). These musical associations carry the mystery and terror of that moment in the second scene ("Three days and nights later he lay in his coffin"), through the moment of revelation in the third scene ("Isn't it written . . ."), and ultimately to the moment in the barracks scene when Wozzeck, haunted

motive B1

motive B2

EX. 9.5   I.2.233–41

Wozzeck: Steht nicht ge-schrie-ben   "Und sich   es ging der

Rauch   auf vom Land,   wie ein Rauch vom O-fen."

254   EX. 9.6   I.3.443–47

Wozzeck: Mein Herr und Gott,

und füh - re uns nicht in Ver - su - chung.

EX. 9.7   2.5.753—58

by an unexpressed awareness of the significance of things, lies abed praying.

As motive B1 evolves from A, and as B2 evolves from B1, so B2 repeatedly leads back to the substance and tone of A. The canon with B2 rises to a phrase that peaks in the highest voice and quickly falls through a whole-tone line (Exx. 9.6–9.8). In the scene with Marie, Wozzeck picks up the whole-tone descent for the recitation from Genesis (Ex. 9.6). In the barracks scene he takes it for the recitation from the Lord's Prayer (Ex. 9.7). The line is achieved through filling in of the upper voice of the chords of the A motive, which come back into focus

EX. 9.8 I.2.241–44

EX. 9.9 I.3.441–43

each time at this point (compare Exx. 9.6–9.8 with 9.1). This return to the point of origin assures our continued awareness of the source of these motives and of the links between their dramatic contents.

There is yet another strand in this network that contributes to the same result. In the third scene Wozzeck's biblical recitation is prepared by an arpeggio solo in the bassoon that eventuates in a *tremolando* on the notes A-flat and B (Ex. 9.9), that same augmented second. It is a sort of intonation for the coming passage, which begins with the same interval. The cello plays such an intonation in the fourth scene, ending again

EX. 9.10   I.4.534–40

EX. 9.11   I.3.466–68

with a *tremolando* on A-flat-B. This time those pitches prepare not the B2 motive but Wozzeck's plaint, "Ach, Marie" (Ex. 9.10). That is of course one of the thematic motives of the opera, always an expression of lamentation and of anxiousness for Marie or the child. Marie sings it in the third scene with the words "Komm, mein Bub." The strings cry it out at the moment of Marie's death. In the third scene it is heard a second time, in association with the equally thematic motive "Wir arme Leut" (Ex. 9.11). The associations among these motives rest on two things: the place of the augmented second in them, and their introduction in association with one another. The dramatic significance of the

EX. 9.12   1.3.372–73 (1.2.250)

association seems clear. The motives of lamentation refer again and again to the hard circumstances of Wozzeck's and Marie's life—there is no getting away from that—but they have their musical source in the mystery and terror of the imagined supernatural. These are then two different manifestations—we might say material and spiritual, or external and psychological—of the forces that press in on Wozzeck and his family. For Wozzeck the two blend into one in his perceptions of a threatening world.

Something like that is expressed again in the melody of Marie's lullaby in the third scene, a moment of melancholy tenderness that falls between the march—which we may reckon as the beginning of the end—and the appearance of Wozzeck with his report about the second scene. The melody comprises two elements: a dotted figure that occurs in several folklike tunes—for example, the accompaniment to Andres's hunting tune in the second scene (see Ex. 9.12, the figure in parentheses), and motive B2 (Ex. 9.12). On the surface, the melody has the qualities of a lullaby. Its full meaning, however, also entails the affect of the lamentation motives and the haunting portentousness that it receives from the context of the B2 motive.

This motivic complex has its final outcome in Wozzeck's death, and after that it is washed away, as we shall see. As the moon "breaks blood-red through the clouds" (Act 3, Scene 4), Wozzeck moans, "But the moon will give me away; the moon is bloody." The strings just then descend in a scale whose intervals derive from the B2 motive, as is made clear by the scoring. Those intervals are identical with the intervals of a six-note chord that pervades the entire scene just as the pitch B pervades the entire scene of Marie's death (Ex. 9.13).

Wozzeck wades into the water to wash the blood away but finds that the water has turned to blood, and he drowns. At that moment the strings rise chromatically, carrying up the six-note chord (Ex. 9.14). The chord is sustained as the Doctor and the Captain stroll by and is left

EX. 9.13   3.4.267–68

EX. 9.14   3.4.284

sounding to the end of the scene. At the very end it is resolved to the chord that begins that great outpouring of sympathy, the D minor orchestral epilogue (Ex. 9.15). The music of the second scene has run its course, just as we may say the prophecy of the second scene has run its ironic course, and it is wiped away, leaving us to contemplate once more that external world on which the first curtain rose.

But the six-note chord of this scene was first heard just after Marie's death. There is a moment's silence, then the orchestra in unison takes up the B that has been sounding throughout the murder scene, makes an enormous crescendo, and crashes down on the six-note chord (Ex. 9.16). The germinal motive of the second scene has reached forward to link both deaths together as its own eventuation.

EX. 9.15   3.4.317–21

EX. 9.16   3.2.109–14

I want finally to describe two musical associations, involving different motivic material, through which meaningful links are established between moments in time and between levels of consciousness. At a certain point in the second scene (m. 286) there begins a lengthy, detailed direction for lighting, with each effect marked exactly with respect to the beat on which it is to occur: "The sun is just setting. The last strong ray bathes the horizon in the most glaring sunlight, which is directly followed by a twilight with the effect of deepest darkness, to which the eye becomes gradually accustomed." What is important here is the immediate juxtaposition of brilliant light and sudden darkness. With the flash of the last strong ray Wozzeck screams, "Ein Feuer! Das fährt von der Erde in den Himmel." In the orchestra a pair of chords crashes up through successive octaves, then falls chromatically to the bottom again (Ex. 9.17). This figure returns in the tavern scene of the second act, as Wozzeck, watching the dancing, screams, "Warum löscht

EX. 9.17   I.2.291–95

EX. 9.18   I.2.274–78

Gott nicht die Sonne aus?" (mm. 517–522). The twilight that Wozzeck
saw as a fire in the second scene now returns to his mind as the con-
flagration before the apocalyptic darkness that he is calling down. This
is for him the moment that was foretold by those signs.

Just before the great lighting display in the second scene, Wozzeck
says to Andres, "Listen! Something down below is moving with us."
The horns are the principal orchestral voice at that moment, and they
rise quickly and hysterically to a climax (Ex. 9.18). In the barracks
scene, describing his nightmare visions to Andres, Wozzeck sings a development of that line. His words are "I keep seeing them and hearing

Wozzeck:

Im-mer zu, Im-mer zu

EX. 9.19 2.5.746—49

Im-mer zu!

EX. 9.20 2.4.546

the fiddles, 'Immer zu, Immer zu'" (Ex. 9.19). With the words "Immer zu" Wozzeck is aping Marie and the Drum Major dancing and singing in the tavern (Ex. 9.20). There the rhythm of those words had fallen right in with the waltz rhythms of the stage band. But now as Wozzeck recalls them, it is in the musical context in which they originated, that fearful moment in the second scene (compare the bracketed notes of Exx. 9.18 and 9.19 with Ex. 9.20). Now we recognize that the waltz has had implanted in it the germ of that earlier music and that the waltzing plays out in Wozzeck's mind what that music portended.

Continuing with the description of his nightmare, Wozzeck sings on with the same music: "Then something flashes repeatedly before my eyes, like a knife, a great knife" (Ex. 9.21). With that the first idea of what must be done enters his mind as the last step in a chain of associa-

EX. 9.21   2.5.750–51

tions which leads from the mysteries of the second scene, through their concretization, to their inevitable consequence. But it is not just an association of ideational contents that is accomplished here. It is a chilling musical projection of the conglomeration of contexts that gives nightmares their disturbing character.

This passage brings us full circle, for it leads directly into motive B1 in the cello (m. 752) and thence to the recitation from the Lord's Prayer with motive B2 (m. 753). With all that has just been shown as crammed together in Wozzeck's mind, the prayer is understandable as the momentary refuge of a terribly frightened man. But with his relentless irony, the tune with which Berg saw fit to provide him is that one he learned in the second scene, singing about a disembodied head and the man who picked it up and was dead three days later.

Wozzeck is a marked man, ground down by the press of circumstances and by the machinations of his own mind. As we reflect on his story, these remarks of Büchner's about his own feelings upon studying the French Revolution become filled with meaning: "I felt crushed under the monstrous fatalism of history . . . The individual mere foam on the wave, greatness a matter of chance, the power of genius a puppet-play, a laughable bout against a law of brass. To comprehend it is the most we can do, to defeat it is impossible . . . 'Must' is one of the curse-words with which man is baptized." [18]

CHAPTER 10

The Lulu Character and the Character of Lulu

The wordplay in the title of this essay is directed toward a way of thinking that I have missed in the published *Lulu* criticism. My inquiry will be about the stage character Lulu, conceived as an artifice, even as a puppet executing its lines and actions in the time and space represented on the stage. But I want to ask about the character, in that sense, as it informs and is informed by the character of the drama. That is a different sort of question than is asked in discussions about the character and motivations of the persons of a drama, as though they might be persons that one would encounter off the stage.[1]

I shall take my perspective from two points of view: the style of the Lulu plays (Frank Wedekind's *Earth Spirit* and *Pandora's Box*) and their adaptation by Alban Berg, and the backgrounds of the several personae that the character presents under its rich array of signs—snake, Pierrot, dancer, whore, prostitute, all those names (Lulu, Eva, Nelly, Mignon).

The difference that I have begun to indicate here has immediate consequences for the critic's choice of moral categories for judging the character's behavior and fate. Consider first Pierre Boulez's commentary provided with the recording of the Paris performance of the opera: "*Lulu* is definitely a morality play, a sort of *Rake's Progress*. The protagonist moves up in society until the murder of her rich protector Dr. Schön. Then she undergoes a progressive degradation down to the wretched state of a London prostitute."[2]

Strong moral judgments are entailed here—in the word "murder," to which I shall return later, and in the phrase "degradation to the wretched state of a prostitute." "Degradation" and "wretched" ride along as natural attributes of "prostitute," as though the view of the prostitute as fallen woman were obligatory. That reflects a widely socialized view, which may indeed be on the whole the most sociologically accurate view that one could take. But sociological accuracy in the portrayal of character is not the only sort of truth to which the theater can aspire, especially the sort of theater that Wedekind was developing. We shall only cloud our view of the Lulu character and of the meanings in the drama if we treat the character as though she had just walked onstage off the street, enveloped in such conventionalized attitudes.

What is striking about the attitude embodied in Boulez's comment is that no one asks the woman herself. In the artistic milieu of the Lulu plays and Berg's opera the position of the prostitute could be seen quite differently, and in a way that claimed to take into account her own interests. An early instance is the prostitute Marie of Nygränd, in Strindberg's novel *The Red Room* (1879). She says that she is not a victim; she has chosen her profession voluntarily because it gives her more freedom than any of the other alternatives open to her. A much more recent one is Luis Buñuel's film *Belle de Jour* (1968), about a middle-class housewife who makes an independent life for herself, free of her ambitious medical-student husband, through daytime prostitution.

During the long love scene between Lulu and Alwa in Act 2, Scene 2, Alwa says, "If it were not for your great childlike eyes I would have to take you for the most cunning whore that ever drove a man to his ruination." Lulu replies, "I wish to God I were that!" As she sings those words, the orchestra intones music that is associated with her throughout the opera (Ex. 10.1). It is heard first in the Prologue, as the stagehand carries "the performer who is to play Lulu in front of the curtain" (Berg's direction), dressed as Pierrot but identified by the Animal Trainer as a snake. It accompanies her major entrances throughout the opera, in particular the entrance, dressed in an "elegant ball-dress, very décolleté," in Act 2, Scene 1, in the midst of her strange masculine coterie of Schigolch, the Athlete, and the Student (Ex. 10.2); and the entrance in Act 2, Scene 2, following her escape from prison. Because of these associations, this radiantly gorgeous music has been called "Lulu's entrance music."[3] But it is not just a sign of her entrances, it is a sign of her identity. Through it she says "This is *me*." It fills the air, as her presence fills the stage. This music, which sings her identity, accompanies Lulu as

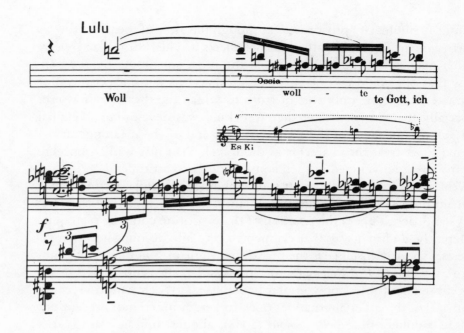

EX. 10.1 2.2.1084–87.

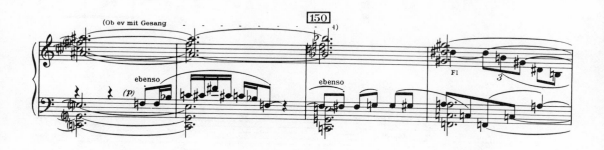

EX. IO.2   2.I.145–53.

she says to Alwa that she wishes she were the cunning whore that he almost takes her for. The great climax of the entrance in Act 2, Scene 2 (just after her escape from prison) is the moment when, dropping her pretended sickly demeanor, she sings "Oh, freedom! Lord God in Heaven!" On the first syllable of "Freiheit" she hits the high point of

EX. 10.3 2.2.1000–1004.

this music, B, a note rich with meaning as well as resonance, as we shall see (Ex. 10.3).

To Lulu as a sexual person, freedom of choice and the fulfillment of her identity are one and the same. In Act 2, Scene 1, when the Marquis attempts to blackmail her into letting herself be sold to a brothel in

Cairo, she says, "I can't sell the only thing I've ever owned." She adds that she can tell "in the dead of night and at a thousand paces whether a man and I are made for each other. And if I find I've sinned against my judgment . . . it takes weeks to overcome my loathing for myself."

Naturalist artists and writers portrayed the prostitute as a fallen woman, all right, albeit with compassion—Dostoevsky's Sonya, Zola's Nana. But at the same time they endowed her with an ultimately superior morality in order to show up the counterfeit righteousness of the bourgeois world of the men for whose pleasure she exists (Fig. 10.1). By contrast Expressionist artists and writers turned a cool and cynical eye on the scene: the woman, neither fallen nor merely submissive, delights in the active play of her sexuality; the man of the world is spellbound, perched on the edge of disaster (Fig. 10.2). The aggressive uncovering of the woman's body in the second image serves as metaphor for the exposure of the brutal dynamic of the whole situation. But some things remain unchanged: the central placement and full view of the woman on display (interestingly enough, our view of the observer is in both images partially occluded); the intensity of the man's gaze, and the precise way it is targeted on the woman's anatomy; and the lie that these details give to the costume he wears as symbol of his worldly respectability and power. Therein lies the social commentary that both images render up.

In *Belle de Jour* the woman carries on her daylight activities in a brothel that has the appearance of an idealized setting for her bourgeois life with her husband. That cinematic *trompe l'oeil* concretizes a favorite metaphor of Expressionist dramatists: the bourgeois household as brothel (and vice versa), the woman suspended between the roles of wife (or sweetheart or mistress) and whore. (Polly Peachum, in Brecht's *Dreigroschenoper,* is the classic case.) In Alwa's remark quoted above, it is only Lulu's "great childlike eyes" that keep her from slipping into the latter role. This thematic idea is evident even in the progression of domestic stage sets in the opera: Act 1, Scene 2, "A very elegant drawing room"; Act 2, Scene 1, "A magnificent room in German Renaissance style"; Act 3, Scene 2, "An attic room without windows [furnished

FIG. 10.1 Edouard Manet. *Nana*

FIG. 10.2 George Grosz. *Near the Limit*

with] tattered mattress, doors which close badly, rickety flower stand, smoking oil lamp . . ." In each of these scenes Lulu is surrounded by what Schön sarcastically calls his "family circle," but what really is Lulu's family circle. The last scene, in which Lulu has become the family provider through open prostitution, comes off as a kind of distillation of what was implicit in all of them. What has been distilled out, ironically, are all the material things that money can buy, and, at her own insistence, the portrait of Lulu as Pierrot. Nothing is more symbolic of Lulu's earlier exploitation for a price than that portrait—but in less direct, more socially acceptable ways. When, in the last scene, she finally sells herself openly, money means little to her.

Since Berg's sketches have become available for study, a brief notation has come to light from which it is evident that this ambivalent idea about the conjugal relationship lived in his mind, too. In several cases Berg assigned to a single singer one role in the first half of the opera and another in the second half. Special meaning derives from the association of each of those pairs, and Berg made cryptic notes hinting at those meanings. One such case is the pairing of the Prince in Act 1, Scene 3, singing of the happiness he anticipates with Lulu as his wife, and the Marquis in Act 3, Scene 1, pressuring her to let herself be sold to a brothel in Cairo. Berg's note is the slogan "Treulich geführt—Bordel ist Ehe" (bordello equals marriage). And into the dense music accompanying the Prince in the earlier of the two scenes he packed most of the tune of the Wedding March from Wagner's *Lohengrin,* which begins with the words "Treulich geführt"[4] (Ex. 10.4; the solo cello begins the tune in mm. 1143–44, and the solo violin picks it up in m. 1146 and carries it through its four notes in m. 1147. But those are the first four notes of Schön's row, into which the violin now continues.).

Susan Seidelman's film *Desperately Seeking Susan* (1985) embroiders this idea into a slick fable of contemporary pop culture, thereby highlighting its archetypical nature. Susan, a whorish drifter portrayed to perfection by the rock star Madonna, communicates through the personal columns of a tabloid paper with her boyfriend Jim, a pop musician. (That an actress named Madonna is so perfectly typecast in this role is a rich coincidence.) The ads are followed with wonder and longing by Roberta, the pretty, sweet, and quintessentially innocent wife of Gary, a mindless salesman of hot tubs. After four years of marriage in

EX. 10.4 I.3.1143–50

their modishly luxurious suburban house in Fort Lee, New Jersey, they have no erotic life together—Roberta sublimates through rich desserts and fantasy, Gary through the hot tub business and a mistress.

Susan and Jim arrange a rendezvous through their ads, and Roberta turns up to watch from a distance. The encounter is brief, as Jim is about to go on tour. Now sinister gangster elements are after Susan in connection with an earlier liaison; they place another ad with Jim's signature in an effort to trap her. She knows that Jim is out of town but Roberta does not, and it is Roberta who turns up for the fake rendezvous. Jim, seeing the ad while on tour, recognizes the trap and calls his friend Des, asking him to be on hand in order to protect Susan.

Roberta, Des, and a gangster all arrive at the same time. The gangster grabs Roberta, Des plows into the gangster with his motor scooter, Roberta is flung against a lamppost and knocked unconscious. She wakes up with amnesia, and with Des standing over her. The amnesia makes her even dumber and more puppetlike. Des takes her to his loft and takes care of her. They fall in love. She gets a job as a magician's assistant in a cheap nightclub, scooped into a minimal costume that she seems always about to overflow; in that role she is a parody of innocent allure. On her first night, the gangster is in the audience and after the show he follows her home through a dark alley (she is still in costume). He grabs her, they scuffle, a police car pulls up with lights flashing, he flees, and the cops pick her up, book her on charges of streetwalking, and fling her into a cell filled with real ladies of the night.

Through a well-designed coincidence, Gary, looking for Roberta, follows a lead that gets him Susan's telephone number. He calls, they meet, one thing leads to another, and Susan happily installs herself for a while in the Fort Lee house. Gary is confused—things have gone out of his control. He learns that Roberta is in jail and arranges for her release. But she chooses to stay with Des. The switch is complete.

It is not really a reversal. Rather, the two female characters, who are presented at the beginning as diametrically opposite types, are developed until each displays the attributes of both types. It is really only the bourgeois male character, Gary, who is thrown off balance by this. He, and the morality that he represents, are the real target of the film's social criticism.

In this brief description I have said virtually all that one *could* say about the main characters in the film. They will strike most viewers as pretty hollow, even two-dimensional, and that can well be a point of criticism. But in the tradition of theater that essentially began with Wedekind, characters are created hollow as a way of keeping them at arm's length from the audience. I spoke at the outset of puppets. In the *Lulu* prologue the Animal Trainer invites the audience "into the menagerie," to see the "soulless creatures" that inhabit it. We are not meant to suffer with such characters, to judge them, to wonder what they did before the drama began, or what will be their fates after it ends. We do not care whether Gary and Susan could live happily together in Fort Lee, and Roberta and Des will make a lasting life together in Manhattan. The story, so far as it concerns us, is complete within the boundaries of the play.

The prologue of *Lulu* establishes the separateness of actors and characters. It sets up in the viewer's mind a perception of the characters as stage creatures. In Berg's setting that is reinforced by the device of the double roles. The curtain that is the backdrop for the Prologue concretizes the separation of realms—the stage and the world of daily life. (To set the Prologue in a circus ring on the stage, as is sometimes done, obscures that essential separation.) Ultimately there is a connection to be made between the two, but that will be in the mind of the viewers, as they contemplate the meaning of what has been played out before them.

The stage is a showplace—part theater, part music hall, part cabaret, part circus—and the drama is a showpiece. Alwa objectifies the action from within, saying one could write an interesting piece about Lulu. For a moment he assumes the voice of the Animal Trainer, even taking up the imagery of the menagerie from the Prologue: as Lulu steps onto the music hall stage in Act 1, Scene 3, he says of the applause and shouts of the audience, "That racket is like the noise in the zoo, when the food is brought in front of the cages." In the opera the effect is still more vivid: The orchestra anticipates Alwa's thought about writing an opera by striking up the beginning of *Wozzeck* (Ex. 10.5).

Such games of hopscotch between the stage and the world outside are characteristic features of Expressionistic theater and cinema—one thinks of the plays of Pirandello, *The Cabinet of Dr. Caligari,* moments in Marx

EX. 10.5 I.3.1095–99.

Brothers films when Groucho turns his face straight to the camera and addresses the audience. That is precisely what Berg's device does. For a moment the music leaps across the proscenium to make a wisecrack to the audience. The citation of Wagner's Wedding March is another such device, but more subtle. Wagner's tune breaks off after the first four notes of the second phrase. But in fact those are the first four notes of Dr. Schön's row in one of its prime transpositions, and the violin simply wanders off into that and plays it out (with an assist from the A-flat of the vibraphone's bell) instead of finishing the *Lohengrin* tune (see Ex. 10.4). The message is clear enough: Lulu's marriage to the Prince is really Schön's project. It pleases him to have Lulu set up in respectable marriages, from which she can join him in occasional liaisons. Still another case is in the scene between Alwa and Lulu in Act 2, Scene 1 (Ex. 10.6). Alwa says "Mignon, ich liebe dich." At the word "liebe" the strings are exposed playing the Tristan chord in its original position. Lulu's reply is "Ich habe deine Mutter vergiftet" (I have poisoned your mother). That calls up the symbolism of the Tristan chord as love potion, for which we should now read "poison" in Berg's language of motives and references.

EX. 10.6   2.1.335–336.

But I meant to return to the moral judgment entailed in Boulez's use of the word "murder" in reference to the death of Dr. Schön. That judgment, even more than the one on Lulu's prostitution, violates the separation of realms that I have been talking about. It distorts the sense of the drama in a fundamental way, and on more than one level. There are three main points to be made.

First, consider it in terms of the criminal code in the world of our experience. A husband, a powerful man of the world, is in a jealous rage at his wife/mistress over the circle of associates and, presumably, lovers she keeps around the house. He presses a gun on her and tries to intimidate her into shooting herself. Protesting that he made her what she is and has every reason to expect such behavior from her, she shoots him instead. A good lawyer would plead self-defense.

It certainly is not premeditated murder. That the action in the second half of the drama has as its premise Lulu's identification as a murderess (she is imprisoned and escapes, the Marquis blackmails her with the threat of turning her over to the police, and so on) is not to be taken as the author's intention that we should see her as a murderess, but as an instance of the hyprocrisy and the double standards on which that world functions. (The Viennese writer Karl Kraus, in a talk introducing the first performance, in 1905, of *Pandora's Box,* the second of the Lulu plays, said, "One of the dramatic conflicts between female nature and some male blockhead placed Lulu in the hands of terrestrial justice, and she would have had nine years in prison during which to reflect that beauty is a punishment from God, had not her devoted slaves of love hatched a romantic plan for her liberation.")[5] This becomes the more apparent, the more we understand that Schön's hatred is based not only on his suspicions of Lulu's infidelity, but more deeply on his recognition that he has lost control of his life—something for which he projects blame onto Lulu. But, as she insists during their long exchange before his death, the choices were his; he could have known what he was getting himself into.

The point here is not to take issue with Boulez. His remark was not made as an assertion about Lulu's guilt; it takes Schön's death as the midpoint of the opera—something that is indisputable—and characterizes it as it is characterized inside the drama. However, the acceptance of it as murder *is* central to much of the prevailing criticism, and that brings me to my second point.

It is a commonplace in much of that criticism that Lulu's death at the hands of Jack the Ripper brings revenge for the deaths of her husbands. That interpretation has seemed especially to be confirmed by the fact that each of the actors in Berg's setting who plays the role of a husband—"victims," they are sometimes called—in the first half is cast as a client in the final scene.

The earliest source for the revenge theme is that introductory talk by Kraus on the occasion of the first performance of *Pandora's Box*. He spoke of the "revenge of the world of men," but then continued "who strove to revenge their own guilt."[6] In focusing on the first phrase, the subsequent criticism has reversed the meaning of the comment; now the clients of the second half—especially Jack the Ripper—are avenging their alter egos for their deaths at Lulu's hands. In the sketches to which I have referred, Berg wrote just "revenge of the world of men" in explaining the double roles of husbands and clients. He heard and was deeply impressed by Kraus's lecture, and his note may have been an abbreviation. Or he may have transformed Kraus's meaning in his own mind. His attitudes about these matters were complicated, as we have begun to see. However that may be, the omission and consequent change of meaning shed light on the attitudes that underlie the criticism, and on aspects of the meaning of the drama itself. I shall return to that as my third point.

The deaths of the men in the drama are brought off with the quick dispatch and matter-of-factness of a comic book or a penny dreadful: the *Medizinalrat* falling dead on the spot with a thud, Alwa felled with one whack of a blackjack, the melodrama of the painter's suicide with a razor at the throat; and—talk about melodrama—Schön's histrionics before he expires. The succession of these deaths is grisly, all right, but no one of them evokes compassion or mourning. It is the succession itself, the rhythm of it, that works its effect. One by one these figures become lifeless. That point is even stronger in Berg's setting, where each death is orchestrated in a precise way. The extreme case is the death of Schön, which Berg took as occasion for a bit of his obsessive numerology: five shots, fired at the climax of an aria with five strophes, which is determined by the number five in various other ways.[7] All the men have already been destroyed in and through their lives; their physical deaths are theatrical events with the emotional charge of the deflation of a dummy.

There is an ineluctability about events presented in such a clinically objective way. It is not the inevitability of actions whose motivations have been carefully provided by the author, as in *Crime and Punishment*.

It is rather more like the inevitability of events in a Greek tragedy—because the world *is* that way, and that is what the author means to show.

Lulu's death has the greatest sense of inevitability, coming, as it does, as the endpoint of a process that informs the whole drama. Lulu dreams her death, and she expects it. She speaks of a recurrent dream in which she falls into the hands of a sex maniac. Of the painter she says that if he had really understood her he would have tied a stone to her neck and thrown her into the sea. To Schön she says, "Strike me! where is your whip? Strike me across the legs!" One critic has called Lulu's movement toward her own death a "Totentanz."[8] Lulu's persona as dancer, whether in the foreground (Act 1, Scene 3) or in the background, has that sense about it.

Over and above the signs for this interpretation in the contents of words and actions, Berg lends an inevitability to Lulu's death as well as those of Schön and Alwa through the formal determinisms of the opera. The three deaths span a harmonic process at the highest level. Each of the opera's three acts ends with a four-note chord, and in the third-act ending the final chords of the first two acts, respectively, precede the very last chord, so that the final ending is a kind of summation (Ex. 10.7). The chords have three common tones, while the upper voice descends chromatically, C-sharp–C–B.

It is in effect a progression that settles into the final chord. Now in the context of these chords the tones C-sharp and C-natural are associated—through row derivations and associations—with Schön and Alwa, respectively.[9] B-natural is associated with Lulu.[10] At the end of Act 1 Schön has just finished writing the letter to his fiancée—dictated by Lulu—in which he breaks off his engagement to her. His will is broken, his future consigned to Lulu, and he sings "Now comes the execution." Act 2 ends with the great love scene between Lulu and Alwa, who sings, "You've robbed me of my reason," to which Lulu responds, "Is this the same sofa on which your father bled to death?" In both cases it is not the death of the male protagonist but his capitulation to lust for Lulu that is the climax of his plot-line. But then, capitulation *is* death in this drama.

The third act ends with the Countess Geschwitz's dying farewell to the dead Lulu—"Lulu, my angel . . ." Lulu's death is a kind of apotheo-

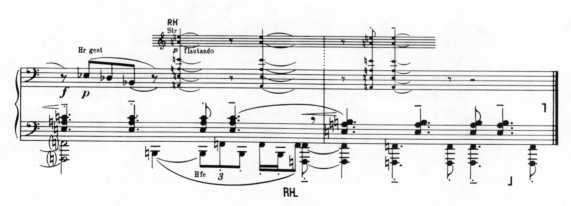

EX. 10.7   1.3.1360–1361
2.2.1149–1150
3.2.1324–26

sis. It is hard to escape the inference that the poet has presented it as her ultimate, and wished-for, liberation, given the way she has walked into it in the last scene, and in reality through the whole second half of the drama. To me that is a major point of inconsistency between the two halves, something to which I shall return very shortly.

In a way this sort of determinism is external to the dramatic structure; one could say that it is in the music alone. It certainly must be understood on one level as a manifestation of Berg's general proclivities for tight formalisms, particularly symmetrical ones. But at the same time this determinism conveys exactly the feeling of imposed necessity about events that Wedekind sought, too; but the music conveys it in a more palpable way. We cannot help feeling the heavy hand of fate in the progression of endings to the three acts. So in this sense Berg's formalisms are not external to the drama, with only their own musical interest. They are perfectly suited to a dramatic style, which we may identify as Expressionist, that depends on the acceptance of actions and events without the expectation that they be motivated from within. It is hard to square these reflections about the deaths of Lulu's husbands and about intentionality and causality in this drama with the concepts of "murder" and "revenge." Lulu is no Don Giovanni being sent to hell for her wanton promiscuity, as one critic has suggested in a comparison that is still further off the mark than the analogy with *The Rake's Progress*.[11]

When it comes to intentionality and morality as against determinism, the obvious comparison to be drawn is with *Wozzeck*. For there, too, the action is an ineluctable process, driven by inescapable human conditions and historical forces. And the sense that events follow a predetermined pattern is immensely enhanced by musical associations and formalisms. One could easily get the impression from these operas alone that Berg's well-known leaning to symmetrically closed forms and tight motivic networks is not a matter of musical inclination alone but a fatalism about life.

———————

The deaths in the opera—and now I mean all of them—are the ravages of socio- and psychosexual struggle. Their formal inevitability on the stage is an objective reflection of the inevitable struggle between Eros and society, and of the implication of death in that struggle. If there is authorial comment it is at that level, not at the level of moral judgment on individual acts. The characteristic paradox of this kind of drama is that we cannot take the characters on the stage seriously as real people. But we are meant to take very seriously the reality of what they have been put on the stage to show us.

Wedekind concretized the paradox. What the Animal Trainer promises to show in the Prologue is characterized not only as "soulless creatures" but also as "das wahre Tier," "the *true* beast, the wild and beautiful beast, not the house pets that inhabit ordinary comedies and tragedies." It belongs to the paradox that Wedekind, who declared himself an antinaturalist, claimed to show his characters in their true and natural state. The Animal Trainer says to Lulu, "You should speak naturally and not unnaturally, for the basic element of every art is that it be self-evident." Lulu says of herself that she is "a product of nature."

These "natural" creatures Wedekind placed in the grotesquely artificial circumstances he designed in order to allow them to act out their natures. They do so without any awareness of the seriousness of what they are in—something that only the audience can see. In a way Schön's long harangue to the Painter, which leads to the latter's suicide, has that as its message: you have been acting without an awareness of the realities of your situation. But that is essentially what Lulu tells Schön before shooting him, when she says, "You knew as well why you took me for your wife, as I knew why I took you for my husband. You fooled your best friends about me; you should have known better than to be fooled yourself."

But this "prodigy of nature," as Lulu calls herself, plays a counterpoint on the stage with a Lulu character that is a complex of roles projected onto it by the men in the drama, out of their own needs, fantasies, and fears about Woman. One of the plot-lines of the drama is Lulu's struggle to establish her own authenticity in the face of that burden. If one is looking for parallels, there is a close one in this respect with Petrouchka: the Pierrot character, through a painful exertion of will, coming into possession of its soul.

The consequences of this struggle are catastrophic and, in a way, tragic. But there is too much irony, too much of the grotesque and the sardonic, too much droll play with the very materials of the drama to identify it as tragedy. It belongs to the Expressionist style that Wedekind, more than anyone else, invented: what Jan Kott, following Eliot, has called "tragic farce."[12] Compared to Strindberg's plays about the ferociousness of sexual conflict (both Wedekind and Berg admired Strindberg very much) *Lulu* is a burlesque. Despite the similarities in the subject matters and their equal seriousness in the end, there is a very great stylistic distance, something like the distance from Edvard Munch to George Grosz. (The closer parallel is really between Munch and Grosz, on one side, and Strindberg and Brecht—by way of Wedekind— on the other.)

Berg entered into Wedekind's sardonic spirit and provided plenty of drollery of his own, playing in all the semiotic registers that he established for himself through the density of motivic and serial associations in which the work is enmeshed, and which could hook into virtually any music outside. The citations from *Lohengrin,* and especially from *Tristan,* are examples. Even without the *Tristan* chord, Lulu's line about the couch first makes one shudder, and then it is funny. But with it the irony is sharpened truly to the point of farce.

The perspective on the Lulu character as a compound of male projections provides one key to the inconsistencies in the character that have been the subject of some discussion. Absolute consistency is not to be expected when Lulu is construed to meet the different needs of her husbands at the same time as she poses the threats that constitute the grounds of their different fears. This will prove to be a central matter for the interpretation of *Lulu,* one that will therefore have to be pursued more fully. But first I want to develop a different sort of interpretation of the inconsistency, at which I have already hinted. It is that it reflects an inconsistency in the style of the two Lulu plays. The characterizations that I have given thus far really pertain more to the first of them, *Earth Spirit,* than to the second, *Pandora's Box. Earth Spirit* is an unflawed masterpiece of Expressionist theater. Its effect is diluted by *Pandora's Box,* which returns part of the way to the manner of the naturalists. One feels this especially in the heavily sentimental treatment of Alwa and of Geschwitz, whom Wedekind identified as the real heroine of the second play. As early as 1920, the critic Paul Fechter called attention to this contrast:

Compared to *Earth Spirit,* the second part of the tragedy is a step backward. It lacks the tight concentration, the sharpness of dialogue . . . *Earth Spirit* is unsentimental, pathos-free to the point of blasphemy . . . It is pure objectivity. An unmoved onlooker, in consciousness of his indifference . . . only points . . . , he does not speak. In *Pandora's Box* his need to become visible shows. The mere setting down of how things are no longer suffices. The poet begins to speak, along with the others.[13]

Early journalistic reviews of the plays are interesting in this regard, for the critics almost unanimously preferred productions of the two parts separately.

The contrast survives, and I would say is magnified, in Berg's setting. The sentimentality in his treatment of Alwa and Geschwitz in the second and third acts borders on the maudlin. But most striking of all in this regard is the musical treatment of Lulu's death. It is of a savagery that overreaches all preparation for it in the opera, and all expectation that one would have from a reading of the second play. The impact is all the greater in a live performance, particularly if one sits close enough to the orchestra to see the ferociousness with which the percussion players must attack their instruments. The violence of the act, as an act done *by* Jack *to* Lulu, focuses attention on his rage and her agony. Wedekind, having brought the play to the point where Lulu's death is required, found a brilliant solution to the problem of how to accomplish it— bring in a famous principal in the sexual warfare of which Lulu is finally a casualty. Everyone knows enough about him to sense the appropriateness of his choice as executioner. There is no curiosity about the mind that has become so twisted as to perform such acts, or about the personal history that resulted in that condition. Wedekind locates the deed offstage. He *reports* it, as Alwa reports that a revolution has broken out in Paris, or as the value of *Jungfrau* stocks is reported in Act 3, Scene 1. With a well-known historical figure as its instrument, Lulu's death is given the aspect of another event in the world on the other side of the proscenium.

But in the musical moment of Lulu's murder, the feelings that Wedekind held off with that device are poured onto the stage in abundance. The musical setting demands a direct participation in the horror that is at most implied in the play. And in the aftermath of the horror, the pathos of Geschwitz's final *cantilena* ("Lulu, my angel") seems as much an authorial commentary on the tragedy of Lulu's death—a signal to feel that tragedy—as a final statement of Geschwitz's undying devotion.

And the confusion is only compounded by Berg's transformation of Jack into a reincarnation of Schön, for it loads that neutral, almost mechanical agent of Lulu's death with all the feelings we have about the despicable and tortured Schön. Lulu's death is in the air throughout the opera as both fated and self-willed. Jack is only the instrument of its execution. To be sure, he is a monster, but his monstrousness has not been provoked by the Lulu character. By making him a Schön persona Berg implicates him in all of her history. Lulu's death becomes a crime of passion, and we are asked to respond to it as *the* tragedy of the drama—as though Berg had determined to repeat in it the death of Marie in *Wozzeck.*

The musical setting of Marie's murder is of an equal savagery, and it is similarly followed by a musical declaration about its pathos (the D-minor interlude, which Berg himself identified as an authorial comment). Marie's death, too, is presented as an ineluctable outcome. But the necessity of it develops before us, in the mind of the male protagonist. The motivation is part jealous rage over Marie's infidelity, part paranoid construction in which Marie comes to stand for all the sinfulness—particularly the sexual debauchery—of the world (see Chapter 9). In identifying Jack the Ripper with Schön, Berg shaped the outcome of *Lulu* in a way very like that of *Wozzeck:* The female protagonist is brutally murdered by a man whose homicidal urge toward her arises at one level out of his very specific sexual rage at her, and at another out of his hatred for some generalized idea of Woman which she symbolizes in his mind. I cannot help associating this striking parallel with Berg's remark "Bordel ist Ehe" and with the extreme brutality in his musical depiction of both murders. What is suggested about Berg's attitudes toward and relationships with women will have to be considered in connection with other aspects of his biography. But those attitudes were certainly active in his work on *Lulu,* vying with his dramatic judgment.[14]

How could it be otherwise for anyone—poet, composer, or critic—working on this subject? In particular, how could critics—especially male critics—fail to be influenced in their interpretations by masculine images of Woman and the relationships between the sexes in view of those images, since these are central themes of the *Lulu* drama? My third point about the judgment on Lulu as a murderess is that it reflects such attitudes as they are held both within and outside of the drama.

In the Prologue, the Animal Trainer lures the members of the audience into the menagerie in order to reflect back to them a true image of themselves. Alwa, hearing the shouts and applause of the audience backstage in Act 1, Scene 3, tells the "real" audience "It sounds like the menagerie at feeding time." Douglas Jarman catches the sense of it well: "the listener in the opera house is forced to realize that he is as much a part of that menagerie as the characters he has come to watch . . . he is forced to recognize the hypocrisy and the capacity for self-deception of both the characters on the stage and himself."[15] Wedekind and Berg address their audience with the ironic attitude of Baudelaire, beckoning his readers into *Les fleurs du mal* (1857). The resonance is sufficient to think of that work as a source:

> If rape and arson, poison and the knife
> have not yet stitched their ludicrous designs
> onto the banal buckram of our fates,
> it is because our souls lack enterprise!
>
> But here among the scorpions and the hounds,
> the jackals, apes and vultures, snakes and wolves,
> monsters that howl and growl and squeal and crawl,
> in all the squalid menagerie of vices, one
> is even uglier and fouler than the rest,
> although the least flamboyant of the lot;
> this beast would gladly undermine the earth
> and swallow all creation in a yawn;
>
> I speak of boredom which with ready tears
> dreams of hangings as it puffs its pipe.
> Reader, you know this squeamish monster well,
> —hypocrite reader,—my alias—my twin![16]

How truly the spectator is reflected in the drama can be read out of the critical literature. Patrice Chéreau, the director of the 1979 Paris production of *Lulu,* goes right to the nub in his commentary provided with the recording. To judge from the criticism with which the work is surrounded, he writes, it would seem that

Berg and Wedekind had well and truly held up to the audience an exact, unflattering mirror. Like Schön they would like Lulu to be an incarnation of Evil ["You beast, dragging me through the mud to an agonized death! . . .

You dark angel! . . . You hangman's noose! You inescapable tormentor! . . . Monster! . . . Murderess! . . . Do you see your bed, with its slaughter victims?"] Like Schön, they see in her only a devourer of men and would, in the last analysis, prefer her to take on the seductive, perverse guise of a star from some imaginary pantheon of the cinema in order to carry out her work of destruction.[17]

Chéreau is right in his choice of the expressions "would like," and "prefer," because the characterizations of the "daemonic" Lulu that commentators have in effect accepted from Schön show not what Lulu *is* but one side of what she, as quintessential Woman, is *held to be* by men on both sides of the curtain. (The Animal Trainer virtually anticipates Schön's words: "She was created to make trouble, to tempt, to seduce, to poison, and to murder.")

Wedekind put on the stage an ambivalent vision of Woman that is probably as old as humankind and that seems endemic in all societies. Schön's daemonic Lulu is one side of that vision. The other is represented by Alwa's famous line in Act 2, Scene 1: "A Soul that will rub the sleep from its eyes in the next world": the passive, innocent, submissive love object, childlike, alluring, and seductive . . . and terrifying; the woman dreamed of, and dreaded. A billboard description of the female protagonist in a 1962 film by Joseph Losey suggests she might be the imagined film goddess in Chéreau's comment: "Mysterious, tantalizing, alluring, wanton, but deep within her burning the violent fires that destroy a man."[18] The character (and the film) are called Eve—the first woman, but hardly in her original innocence. Eve is one of the Painter's names for Lulu. That has to be read as ironic sign for his complex perception of her.

Tilly Wedekind, the playwright's wife, was the first stage Lulu. In her memoir about the role, she reports her husband's impression about the critical commentaries, and it is strikingly similar to Chéreau's: "He apparently wanted Lulu played like a Madonna. But the critics who wrote about the production were of a different opinion, and to this day [1969] many of them cling to the conception that Lulu must be portrayed as a wild animal who has already devoured a couple of men for breakfast. 'It is no longer possible to take the play seriously if the part is played like that,' Wedekind used to say. And men get out of the way of that sort of woman."[19]

The association of Lulu and Madonna can seem ironic, like the name Madonna for an aggressively sexy pop singer. But it is more profound than that. Edvard Munch made one oil painting and two lithographs entitled "Madonna" that make plausible a figure that can be voluptuous in its purity and innocence (Figs. 10.3–10.5). The face in the third of the Madonna images (Fig. 10.5) is virtually repeated in another lithograph, which Munch entitled "Salome" (Fig. 10.6; the face of John the Baptist is a self-portrait; the two women's faces have the same model, the artist's mistress Eva Mudocci).

Mystery—the first attribute in the characterization of the Eve in the Losey film—is of the essence in this conception of Woman. Lulu is a shadowy character. There is vagueness about her age, her parentage, her name. Schön and Alwa call her Mignon, and they have presumably called her that since Schön picked her up, a child of twelve, in front of the Alhambra Cafe. I imagine the name derives from the character Mignon, the twelve-year-old dancer in Goethe's *Wilhelm Meister*. Thomas Carlyle described her in the preface of his English translation of 1826 in a way that might almost have inspired the title of Wedekind's first Lulu play: "The daughter of enthusiasm, rapture, passion and despair, she is of the earth, but not earthly . . . When she glides before us through the light images of her dances we could almost fancy her an ethereal spirit."[20] Goethe's Mignon dances herself to death; so does Lulu, in a way.

The names Lulu and Eve must be understood in terms of one another. Schigolch says he has always called her Lulu, and he is the person who has known her longest (there are even intimations from Schön that Schigolch is her father). "Lulu" is a thinly veiled transformation of "Lilith," the mythological demon-woman of that name whom we encounter first in an apocalpytic poem in the Book of Isaiah, which describes the end of the kingdom of Edom and the return of the earth to the chaos of the beginning. Probably Wedekind's direct source was Goethe's *Faust,* where Lilith is mentioned in the *Walpurgisnacht* of Part 1. Mephistopheles points her out to Faust.

> Lilith, the first wife of Adam
> Beware of her fair hair, for she excels
> All women in the magic of her locks
> And when she winds them around a young man's neck
> She will not ever set him free again.

FIG. 10.3 Edvard Munch. *Madonna* (oil)

FIG. 10.4　Edvard Munch. *Madonna* (lithograph)

FIG. 10.5 Edvard Munch. *Madonna* (lithograph)

FIG. 10.6 Edvard Munch. *Salome*

That she is the first wife of Adam derives from Jewish biblical commentaries, where she is also identified as the incarnation of the dark side of Eve. I believe that is how we must understand the relationship between the names Eve and Lulu. There is an important difference in their origins, according to these sources: Lilith was made of the same dust as Adam and considered herself his equal. She fled from the Garden of Eden when Adam ordered her to lie beneath him. He begged God for another partner and God gave him Eve, made this time from Adam's rib. In Christian commentaries Lilith is the daughter of Satan, and is identified with the serpent in the Garden of Eden. As a snake with a woman's head she is a common nineteenth-century image—hence Lulu's presentation as a serpent in the Prologue.[21]

Lilith's identification as Satan's daughter inevitably calls up the hints that Schigolch is Lulu's father. He, too, is a shadowy figure who, like Lulu, seems to have no beginning to his life history, and he is the only one of the main characters whose life has no end within the drama; he slips out for a drink just before the final slaughter. There is something primeval about him, which Berg magnified. Among the animals mentioned by the Animal Trainer in the Prologue is the *Molch* (lizard). Berg picked up on the sound association between *Molch* and Schigolch, and he accompanied the Animal Trainer as he speaks of reptiles and lizards with music that becomes associated with Schigolch—slithery, chromatic music (Ex. 10.8). The way he drags his feet, the way he acts the man of the world who has seen better days, his cynicism, his agelessness, his ugliness, all suggest a Mephistopheles figure. In *Wilhelm Meister,* the first master of Mignon is a showman known as "The Great Devil." Recognizing this aspect of Schigolch, we can appreciate a wonderfully ironic touch in Act 3, Scene 2. Lulu is desperate to get the Athlete off her back, and she promises Schigolch her favors (not for the first time, we gather) if he will throw the pest out the window. He agrees, she insists he swear; he says "by all that's holy," and Berg has him punctuate with an asthmatic gasp.

––––––––––

It is in the first scene that the Painter, enraptured by Lulu, calls her Eve. The exchange goes like this:

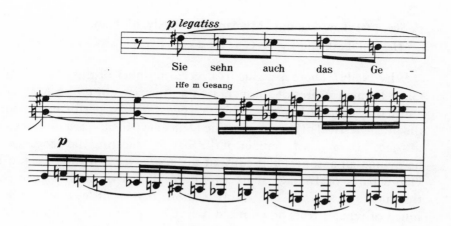

EX. 10.8 Prologue, 33–36

He: "No pity . . ." (sits down by Lulu's side and covers her hands with kisses) "How do you feel?"

She: (with closed eyes) "My husband will be coming soon . . ."

He: "I love you!"

She: (still with closed eyes) "Once I loved a student with 175 dueling scars . . ."

He: (calling her) "Nelly . . ."

She: (as if awakening) "My name isn't Nelly, it's Lulu."

He: "I'll call you Eve.—Give me a kiss, Eve!"

Why Nelly? There is a clue in a recent number of the *Musical Times*. Clive Bennett writes of an opera by the Austrian composer Max Brand entitled *Maschinist Hopkins,* which received its first performance during the music festival of the Allgemeine Deutsche Musikverein in Duisburg, in 1929.[22] Berg was a member of the jury for selecting the program, and he owned an autographed copy of the score. It is Bennett's claim that "large parts of Brand's score prefigure almost uncannily events and treatments in *Lulu*." The claim is more than a little misleading, for much of what it rests on comes down to similarities of plot and character between Brand's opera and Wedekind's Lulu plays, which, after, all, Berg took over. It is the possibility of reading Brand as a gloss of Wedekind that interests me at this point, although this is a perspective that Bennett did not take. He writes "The plot of *Lulu* [is] strikingly similar to that of *Maschinist Hopkins.* In both, the heroine moves from being a working-class girl of few morals to a rich industrialist's lover and at her apogee a nightclub singer. In both she is blackmailed by someone with designs on her and also a grudge towards her, and resorts to prostitution, only to be murdered by the man she loved but betrayed." Putting aside all questions about the aptness of that description of *Lulu,* it is yet of interest that Brand's heroine is named Nelly. It also happens that Hopkins is the name Wedekind gave in the first edition of the Lulu plays (1895) to the character he later renamed Dr. Hunidei, and who survives in the opera as the Professor (whom Berg associated in a double role with the *Medizinalrat*). So it is easy enough to think of the Lulu plays as a source for Brand; they were certainly notorious enough before Berg adapted them. But whether we can read Brand's Nelly back into Wedekind's brief use of that name is another question. I think we can, if only obliquely. Nelly was a name often taken by showgirls and prostitutes. That the painter calls Lulu Nelly first, and then Eve, focuses exactly on the ambivalence that I have been talking about. Then we should carry our understanding of that ambivalence into the second scene, where the Painter has set Lulu up in a sort of *Doll's House* scenario, and set himself up for disillusionment and suicide.

The universal female pantheon is everywhere bipolar, showing protective and nourishing figures on one side, and threatening and destroying ones on the other. Individual figures may combine these antithetical properties. Mary is the unambiguous opposite of the demon goddesses through virtually the whole tradition of Marian images, but in Munch's representations, as we saw, she shows that seductive quality that is the beginning of what is threatening about those godesses. Eve, whom Mary resembles, embodies an antithesis of the spiritual and the carnal. And Eve herself has her double, who is Lilith. These images represent ambivalent masculine conceptions about Woman: as lover and whore, as nourisher and devourer, as seductress and destroyer.

The type of figure that embodies these opposite attributes was widely known in the Romantic era as the femme fatale, but it is recognizable in the art, literature, and mythology of virtually all times and places.[23] The Salome we saw in Munch's lithograph exemplifies the continuing preoccupation with the type. Next to it in Munch's gallery of female images belongs his *Vampire* (Fig. 10.7). The interpretation of the vampire legend in the sense of the seductive woman sapping the male of his life's blood was prominent enough to have generated the word "vamp." The Eurydice of the Orpheus legend is a character of this type—especially in Cocteau's *Orphée*. The Lorelei and Rusalka of German and Russian mythology, respectively, are such figures, as is the Queen of the Night—especially in Ingmar Bergman's *Magic Flute*; Lola Lola, of *The Blue Angel*; Medea. That is the sisterhood to which Lulu belongs.[24]

There can be something misleading about the recognition that a character, in this instance Lulu, belongs to a certain archetype—the femme fatale—that is represented over a broad range of literature and mythology. It tends to imply an explanation. By showing that the author has created a character that follows a certain tradition it can seem to ascribe to tradition the author's particular way of displaying psychological states that arise from the intersection of the universal human condition and the social and economic conditions of the culture that he reflects and comments upon in his work. The robustness of the archetype in mythology and literature is a reflection of the constancy and urgency of the conditions that generate it. To be sure, in a culture with an active and self-conscious literary tradition, such as the European culture of Romanticism, genres and types are perpetuated for their own sake, and that was surely the case with the type of the femme fatale. But that is not a purely literary phenomenon; it reflects a preoccupation with the psychological conditions, and the particular role of the femme fatale in

FIG. 10.7 Edvard Munch. *Vampire* (oil)

the social ecology of the literature in which she is situated demands understanding in terms of the social dynamics of the time.

As a clue to the nature of those conditions it is worth thinking about the fact that we do not identify a corresponding type of the *homme fatal* in literature, and wonder why that is the case. A possible contender is the Don Juan figure.[25] But the virile, aggressive, and restless seducer is hardly the counterpart of the alluring, passive beauty for whose possession men are led to their destruction. Accordingly it is the femme fatale who is despised as the "Death Angel" (Schön's epithet for Lulu). If women are ruined by a Don Juan, they usually suffer sexual use and abandonment. But the ruination of men by the femme fatale means their death (why, after all, is she called that?); men are not thought to be ruined by being sexually used and abandoned. The fatal woman is not satisfied to love them and leave them. She craves the destruction of men, like the female spider or praying mantis. Not so the Don Juan. The killer of women—Jack the Ripper, the Boston Strangler—is a different type altogether. He acts, ultimately, in rage against an idea of Woman that may be represented by the femme fatale. He has no female counterpart in literature or myth, or for that matter in life. These differences are symptoms of the alignment of sexual roles and identities, not only in the Romantic European culture that identified and was obsessed with the femme fatale, but in all cultures whose iconologies feature such an ambivalent image of Woman. That image must constitute a background for reading *Lulu*.

The femme fatale has only to *be*, she does not have to *act*, in order to activate men's fear of women in a male-dominated society. What is at risk is the loss of control in the one domain in which male control is most vulnerable. The metaphor of wife or lover as whore is not, then, just a display of cynicism or ambivalence, but an amelioration, for it is a way of regaining control; but it has its threatening side as well. Loss of control in that one domain can mean loss of control in the world altogether, and even loss of life. In the type of drama of which *Lulu* is an instance, that threat reveals the masochist in Man, and the corresponding androgynous aspect of Woman. In *Lulu* the male protagonists invest in Lulu the attribute of unrestrained sexuality—an attribute they cannot allow for themselves because of its inconsistency with the conduct of a responsible life in the masculine world of power. Having done that, they then try to invent a tamed persona for her. But Lulu senses the duplicity in this as an animal senses a trap, and she refuses to cooperate. The failure of the illusion results in their destruction. It shows how irrelevant the "revenge" motif is, and how much more to the point it is to see Lulu as a scapegoat. Wedekind showed great depth of insight in producing, as the final match for Lulu, a figure whose madness put him beyond vulnerability.

In *Lulu* the tragedy inherent in these configurations is forced to the surface by Lulu's own resistance to all such role manipulations. The issue is focused in the pitched battle between Lulu and Schön—between the snake and the tiger—in Act 2, Scene 1, a battle so ferocious that it makes the political revolution in Paris that Alwa reports seem trivial. Lulu's death at the hands of Jack is another battle in the same war. She plays with death in her effort to break free. The stakes are that high, higher than those in the various money transactions that are always in the background of the drama. Jack is himself a casualty of the same war. If we associate him with Schön, it should be not as avenger but as mindless parody.

Jungian psychology interprets the femme fatale figure as the projection of an inner image, the anima, which is the female personification of the masculine unconscious. This image is always a product of the childhood relationship with the mother; the femme fatale reflects the case where that relationship is a threatening and fearful one, and the widespread appearance of that image in literature is a measure of the prevalence of that condition in the culture.[26] Before Jung described it, Strindberg exemplified it, in his play *The Father.* The Captain, who is the play's male protagonist, first enters into the relationship with the woman he is to marry almost as child to mother. As she becomes his lover and wife the relationship becomes increasingly threatening to him because of its implicitly incestuous character, and he reacts defensively with growing hostility toward her.

The most palpable sign for the Lulu character as a creation of male desires is the Pierrot portrait. Berg made quite a point of showing the Pierrot persona as a source for the character. His directions (not Wedekind's) have Lulu appear in the Prologue in her Pierrot costume; and in that arcane semiotic register in which he seems to address musical analysts, or perhaps himself, he derives Lulu's characteristic tone row from the series of chords that he associates initially with the portrait. Like the Eve-Lilith symbolism, the Pierrot portrait connects to a shatteringly ambivalent attitude about Woman. But it is at the same time a symbolism that allows the poet and composer to show the Lulu character struggling against that attitude to gain her own authenticity, a struggle that reflects the struggle of sex roles from another side.

In the last scene of the opera Geschwitz brings in the portrait, which she has salvaged. Lulu screams, "My portrait! Out of my sight! Throw it out the window!" Alwa interrupts, "But why not? In the face of this portrait I can regain my self-respect. It makes my fate understandable.

EX. 10.9 3.2.1270–75.

Whoever can feel secure in his bourgeois position in the face of these blossoming, swelling lips, these great, innocent child's eyes, this rosy-white exuberant body—let him cast the first stone."

But by this time Lulu wants no more of that sort of responsibility. She wants love without entanglements. Berg makes that audibly clear in his setting of the encounter with Jack. As Jack is admiring her, the orchestra intones the music that had been associated with Schön's entrapment in the relationship with Lulu. But as she puts her arms about him and says, "I like you so; don't let me beg any longer," that music gives way to the music that has become familiar as the sign of her identity, and that has been associated with her aspiration to freedom (Ex. 10.9). One of the dimensions of this drama is the story of Lulu's fatal progression from character to person (think, again, of Petrouchka). But that is the symbolism of Pierrot.[27]

In the portrait, as in the music hall scene, Lulu is presented as the essential actress, the role player, the person on display, passively at the disposition of the paying onlooker. In her Pierrot costume she conveys the ironic conceit that had become so enormously important in the art and literature of the turn of the century—that essential and ultimate truth is to be found in the illusions of such otherworldly and artificial settings as the popular theater, circus, or cabaret. That is in effect what Alwa says in his reaction to the portrait in the final scene of the opera.

But there is often a darker penumbra about such images, an elusive edge of the melancholy and even the macabre, that gives them a threatening quality on which Wedekind and Berg played. They represent illusion and play, but at the same time disillusion, dejection. They are soulfull, but soulless. The double aspect of their appealing character and otherworldliness can be deadly, for they cannot safely mix with ordinary creatures of the daily world. This double aspect reflects the androgynous character of the images. They unite the passive beauty that draws the spectator to their subject (think again of Alwa's lyric about the portrait near the end) with the active and threatening persona (think of Lulu/Pierrot in the beginning, provoking the Painter, evading him, ensnaring him, and leading him straight to his self-destruction). This bipolar creature of the masculine imagination is a different, highly specialized expression of what is embodied in the femme fatale.

It is on this point that a rather more meaningful parallel with *The Rake's Progress* emerges. The attributes of the bipolar, androgynous Pierrot figure are invested separately in the characters of Anne Truelove and Baba the Turk. Baba is a parody, of course, and her appeal for Tom Rakewell lies precisely in her lack of appeal. But his coupling with her is the fullest expression of his ruination. The sharpness of the separation and the palpably symbolic nature of the two figures are of the essence in this opera; Boulez is right that it is a morality play. The female characters are matched in that respect by the two main male characters, Rakewell and his (Nick) Shadow, whose identity as the trickster in the Jungian picture of the unconscious is hardly disguised.

Tilly Wedekind remarked about the Lulu portrait: "It is painted during the first act of *Earth Spirit* and, as a result, the painter becomes infatuated with his model. In the following act and in the last act, the picture is on stage, and each time a man is ruined by his passion for Lulu."[28] In this brief remark Tilly Wedekind displayed her deep understanding of the sinister symbolism of the Pierrot portrait: not only as sign of seduction and doom for each of those men, but as reminder that it is not Lulu but their own desire that brings them down.

―――――――

I shall exit through the gallery of Munch, with wordless reflection on two other lithographs: his interpretation of Carmen, the one figure we have neglected so far (Fig. 10.8), and one entitled simply "Hands" (Fig. 10.9).

FIG. 10.8 Edvard Munch. *The Alley (Carmen)*

FIG. 10.9   Edvard Munch. *Hands*

Notes

Introduction

1. Hans Georg Gadamer, *Philosophical Hermeneutics,* ed. and trans. David G. Linge (Berkeley, Calif., 1977).
2. "On Relevance and Responsibility in the Humanities," *Daedalus,* 98 (1969), 844–52.
3. Fred Evans, "Children of Light: The Volunteer's Narrative in Laos," unpublished paper presented to the Conference of Culture and Communication, Philadelphia, 1987. I am grateful to the author for providing me with a copy.
4. See Leo Treitler, "Reading and Singing: On the Genesis of Occidental Music-Writing," *Early Music History,* 4 (1984), 160–61.
5. Title of Polanyi's major work of epistemology (Chicago, 1958).
6. *Saint Augustine: Confessions,* trans. R. S. Pine-Coffin (Harmondsworth, England, 1961), book 10, chap. 33, pp. 238–39.
7. *Phaedrus,* 245B.
8. *Republic,* 514.
9. *Timaeus,* 50D.
10. See Genevieve Lloyd, *The Man of Reason: "Male" and "Female" in Western Philosophy* (Minneapolis, 1984), pp. 22–28.
11. This phrase is borrowed from Chapter 2.
12. See Robert Jay Lifton and Richard Falk, *Indefensible Weapons: The Political and Psychological Case against Nuclearism* (New York, 1982).
13. Robert S. McNamara, "The Military Role of Nuclear Weapons: Perceptions and Misperceptions," *Foreign Affairs,* 62 (1983), 59–80.
14. Robert Jay Lifton, *The Future of Immortality* (New York, 1987), p. 25.
15. My remarks are based on Susan Bordo, "The Cartesian Masculinization of Thought," in Sandra Harding and Jean F. O'Barr, eds., *Sex and Scientific Inquiry* (Chicago, 1975).

16. Owen Barfield, *Saving the Appearances: A Study in Idolatry* (New York, 1965), p. 78. The brackets indicate the removal of the generic masculine. That Barfield uses the form so consistently has a certain irony, for the very world that he describes was not polarized by gender nearly to the degree and with the consistency of the post-Cartesian world, from what we can gather about the education of women, their role in the arts, their rights of inheritance, and so on. The fact is surely related directly to the character of the culture as Barfield has portrayed it.

17. Bordo, p. 259.

18. See Evelyn Fox Keller, *Reflections on Gender and Science* (New Haven, Conn., 1985), chap. 2; and Lloyd, pp. 10–17.

19. Nino Pirrotta, *Music and Culture in Italy from the Middle Ages to the Baroque* (Cambridge, Mass., 1984), p. 26.

1. History, Criticism, and Beethoven's Ninth Symphony

The original publication of this essay was dedicated to the memory of the composer Seymour Shifrin, whose sympathetic understanding and support through the ten years of our friendship helped me immensely in the work on this subject as well as others.

1. This sort of stagelike space is a new dimension for concert music. Romantic composers, for example Mahler, made much of it, as in the first movement of the Third Symphony, in which the music takes up a position in center stage and makes a real beginning only after the movement has been under way for three hundred measures (rehearsal no. 26).

2. Thus Nietzsche: "The thinker feels himself floating above the earth in an astral dome, with the dream of immortality in his heart: all the stars seem to glimmer about him, and the earth seems to sink ever further downward" (*Menschliches Allzumenschliches,* 1878).

3. Carl Dahlhaus, *Die Idee der absoluten Musik* (Kassel, 1978).

4. Donald Francis Tovey, *Essays in Musical Analysis* (London, 1935). The large essay on the Ninth Symphony is in vol. 2, pp. 1–44.

5. See Charles Rosen, *The Classical Style* (London, 1971), p. 440.

6. The theme of the *Choral Fantasy* is of a similar form and character. It is presented in similar fashion, with quite the same rousing effect. Neither of these sets of variations, on the other hand, has very much in common with the Diabelli Variations; they show rather more of a Handelian conception. In any case it would seem that such assessments of the designs that a work or a passage makes upon the listener would be required if one wishes to have an understanding of its place in the history of the genre.

7. The most authoritative is E. H. Gombrich, *Art and Illusion,* 2nd ed. (Prince-

ton, N.J., 1962). For the history of literature such a theory has been pro-pounded by the Russian Formalist school. There is discussion of that theory in Carl Dahlhaus, *Grundlagen der Musikgeschichte* (Cologne, 1977), pp. 202–204 (see Chapter 6).

8. Heinrich Schenker, *Beethoven, Neunte Sinfonie: Eine Darstellung des musi-kalischen Inhaltes unter fortlaufender Berücksichtigung auch des Vortrags und der Literatur* (reprinted Vienna, 1969).

9. "Beethoven's Dritte Sinfonie zum erstenmal in ihrem wahren Inhalt dar-gestellt," in *Das Meisterwerk in der Musik: Ein Jahrbuch von Heinrich Schenker* (Munich, 1930), III, 25–101.

10. Schenker's claims about the listener are of no consequence one way or the other for his theories. But nowadays claims about "how one hears" are made in earnest as fulfillments of the aims of music theory, and that raises questions about what theory can and cannot accomplish. It *can* "describe the ways in which, given a certain body of literature, composers and lis-teners appear to have accepted sound as conceptually structured, cate-gorically *prior to any one specific piece*" (David Lewin, "Behind the Beyond: Response to Edward T. Cone," *Perspectives of New Music,* 7 [1969], 61). It *cannot* provide a sufficient account of the fact that "an educated listener . . . is able . . . to comprehend *a piece* within an idiom" (Fred Lerdahl and Ray Jackendoff, "Toward a Formal Theory of Tonal Music," *Journal of Music Theory,* 21 [1977], 11–171; italics mine). This claim is as naive as it is ex-travagant. The model is of course Noam Chomsky's statement of the goals of a theory of language, but in that domain no one seriously claims that an account of our ability to understand any well-formed sentence in a lan-guage will also account for our ability to understand some of those sen-tences as poems. Lerdahl and Jackendoff consistently treat "sentence" and "piece" as analogues. But surely the only possible analogues would be "sentence"/"*Satz*" and "poem"/"piece." A more realistic statement of goals is given by Björn Lindblom and Johan Sundberg, "Toward a Genera-tive Theory of Melody," *Swedish Journal of Musicology,* 52 (1970), 71–88.

11. See Stephen C. Pepper, *World Hypotheses: A Study in Evidence* (Berkeley and Los Angeles, 1961), chap. 11, "Organicism." Studies of the concept of organic form in literature and the history of ideas are collected in G. S. Rousseau, ed., *Organic Form: The Life of an Idea* (London, 1972). Lewis Lockwood has recognized the importance that this idea assumed in ana-lytical procedures during the nineteenth century; see "'Eroica' Perspec-tives: Strategy and Design in the First Movement," in *Beethoven Studies,* vol. 3, ed. Alan Tyson (Cambridge, Mass., 1982).

12. Kretzschmar called his mode of interpretation "musical hermeneutics" (see Dahlhaus, *Die Idee der absoluten Musik*).

13. H. H. Eggebrecht, *Zur Geschichte der Beethoven-Rezeption* (Mainz, 1972).

14. Eggebrecht, *Beethoven-Rezeption,* p. 8, gives citations for this and other characteristic remarks of Busoni.

15. Wilhelm Windelband, "Geschichte und Naturwissenschaft" (1894), in *Präludien, Aufsätze, und Reden zur Philosophie und ihrer Geschichte* (Tübingen, 1915), II, 136–60.

16. To put this in language cited in Note 10, an analysis is a demonstration that, and how, a particular piece is an instance of a sound system whose conceptual structuring is described in a theory (it would correspond more or less to an explanation in science). Now Lewin does not say this. What he does say about analysis tends in the direction of what I say about criticism. That leaves him with not very much to say about criticism, except that it describes such responses as "I like this," or "this engages me." I do not aim to provoke an a priori terminological dispute here. But it is my impression that Schenker's shortfall in dealing with the individual qualities of the Ninth Symphony remains characteristic of much writing and teaching in what is called analysis. What is important is not to brush it under the carpet as "bad analysis," but to recognize that it is perfectly consistent with the aims of analysis in relation to a theory. That is why we need such a practice as what I call criticism. In calling it criticism I simply use the term that students of literature and history have had for it for a long time.

17. Jonathan Culler, *Structuralist Poetics* (Ithaca, N.Y., 1975), pp. 74, 31. A similar conclusion about the limited usefulness of linguistics for the analysis of meaning is a consequence of the views of John Searle, set forth in his book *Speech Acts* (Cambridge, 1969). I have discussed those views and their relevance to music criticism and analysis in my contribution to the round table discussion "Current Methods of Stylistic Analysis," *International Musicological Society, Report of the 11th Congress, Copenhagen 1972* (Copenhagen, 1973), pp. 61–70.

18. See Allan Keiler, "Bernstein's *The Unanswered Question* and the Problem of Musical Competence," *Musical Quarterly,* 64 (1978), 195–222.

19. Culler, *Structuralist Poetics,* p. 8.

20. Treitler, "Current Methods of Stylistic Analysis."

21. Ibid.

22. Claudio Guillén, *Literature as System* (Princeton, 1971), 390.

23. Culler, p. 137.

24. T. S. Eliot, *Poetry and Drama* (Cambridge, Mass., 1951).

25. Culler, p. 116.

26. The phrase is that of the great German historian and historiographer Leopold von Ranke (1795–1886). See the preface to his *Geschichten der romanischen und germanischen Völker* (Berlin, 1824). The misunderstanding arises when this remark is interpreted as indicative of a belief in the priority and possibility of objective, verifiable knowledge of the past. (I am

among those guilty of this misreading; see Chapter 3.) But Ranke's notion of "reality" in history reflected a different sort of emphasis, the idea that what is real in history is what pertains to the individual and particular in view of its own context, not, as in the ideas that were dominant when he began his work, what transcends the particular in the philosophical view of the historian. See Friedrich Meinecke, *Die Entstehung des Historismus* (Munich and Berlin, 1936).

27. See Charles Rosen, "The Ruins of Walter Benjamin," *New York Review of Books,* 27 October 1977, pp. 31–40, and "The Origins of Walter Benjamin," *New York Review of Books,* 10 November 1977, pp. 30–38.

28. *The Works of Thomas Carlyle* (New York, 1904), vol. 3.

29. Claude Lévi-Strauss, "History and Dialectic," reprinted in R. DeGeorge and F. DeGeorge, eds., *The Structuralists from Marx to Lévi-Strauss* (New York, 1962), pp. 209–37.

30. See Hayden White, "Interpretation in History," *New Literary History,* 4 (1973), 281–314.

31. See Karl Löwith, *Jacob Burckhardt: Der Mensch inmitten der Geschichte* (Stuttgart, 1966).

32. Johann Gustav Droysen, *Historik* (Munich and Berlin, 1937). Droysen's *Grundriss der Historik* (Jena, 1858) is essentially a summary in outline form of the larger work. An English translation by E. Benjamin Andrews was published as *Principles of History* (Boston, 1893).

33. Wilhelm Dilthey, *Die Entstehung der Hermeneutik,* in *Gesammelte Schriften* (Stuttgart and Göttingen, 1924). An English translation by Frederic Jameson is available as "The Rise of Hermeneutics," *New Literary History,* 3 (1971), 229ff. For a general exposition of Dilthey's ideas, see H. A. Hodges, *The Philosophy of Wilhelm Dilthey* (London, 1952). See also Dilthey, "The Understanding of Other Persons and Their Life-Expressions," in Patrick Gardiner, ed., *Theories of History* (New York, 1959), pp. 213–25.

34. R. G. Collingwood, *The Idea of History,* ed. T. M. Knox (Oxford, 1956). Collingwood's ideas about history are scattered throughout his writings. Two general expositions are recommended: Louis O. Mink, "Collingwood's Dialectic of History," *History and Theory,* 7 (1968), 3–37; and Leon J. Goldstein, "Collingwood's Theory of Historical Knowing," *History and Theory,* 9 (1970), 3–36.

35. Benedetto Croce, *Teoria e storia della storiografia* (Bari, 1920); English translation by Douglas Ainslee, *History: Its Theory and Practice* (New York, 1960). Two extracts are published in Gardiner, *Theories of History.*

36. T. S. Eliot, "Tradition and the Individual Talent." Available in numerous collections, earliest in *The Sacred Wood: Essays on Poetry and Criticism* (London, 1920).

37. Friedrich Meinecke, *Die Entstehung des Historismus.* The position I have

been describing is indeed known in the historiographical literature as "historicism" (German *Historismus*). But the term has been used in several senses, some diametrically opposed. So it has lost its usefulness, at least for the nonspecialist, and I have avoided it in my main text.

38. See Rudolf A. Makkreel, "Wilhelm Dilthey and the Neo-Kantians: The Distinction of the *Geisteswissenschaften* and the *Kulturwissenschaften*," *Journal of the History of Philosophy*, 4 (October 1969), 423–40.

39. This very live issue was the stage on which Georg Büchner's *Woyzeck* was played. The play may be understood as a dramatization of Droysen's position, and as a powerful protest against the degrading and the belittling of the individual in the reckoning of the forces that count in history, and in the determination of moral judgments. In this Büchner projected attitudes that were plainly set out a generation later by Kierkegaard and Nietzsche. See Chapter 9.

40. The objections to the concept of intention in criticism are dealt with in my own paper, "Stylistic Analysis" (see note 14), and in Chapter 3.

41. Carl Hempel, "The Function of General Laws in History," in Gardiner, *Theories of History*, pp. 344–56. The central argument in this essay is that historical understanding aims at the explanation of the historian's subject, and that explanation in history, like explanation in every empirical science, is based upon general laws that are subject to confirmation or disconfirmation through empirical findings. The essay is generally taken as the authoritative statement of the standard to which historians should aspire in casting their accounts as causal explanations. But it can also be read as an argument for the view that the standard itself is an inappropriate one for history, for Hempel shows that it is a standard which history could not conceivably attain.

2. "To Worship That Celestial Sound"

1. Peter Kivy, *The Corded Shell* (Princeton, 1980). As a motto for the book Kivy prints the second stanza of John Dryden's *A Song for St. Cecilia's Day:*

> What Passion cannot MUSIC raise and quell!
> When *Jubal* struck the corded Shell,
> His list'ning Brethren stood around
> And wond'ring on their Faces fell
> To worship that Celestial Sound.
> Less than a God they thought there cou'd not dwell
> Within the hollow of that Shell
> That spoke so sweetly and so well.
> What Passion cannot MUSIC raise and quell!

2. Another has been Stanley Cavell. See *Must We Mean What We Say?* (New York, 1969).

3. Guido Adler, *Der Stil in der Musik,* vol. 1 (Leipzig, 1911).

4. Regarding the several senses of "historicism" see Wesley Morris, *Toward a New Historicism* (Princeton, 1977), chap. 1.

5. Gadamer's major work is *Wahrheit und Methode* (Tübingen, 1975); English translation, *Truth and Method* (New York, 1975). An excellent introduction to Gadamer's thought is provided by David Linge, the editor of the collection of essays published under the title *Philosophical Hermeneutics* (Berkeley, 1976).

6. Oliver Strunk, ed., *Source Readings in Music History* (New York, 1950), pp. 152–53.

7. "Analysis," in *The New Grove Dictionary of Music and Musicians,* I, 341–88.

8. Ruth Solie, "The Living Work: Organicism and Musical Analysis," *19th Century Music,* 4 (1980), 147–56.

9. Knud Jeppesen, *Palestrina and the Style of the Dissonance* (New York and London, 1946); Jan LaRue, *Guidelines for Style Analysis* (New York, 1970).

10. Willi Apel, *Gregorian Chant* (Bloomington, In., 1958).

11. Joseph Kerman, "How We Got into Analysis, and How to Get Out," *Critical Inquiry,* 7 (1980), 311–31.

12. Eric Sams, *The Songs of Robert Schumann* (London, 1969).

13. Friedrich Blume, "Renaissance," in *Die Musik in Geschichte und Gegenwart,* ed. Blume et al. (Kassel, 1949–1986).

14. The discussion of Gregorian Chant occurs in Schenker's *Neue Musikalische Theorien und Phantasien* of 1906, published in English as *Harmony* (Chicago, 1954). It is worth quoting some of his language: "musical instinct, to begin with, was totally inartistic and only rose from a chaos of fog to a principle of art . . . We have to accept the fact that the majority of Gregorian chants lacked any guiding principle, thus placing themselves outside the scope of art in the intrinsically musical and formally technical sense." The discussion of Wagner occurs in *Neue Musikalische Theorien und Phantasien,* vol. 2, *Kontrapunkt* (Stuttgart and Berlin, 1910), p. viii.

15. Howard M. Brown, *Music in the Renaissance* (New York, 1976), p. 79.

16. Charles van den Borren, *Etudes sur le quinzième siècle musicale* (Antwerp, 1941), p. 168.

17. Manfred Bukofzer, "*Caput:* A Liturgico-Musical Study," in *Studies in Medieval and Renaissance Music* (New York, 1950), pp. 291–92.

18. Brown, *Music in the Renaissance,* p. 80.

19. David G. Hughes, *A History of Western Music* (New York, 1974), p. 118.

20. Brown, *Music in the Renaissance,* p. 66.

21. Forced, that is, by the revelation that the works on which that earlier impression was based do not predominate in the Composer's canon. See Leeman Perkins's article "Ockeghem," in *The New Grove.*

22. See Carl Dahlhaus, "Die Termini Dur und Moll," *Archiv für Musik-forschung,* 12 (1955), 280–96, and Eric Chafe, "Key Structure and Tonal Allegory in the Passions of J. S. Bach: an Introduction," *Current Musicology,* 31 (1981), 39–54.

23. Friedrich Nietzsche, *Menschliches Allzumenschliches* (1878).

24. Ibid. Walter Wiora has written about this phenomenon in "Religioso: Triviale Zonen in der religiösen Kunst des 19. Jahrhunderts," in *Studien zur Philosophie und Literatur des Neunzehnten Jahrhunderts,* vol. 15 (Frankfurt, 1971).

25. See, for example, Maynard Solomon, *Beethoven Essays* (Cambridge, Mass., 1988), chap. 9.

26. Anton Schindler, *Biographie Ludwig van Beethovens* (Münster, 1840). Christian Schubart, *Ideen zu einer Ästhetic der Tonkunst,* completed 1784 (Vienna, 1804).

27. Alf Kalischer, ed., *The Letters of Ludwig van Beethoven* (New York, 1909; reprint, New York, 1969).

3. *Music Analysis in a Historical Context*

1. See Joseph Kerman, "A Profile for American Musicology," *Journal of the American Musicological Society,* 18 (1965), 65–69; Edward E. Lowinsky, "Character and Purposes of American Musicology: A Reply to Joseph Kerman," 222–34; communication from Joseph Kerman, 426–27.

2. In using the terms "analysis" and "criticism" I do not presuppose the hierarchy—with criticism at the top—that is suggested by Kerman. It is admittedly difficult for musical scholars to agree on the meaning of the word "criticism," for, as Kerman has observed, it is a foreign word in the language of our discipline. But the study of music, considered as art rather than as document of history (the latter is possible and legitimate, but it presupposes the former) is in any case criticism. On the other hand, to put criticism at the end of the scholarly process, as Lowinsky does in writing of "the enormous work that needs to be done before fruitful and responsible criticism can be practiced in all areas of music history" is to suggest the procedure of the young piano pupil who learns the notes first and puts in the feeling afterwards.

   In any case, a belief in the separability of the observational from the interpretive and the evaluative seems to be a minimal commitment in maintaining such distinctions. The following is meant to question seriously the soundness of that position. For now, I should merely like to ask whether an analysis that does not attain the level of criticism fails in a radically different way than does, let us say, an analysis that is made from an incomplete score. For it seems inescapable that any analysis—even the choice of one system of analysis over another—will embody judgments that must be regarded as "critical."

3. The quotation is taken from Georgio Vasari, *Lives of the Most Eminent Painters, Sculptors, and Architects,* (London, 1892), V, 239.

4. Henrich Wölfflin, *Die Jugendwerke des Michelangelo* (Munich, 1891), p. 23. Translation mine.

5. Ernst Gombrich, *Art and Illusion.* 2d. rev. ed. (New York, 1961), pp. 359–60. Gombrich's thesis—that the inventions of artists are accompanied by an evolution in the reading of images—has not, I believe, had any parallel expression in music criticism. But it seems clear that responses to musical sounds have changed through the history of the species. We may consider a single example. While it is certain that during the Middle Ages the octave—considered as an interval—was heard as we hear it today, it is also clear from medieval melody that our doctrine of octave equivalence was not in effect (i.e., two members of a pitch-class could not have been heard to share the same function). Similarly, it was through Rameau's teaching that we learned to hear inverted triads functioning as versions of their root positions.

6. *The Elements of Drawing,* in *The Works of John Ruskin,* ed. E. T. Cook and Alexander Wedderburn (London and New York, 1903–1912).

7. See Monroe C. Beardsley and W. K. Wimsatt, Jr., "The Intentional Fallacy," in the latter's *The Verbal Icon* (Lexington, Ky., 1954).

8. Allen Forte, *The Compositional Matrix* (Baldwin, N.Y., 1961), p. 15. I am glad to note, twenty-two years after the writing of this essay, how far the project of the analysis of the Beethoven sketches has been realized.

9. "Tone System in the Secular Works of Dufay," *JAMS,* 18 (1965), 132–69.

10. Heinrich Besseler, *Bourdon und Fauxbourdon* (Leipzig, 1950), p. 72.

11. Quoted by Rudolph Arnheim in *Picasso's Guernica* (Berkeley and Los Angeles, 1962), p. 12.

12. Frank Harrison, *Musicology* (Englewood Cliffs, N.J., 1963), p. 80.

13. Milton Babbitt, review of *Structural Hearing* by Felix Salzer, *JAMS,* 5 (1952), 260–65.

14. J. K. Randall, "Haydn's String Quartet in D Major, Opus 76, No. 5," *Music Review,* 21 (1960).

15. Examples: the original progression D–b–G–e–D; its retrograde form is D–e–G–b–D; the upward transposition by minor third of the retrograde, beginning with the fourth element, d–F–g–B-flat–d.

16. Arnheim, pp. 1–2.

17. In this instance it might be a question about whether Randall's statement of the tonal relationships in the work in question—attractive as it is for its own elegance—is as significant as would be one in which symmetrical progression by thirds (retrogression and rotation follow readily from that

as first principle), with consequent emphasis of the subdominant, is seen as an alternative to progressions based on the dominant relationship. Then the non-unique case of the Haydn quartet would be illuminated by consideration of other tonal works—e.g., Beethoven's *Hammerklavier* Sonata, the Ninth Symphony, Brahm's Fourth Symphony.

4. On Historical Criticism

1. William Arrowsmith, "The Shame of Our Graduate Schools," *Harper's Magazine,* March 1966, pp. 51–59. Symptomatic though it may be, Arrowsmith's broadside was not altogether well informed. Thus his linking of classics and musicology as the most backward of the humanistic disciplines was surely ill-advised considering the enormous differences in the background and the current state of the two.
2. Eric Larabee, "Saving the Humanities," *Commentary,* December 1966, pp. 53–60.
3. Charles Rosen, "The Proper Study of Music," *Perspectives of New Music,* 1 (1962), 80–88; Joseph Kerman, "The Proper Study of Music: A Reply," *Perspectives,* 2 (1963), 151–59; Kerman, "A Profile for American Musicology," Edward E. Lowinsky, "Character and Purposes of American Musicology: A Reply to Joseph Kerman," and communication from Kerman, *JAMS,* 18 (1965), 65–69, 222–34, 426–27.
4. Warren Allen, *Philosophies of Music History* (New York, 1962); Frank L. Harrison, Mantle Hood, and Claude V. Palisca, *Musicology* (Englewood Cliffs, N.J., 1963); Lewis Lockwood's review of the latter, *Perspectives,* 3 (1964), 119–27; Harold S. Powers, review of Allan Merriam, "The Anthropology of Music," *Perspectives,* 5 (1966), 161–71.
5. Some principal writings: James Ackerman, "A Theory of Style," *Journal of Aesthetics and Art Criticism,* 20 (1961), 227–37; Ackerman, with Rhys Carpenter, *Art and Archeology* (Englewood Cliffs, N.J., 1963); Ernst Gombrich, *Art and Illusion,* 2d. rev. ed. (New York, 1961); Gombrich, *Meditations on a Hobby Horse and Other Essays on the Theory of Art* (London, 1963); Erwin Panofsky, "Das Problem des Stils in der bildenden Kunst," *Zeitschrift für Aesthetik,* 10 (1915), 460–67; the discussion of the latter is continued in "Der Begriff des Kunstwollens," *Zeitschrift für Aesthetik,* 14 (1919–20), 21–39; Panofsky, *Meaning in the Visual Arts: Papers in and on Art History* (New York, 1955); Meyer Schapiro, "Style," reprinted in Morris Philipson, ed., *Aesthetics Today* (New York, 1961); Schapiro, "On Perfection, Coherence, and Unity of Form and Content," in Sidney Hook, ed., *Art and Philosophy* (New York, 1966), 3–15.
6. Panofsky, "Der Begriff des Kunstwollens."

7. This point of view has been restated by Edward Lippman in "The Problem of Musical Hermeneutics: A Protest and Analysis," In Hook, ed., *Art and Philosophy,* 307–35.

8. This apparently innocent distinction in meanings for our word "understand" rests on the ancient epistemological split between subjective and objective knowledge, that is to say, the dissociation of the knower from what is known. It harbors issues of great importance and ultimate relevance that must be mentioned here, even though these remarks may not appear to be immediately basic to the argument that is to follow. From the point of view that I have been sketching above, statements must derive their validity from either factual correctness (verifiability) or formal consistency (as in a definition or mathematical equation). "Subjective" statements can do neither, and are therefore disqualified from the status of knowledge and relegated to the category of expressions that includes also cries of pain and ecstasy. The language of formal logic represents, then, a distillation of the substantive content of rational, "objective" statements, and, by corollary, statements that are not reducible to the notation of formal logic are not "objective." These remarks apply with equal force to long-term intellectual processes, such as experimentation and theory development, and, relevant to this discussion, causal explanation.

This canon forms the basis of the scientism to which the humanities and social sciences have aspired since the nineteenth century, and it now informs a good deal of music-historical and music-theoretical writing. That being the case, it is necessary to note at once that, as a model for rational discourse, this bipartite reduction of knowledge, with its methodological consequences, has come to be widely regarded as an oversimplification and even as a delusion. I quote Michael Polanyi: "I start by rejecting the ideal of scientific detachment. In the exact sciences, this false ideal is perhaps harmless, for it is in fact disregarded there by scientists. But we shall see that it exercises a destructive influence in biology, psychology, and sociology, and falsifies our whole outlook far beyond the domain of science" (*Personal Knowledge* [Chicago, 1958], p. viii). And on the principal subject of this discussion, Mario Bunge wrote: "The reduction of lawfulness [orderliness] to causality is a mistake in scientific method and, like other mistakes of this sort, it is liable to have noxious consequences for every general world outlook that claims to be based on science" (*Causality* [Cambridge, Mass., 1959], p. 262).

The opposition is voiced in diverse fields—linguistic and analytic philosophy, the philosophy of history, the philosophy of science, gestalt psychology, anthropology, the theory of art—and it is not coordinated. It is impossible to formulate alternate views in this space, but a number of central principles should be mentioned: (1) Knowing is an active process of assimilation that incorporates an act of appraisal. It is like skill and connoisseurship in being partly inarticulate and inarticulable. (2) Theory—seen as interpretive patterns or structures—is in effect a screen between the knower and the things known. We do not regard facts as being true except as they have a place in some theoretical framework. Particulars are meaningless if we lose sight of the pattern they jointly constitute. Observation and theory are related in an interplay, not a hierarchy or a strictly ordered time sequence. (3) Verifiability as the measure of lawfulness yields ground to intelligibility, coherence, potential explanatory power. (4) The knower finds himself within a continuous matrix that connects the world of "objective" reality, directly given through experience and activity, with consciousness. (5) Formal logic is not identical with meaningful discourse; it is one—highly specialized and selective—among several varieties thereof.

9. This is one of the most vulnerable points in this view of explanation. It has been argued that, although explanation and prediction may show parallel formal structures, they do not always turn out to be reversible. The basis for the argument is the assertion that each of the terms "cause," "law," "explanation," and "prediction" in fact covers a wider range of referents than is recognized by the covering-law model. See William Dray, *Laws and Explanation in History* (London, 1957), chap. 3, pp. 58–85, and Bunge, pp. 307–32. A minute example: The statement "Lions are fierce" provides the basis for a prediction on which one's life may depend, but it would not explain a single manifestation of a particular lion's fierceness. I shall want to consider the status of such "explanations" in music history further on.

As students of music especially, we should not be surprised by this lack of symmetry between explanation and prediction. The analysis of music, like the analysis of narrative or dramatic fiction, comes down very much to a detailed demonstration of the way in which the events of the work are motivated. Being convinced by such a demonstration we do not, however, go on to claim that it was all predictable. On the contrary, we would say that it is just within this gap between explanation and prediction that artistic excellence is located.

10. Carl Hempel, "The Function of General Laws in History," *Journal of Philosophy,* 39 (1942), reprinted in Feigl and Sellars, eds., *Readings in Philosophical Analysis* (New York, 1949), and Patrick Gardiner, ed., *Theories of History* (New York, 1959).

11. Arthur Mendel, "Evidence and Explanation," *International Musicological Society Report of the Eighth Congress, New York, 1961* (Kassel, 1962), pp. 3–18. The reader will find there a far more detailed and thoughtful exposition of this point of view than space allows here.

12. This question is not raised here for the first time. The following brief review incorporates some of my own arguments, but it owes much to the selections from a very extensive literature that I list here and cite specifically in the context of my discussion.

H. Butterfield, *The Whig Interpretation of History* (London, 1931); Arthur Child, "Thoughts on the Historiology of Neo-Positivism," *Journal of Philosophy,* 57 (1960), 665; Benedetto Croce, "Historical Determinism and Philosophy of History," reprinted in Gardiner, *Theories;* Alan Donagan, "Explanation in History," in Gardiner, *Theories;* William Dray, *Laws and Explanations in History,* "Explaining What," in Gardiner, *Theories,* and "Explanatory Narrative in History," *Philosophical Quarterly* (1954), 15–27; Charles Frankel, "Explanation and Interpretation in History," in Gardiner, *Theories;* Patrick Gardiner, *The Nature of Historical Explanation* (London, 1952); Michael Scriven, "Truisms as the Grounds for Historical Explanation," in Gardiner, *Theories;* W. H. Walsh, "The Intelligibility of History," *Philosophy* (1942), 129–43.

Mendel supports Hempel's thesis, and in rejecting the arguments presented by the latter's opponents he shows that the conditions of history that are alleged to stand in the way of a scientific methodology—e.g., the uniqueness of historical events, the elusiveness of causal laws—obtain in science as well. Indeed the following arguments are not intended to support the doctrine that history is sui generis in its methods. But then the general conclusion must be that "it is desirable to dispense with a nomenclature attached to an outdated philosophy of science, namely that asserting the coextensiveness of science and causality" (Bunge, p. 277). This is to say that the identification of all knowledge as *causal* is as unsatisfactory in science as it is in history.

13. Gustave Reese, *Music in the Middle Ages* (New York, 1940), p. 403.

14. The example is from Dray, *Laws and Explanations,* p. 39ff.

15. Walsh; Child; Butterfield; Dray, "Explaining What" (Gardiner, *The Nature of Historical Explanation,* chap. 2).

16. Quoted by Croce, p. 239. As an antidote to Taine's maxim I refer the reader to Norwood Hanson, *Patterns of Discovery* (Cambridge, 1958).

17. Child, p. 665; Butterfield, p. 22; Frankel, p. 411.

18. Hempel, in Gardiner, *Theories,* pp. 344–59.

19. Dray, *Laws and Explanation,* pp. 25–31.

20. Guido Adler, *Methode der Musikgeschichte* (Leipzig, 1919), p. 9.

21. Quoted from the Oxford translation, edited by W. D. Ross, *Physics:* Bk. 2, ch. 8, p. 199b, ll. 15–19; p. 199a, ll. 15–16. *Poetics:* ch. 4, p. 1449a, ll. 14–15.

22. Leo Schrade, "Renaissance: The Historical Conception of an Epoch,"

International Musicological Society, Report of the 5th Congress, Utrecht, 1952 (Kassel, 1953), 19–32.

23. Kant, "The Idea of a Cosmo-Political History," trans. W. Hastie, in *Eternal Peace and Other International Essays* (Boston, 1914).

24. Hegel, *Lectures on the Philosophy of History,* excerpted in J. Loewenberg, ed., *Hegel Selections* (New York, 1929), p. 409.

25. Herder, "Ideas toward a Philosophy of the History of Man," trans. T. Churchill, in Gardiner, *Theories,* pp. 35–51.

26. Winckelmann, *History of Ancient Art,* trans. G. Henry Lodge (Boston, 1873), pp. 191–92.

27. Ernst Gombrich, *The Ideas of Progress and Their Impact on Art* (New York, 1971).

28. Alfred Einstein, *A Short History of Music,* 4th American ed., rev. (New York, 1956), p. 164.

29. Donald Jay Grout, *A History of Western Music* (New York, 1960), p. 297.

30. Richard Crocker, *A History of Musical Style* (New York, 1966), p. 525.

31. John Mueller, "Baroque: Is It Datum, Hypothesis, or Tautology?" *Journal of Aesthetics and Art Criticism,* 12 (1954), 421–37.

32. Manfred Bukofzer, "The Baroque in Music History," *Journal of Aesthetics and Art Criticism,* 14 (1955), 152–56.

33. Paul Henry Lang, *Music in Western Civilization* (New York, 1941), p. 529.

34. Karl Popper, *The Poverty of Historicism,* 3rd ed. (New York, 1961), pp. 26–34.

35. "Allzuvieles Fragen nach den Ursachen sei gefährlich; man solle lieber an die Erscheinungen als gegebene Tatsache halten." Quoted by H. J. Moser in "Zur Methodik der musikalischen Geschichtschreibung," *Zeitschrift für Aesthetik,* 14 (1920), 130–45.

36. Howard Brofsky, "The Symphonies of Padre Martini," *The Musical Quarterly,* 51 (1965), 649–73.

37. "Symphonie," in *Die Musik in Geschichte und Gegenwart* (Kassel, 1965), vol. 12, cols. 1803–99.

38. Hegel, *Lectures on the Philosophy of History,* trans. J. Sibree (London, 1894). The passage quoted is from the author's introduction.

39. Oswald Spengler marked the beginning of the decline of Western music with Beethoven, on grounds very like those laid down by Winckelmann: profusion and the consequent disruption of form. Alfred Einstein argued that, on the contrary, Beethoven represents a peak in that he brought about the full realization of the potentials of sonata form. They assess their man differently, but only because he occupies different positions in their respective schemes of development. Spengler, *The Decline of the West,* trans. Charles F. Atkinson (New York, 1926 and 1928), I, 291ff; Einstein,

"Oswald Spengler und die Musikgeschichte," *Zeitschrift für Musikwissen-schaft,* 3 (1920), 30–32.

40. H. C. Robbins Landon, *The Symphonies of Joseph Haydn* (London, 1955), pp. 552, 573.

5. The Present as History

1. Jacques Chailley, *40,000 Years of Music,* trans. Rollo Myers (Paris, 1961; London, 1964); Walter Wiora, *The Four Ages of Music,* trans. M. D. Herter Norton (Stuttgart, 1965; New York, 1965); Richard L. Crocker, *A History of Musical Style* (New York, 1966); Leonard B. Meyer, *Music/The Arts/and Ideas: Patterns and Predictions in Twentieth-Century Culture* (Chicago, 1967).

2. After the completion of this essay in the summer of 1968 a new version of Ranke's slogan became a commonplace: "Tell it like it is." One's first impulse is to pull out the phrase, with the attitude of the lady whose St. Laurent original is suddenly mass-produced for distribution through Macy's. But I leave it, for its new currency points straight to the inherent naiveté of the idea when it is expressed under any circumstances. "Tell it like it is" says, "Stop favoring your view of the case by the way you frame your report." As though telling from a particular point of view could be turned on and off at will! (But see Chapter 1, note 26.)

3. Milton Babbitt, "Who Cares If You Listen?" and John Cage, "Interview with Roger Reynolds," in Elliott Schwartz and Barney Childs, eds., *Contemporary Composers on Contemporary Music* (New York, 1967).

4. James Johnson Sweeney, *Vision and Image* (New York, 1968).

5. Northrop Frye, *The Modern Century* (Toronto, 1967).

6. The significance of this symbiotic relationship is discussed in some depth by Stanley Cavell in "Music Discomposed," in *Must We Mean What We Say?* (New York, 1969). But I know of no more direct a demonstration of it than J. K. Randall's discussion of Godfrey Winham's *Composition for Orchestra* in *Perspectives of New Music,* 2, (1963), 102–13. Looking at the musical examples alone, one is likely to be misled about the nature of the composer's achievement, for they seem deceptively simple and familiar in style. What is demonstrated is that such discussions take place in a realm of discourse that does not at all necessarily include the work's stylistic or aesthetic surface.

7. René Wellek, "The Crisis of Comparative Literature," *Proceedings of the International Comparative Literature Association,* 1 (1959), 149–59.

8. Claudio Guillén, "The Aesthetics of Influence Studies in Comparative Literature," ibid., pp. 175–91.

9. Henri Peyre, "A Glance at Comparative Literature in America," *Yearbook of Comparative and General Literature,* 6 (1952), 1–16.

10. William Dray, "Explaining What," in Patrick Gardiner, *Theories of History* (New York, 1959).

11. Maurice Mandelbaum, "A Note on History as Narrative," *History and Theory,* 6 (1967), 413–19.

12. Felix Salzer, "Tonality in Early Medieval Polyphony: Towards a History of Tonality," and Peter Bergquist, "Mode and Polyphony around 1500: Theory and Practice," both in *Music Forum,* 1 (1967).

13. David Lewin, "Inversional Balance as an Organizing Force in Schoenberg's Music and Thought," *Perspectives of New Music,* 6 (1968), 1–21.

14. Compare Lewin's analysis of the first movement of the Fantasy with my analysis of the first movement of Bartók's Fourth Quartet in "Harmonic Procedure in the Fourth Quartet of Bela Bartók," *Journal of Music Theory,* 3 (1959), 292–98.

15. Ludwig Wittgenstein, *Philosophical Investigations,* trans. G. E. M. Anscombe, 2nd ed. (New York, 1958).

16. Thomas Munro, *Evolution in the Arts* (Cleveland, 1963).

17. Norwood R. Hanson, *Patterns of Discovery* (Cambridge, 1958); Thomas S. Kuhn, *The Structure of Scientific Revolutions* (Chicago, 1962); Michael Polanyi, *Personal Knowledge* (Chicago, 1958).

18. Cavell, "Music Discomposed." This thought is considered during the course of an argument. It does not express Cavell's ultimate wish, nor, for that matter, mine.

19. Lewin, "Inversional Balance."

20. James Ackerman, "Art and Evolution," in Gyorgy Kepes, ed., *The Nature and Art of Motion* (New York, 1965).

21. See Patricia Carpenter, "The Musical Object," *Current Musicology,* 5 (1967).

22. See, for example, Irving Howe, "The Culture of Modernism," *Commentary,* 44 (November 1967).

6. What Kind of Story Is History?

1. Chapter 1 of this book.

2. Gordon S. Wood, "Star-Spangled History," *New York Review of Books,* 12 August 1982, pp. 4–9; Bernard Bailyn, "The Challenge to Modern Historiography," *American Historical Review,* 87 (1982), 1–24.

3. Carl Schorske, *Fin-de-Siècle Vienna: Politics and Culture* (New York, 1980).

4. *Oxford History of the United States* (Oxford, 1982), vol. 2.

5. See, for example, Ernst Breisach, *Historiography: Ancient, Medieval and Modern* (Chicago, 1983), p. 250ff.

6. Wood, "Star-Spangled History."

7. Marshall Sahlins, *Historical Metaphors and Mythical Realities: Structure in the Early History of the Sandwich Islands Kingdom* (Ann Arbor, 1981).

8. E. E. Evans-Pritchard, "Anthropology and History," in *Essays in Social Anthropology* (New York, 1963), pp. 46–65.

9. Leo Treitler, "Reading and Singing: On the Genesis of Occidental Music Writing," *Early Music History*, 4 (1984), 135–208.

10. R. G. Collingwood. For discussion and citation of the literature, see Chapter 1, esp. note 34.

11. Bernard Bischoff, "Panorama der Handschriftenüberlieferung aus der Zeit Karls des Grossen," in W. Braunfels, ed., *Karl der Grosse: Lebenswerk und Nachleben* (Düsseldorf, 1965–1967), II, 234–54.

12. F. L. Ganshof, *The Carolingians and the Frankish Monarchy* (London, 1971), p. 29.

13. Luitpold Wallach, ed., *Alcuin and Charlemagne: Studies in Carolingian History and Literature* (Ithaca, N.Y., 1959), pp. 202–204.

14. Walter J. Ong, *Orality and Literacy: The Technologizing of the Word* (London and New York, 1982).

15. Peter Wagner, *Einführung in die Gregorianischen Melodien* (Leipzig, 1912; reprinted Hildesheim, 1963), II, 264–67.

16. R. C. Lewontin, "Darwin's Real Revolution," *New York Review of Books,* 16 June 1983, pp. 21–27. Music historians who are tempted to write of "evolution" can get an accurate sense of what Darwin really said, and his place in the history of theorizing about evolution, from Jonathan Miller's delightful illustrated book *Darwin for Beginners* (London, 1982).

17. Carl Dahlhaus, *Foundations of Music History* (Cambridge, England, 1983).

18. Erwin Panofsky, "The History of Arts as a Humanistic Discipline," in *Meaning in the Visual Arts: Papers in and on Art History* (Garden City, N.Y., 1955), pp. 1–25.

19. Dahlhaus, *Foundations of Music History,* "Translator's Preface."

20. Joseph Kerman, "A Few Canonic Variations," *Critical Inquiry,* 10 (1983), 107–26.

21. Hayden White, "Interpretation in History," *New Literary History,* 4 (1973), pp. 281–314.

22. See Victor Erlich, *Russian Formalism: History-Doctrine,* 3rd ed. (New Haven and London, 1981).

23. E. H. Gombrich, *Art and Illusion* (London, 1960).

7. Mozart and the Idea of Absolute Music

1. E. T. A. Hoffman, *Schriften zur Musik,* ed. Friedrich Schnapp (Munich, 1963), p. 145.

2. Carl Dahlhaus, *Die Idee der absoluten Musik* (Munich, 1978).

3. John Neubauer, *The Emancipation of Music from Language* (New Haven, Ct., 1986).

4. Richard Wagner, *Gesammelte Schriften und Dichtungen,* ed. Wolfgang Golther (Berlin and Leipzig, no date), II, 61.

5. Wilhelm Heinrich Wackenroder, *Werke und Briefe* (Heidelberg, 1967), pp. 254–55.

6. Stéphane Mallarmé, *Oeuvres complètes* (Paris, 1945), p. 870.

7. The quotations about Wordsworth and Friedrich are from Charles Rosen and Henri Zerner, *Romanticism and Realism: The Mythology of Nineteenth-Century Art* (New York, 1984), pp. 57, 59, 63.

8. To interpret "the emergence of the new aesthetics as breaking the ground for abstract art" is an express purpose of Neubauer's book; see p. 2.

9. Roman Jakobson, "Language in Relation to Other Communications Systems," *Selected Writings,* vol. 2 (The Hague, 1971), p. 705.

10. T. S. Eliot, *Poetry and Drama* (Cambridge, Mass., 1951), pp. 42–43.

11. Quoted by Neubauer, p. 1.

12. Charles Rosen, *The Classical Style* (New York, 1972).

13. Dahlhaus, whose book (see note 2) has been an invaluable source for this essay, develops absolute music as an *a priori* idea in the context of the history of aesthetic philosophy. He makes no attempt to regard it as a critical theory with reference to a particular musical practice. On the other side contemporary music criticism tends to approach "the classical style" from the standpoint of stylistic language, with little regard for the aesthetic that it serves. Something essential is lost by this isolation of style and aesthetics from one another.

14. Wolfgang Hildesheimer, *Mozart,* trans. Marion Faber (New York, 1982).

15. Hildesheimer, p. 279.

16. Hildesheimer, pp. 227, 241.

17. Hildesheimer, pp. 241, 242.

18. Edward T. Cone, "Schubert's Promissory Note: An Exercise in Musical Hermeneutics," *19th Century Music,* 5 (1982), 233–41.

19. Ex. 7.2, the passage following (N), and its counterparts.

20. Wackenroder, pp. 254–55.

21. Hoffmann, p. 145. Wackenroder (pp. 226 and 255) characterizes the symphony as a "drama of instruments."

22. Novalis, *Schriften,* ed. Richard Samuel, 2nd ed. (Stuttgart, 1975), III, 458.

23. Christian Gottfried Körner, "Über Charakterdarstellung in der Musik," *Die Horen,* 5 (1795), 99, paraphrased by Neubauer, p. 196.

24. Wackenroder, pp. 254–55.

25. The phrase *musique naturel* comes from Eustache Deschamps, author of the sole theoretical tract on poetry surviving from that time. For details see John Stevens, *Words and Music in the Middle Ages* (Cambridge, England, 1986).

26. Wackenroder, p. 250.

27. Novalis, III, 572.

28. Friedrich Schlegel, *Charakteristiken und Kritiken,* 1, in *Kritische Friedrich-Schlegel-Ausgabe,* vol. 2, ed. Hans Eichner (Munich, 1967), p. 254.

29. Hildesheimer, p. 28.

30. Hildesheimer, p. 38, 57.

31. Hildesheimer, pp. 40–41.

32. Quoted from Nelson Goodman, "Twisted Tales; or, Story, Study, and Symphony," in W. J. T. Mitchell, ed., *On Narrative* (Chicago, 1981), p. 255.

33. Frank Kermode, "Secrets and Narrative Sequence," in *On Narrative,* p. 82.

34. Donald Francis Tovey, *Essays in Musical Analysis,* vol. 1 (Oxford, 1935), p. 68.

35. *The New Grove Dictionary of Music and Musicians* (New York, 1980), XII, 713; Tovey, I, 189.

36. *"Tönend bewegte Formen";* Eduard Hanslick, *Vom musikalisch-Schönen* (Leipzig, 1854), p. 32. This translation is William Austin's, from Carl Dahlhaus, *Esthetics of Music* (Cambridge, England, 1982), p. 52.

37. Dahlhaus, in *Die Idee der absoluten Musik* (p. 41), writes, "The restriction of the term 'absolute music' to the architectonic form of instrumental music is owing to Ottokar Hostinsky." Hostinsky was the author of *Das Musikalisch-Schöne und das Gesammtkunstwerk vom Standpunkt der formalen Aesthetik* (Leipzig, 1877). What this amounts to is the transformation of the absolute music concept from its reference to the condition and expressive potency of music, in the context of a particular aesthetic doctrine, to an analytical stance toward music in general, with implications for what is to count as music altogether (i.e., only that which is susceptible to analysis in terms of its architectonic form). This is the pathway from the absolute music concept to the formalist doctrine with which it is often associated nowadays. A similar route has sometimes been traced by painting: from the general aesthetic ideal embodied in the absolute music concept to formalism, by way of abstraction.

38. Columbia ML 5014 (1956); L'Oiseau-Lyre 410233-1 OH (1983).

39. RCA Victor LM 2001 (1956).

40. Neal Zaslaw, "Mozart's Tempo Conventions," in *International Musicological Society, Report of the Eleventh Congress, Copenhagen 1972* (Copenhagen, 1974), 720–33.

8. Dufay the Progressive

1. Arnold Schoenberg, "Brahms the Progressive," in *Style and Idea* (New York, 1950).

2. Schoenberg's reckoning of progress in music in terms of the development

of an "unrestricted musical language" was one of the thematic elements in his historical view. And it is one of the points at which the Hegelian cast of his thinking is especially clear, for it corresponds exactly to Hegel's notion of historical progress as the working out of the idea of freedom: "The final cause of the world is the realization of its own freedom by Spirit." But to understand Schoenberg's concept of "unrestricted," it is helpful to think of Hegel's dictum that "Freedom is nothing other than the recognition and adoption of . . . Right and Law." See G. W. F. Hegel, *Philosophy of History,* trans. J. Sibree (New York, 1902), esp. pp. 61–65 of the Introduction.

3. Heinrich Besseler, *Guglielmi Dufay: Opera Omnia,* III (Rome, 1951). In the interest of economy the texts have been omitted from the examples, as they do not directly pertain to what is being discussed. Readers will find it in any case more convenient to follow the discussion with the Besseler edition at hand, if they have access to it.

4. Leo Treitler, "Tone System in the Secular Works of Guillaume Dufay," *Journal of the American Musicological Society,* 18 (1965), 131–69; Leeman Perkins, "Mode and Structure in the Masses of Josquin," *Journal of the American Musicological Society,* 26 (1973), 190–239.

5. The reader may consult Besseler's critical notes for details about the transmission with respect to the signature of the superius part. There is no reason to challenge Besseler's judgment regarding the authority of the version without B-flat. The observations offered here about the role of the superius in the polyphony are in support of that judgment.

9. Wozzeck *and the Apocalypse*

1. Letter to his family, February 1834: "I scorn no one, least of all because of his understanding or his education, for it lies in no one's power not to become a dumbbell or a criminal—because we have all become alike through like circumstances, and because the circumstances lie outside of ourselves . . ." Werner Lehmann, *Georg Büchner: Sämtliche Werke und Briefe* (Hamburg, 1971), II, 422.

2. See Lehmann, I, 338ff. Berg's libretto follows the scenic order of the first edition by Franzos; see George Perle, "*Woyzeck* and *Wozzeck,*" *Musical Quarterly,* 53 (1967), 206–19. In both versions the scene in the field is followed immediately by the scene that opens with Marie ogling the Drum Major. That fact seems most essential, for it is the latter act that initiates the chain of events which Wozzeck comes to interpret as the fulfillment of the prophecy revealed to him through the signs in the field. The question arises: What understanding can we have of the first scene if the essential process of the drama appears to begin in the second? The drama runs its

course in two settings at once, really: the predatory external world of the first scene and the haunted world of Wozzeck's mind, introduced in the second. In the first scene Wozzeck is shown as the victim of conditions that are responsible for the state of his mind and for what unfolds subsequent to the second scene. The last scene of the opera, too, is outside the process that begins in the second. It is in a way the ultimate statement about the condition of the external world.

3. I refer here to Marie's monologue in Act 3, Scene 1.

4. Lehmann, I, 427.

5. G. W. F. Hegel, *Reason in History*, trans. Robert S. Hartman (Indianapolis and New York, 1953), p. 18.

6. Lehmann, II, 291ff.

7. Letter to his family, 28 July 1835: "The dramatic poet is in my eyes nothing other than a writer of history . . . His highest task is to come as near as possible to history as it really transpired." Lehmann, II, 443.

8. Hegel, *Reason in History*, pp. 46–47.

9. Immanuel Kant, "The Idea of a Cosmo-Political History," trans. W. Hastie, in *Eternal Peace and Other International Essays* (Boston, 1914).

10. Regarding the interpretation of Enlightenment historiography as secularization of Christian doctrine, see Karl Löwith, *Meaning in History* (Chicago, 1949) and W. J. Walsh, "'Meaning' in History," in Patrick Gardiner, ed., *Theories of History* (Glencoe, Ill., 1959).

11. Hegel, "Die Vernunft in der Geschichte," trans. Walter Kaufmann, in *Hegel: A Reinterpretation* (New York, 1965) p. 251. See Kaufmann's bibliographical note, p. 383, regarding the relation between his text and Hartman's.

12. I cite just one other contemporary declaration of despair with the religion of progress in order to show something of the climate of controversy: "From all the signs that have been staring us in the face during the past year, I believe it is safe to say that all progress must lead not to further progress, but finally to the negation of progress, a return to the point of departure . . . Is it not very clear that progress, that is to say, the onward march of things, good as well as evil, has brought our civilization to the brink of an abyss into which it may very possibly fall, giving place to utter barbarism?" *The Journal of Eugène Delacroix,* trans. Lucy Norton (London, 1951). The passage is cited in E. H. Gombrich, *The Ideas of Progress and Their Impact on Art* (New York, 1971).

13. Hegel, *Reason in History*, p. 45.

14. Lehmann, I, 411.

15. The report of Clarus is printed in Lehmann, I, 487ff. In March 1929 Berg presented a lecture on *Wozzeck* in connection with the performance of the opera in Oldenburg. About the scene-changing music between the fourth

and fifth scenes of Act 3 he said this: "From the dramatic standpoint it should be conceived as an 'Epilogue' to Wozzeck's suicide, as a declaration of the author who, stepping outside the action on the stage, issues an appeal to the audience, regarded as the representatives of humanity." H. Redlich, *Alban Berg: Versuch einer Würdigung* (Vienna, 1957), pp. 311–27.

16. This is not the first time that attention has been drawn to the motivic tautness of Berg's music. With respect to *Wozzeck,* see esp. George Perle, "Representation and Symbol in the Music of *Wozzeck,*" *Music Review,* 32 (1971), 281–308, and "The Musical Language of *Wozzeck,*" *Music Forum,* 1 (1967), 204ff. From this point on the reader can best follow the argument by referring to a score and a recording.

17. The upper voice of motive *a* is marked H in the score (*Hauptstimme,* or principal voice). That is the case with every strand of the motivic network I am describing here, something I take to be an indication of Berg's intentions with respect to the rank of these motives.

18. Letter to his fiancée, after 10 March 1834. Lehmann, II, 425–26.

10. The Lulu Character and the Character of Lulu

The work on this subject has benefited in numerous ways from conversations with the great drama critic Jan Kott. I offer it in appreciation for his help and for his work in general.

1. Such is the discussion between Donald Mitchell, in "The Character of Lulu: Wedekind's and Berg's Conceptions Compared," *Music Review,* 15 (1954), 268–74, and George Perle, "The Character of Lulu: A Sequel," *Music Review,* 25 (1964), 311–19.

2. Program booklet, *Deutsche Grammophon Gesellschaft* no. 3308345-48 (1979), pp. 4–5.

3. George Perle, *The Operas of Alban Berg,* vol. 2, *Lulu* (Berkeley, 1985), p. 69.

4. The sketches are reproduced and discussed in Patricia Hall, "Role and Form in Berg's Sketches for *Lulu,*" in R. Morgan and D. Gable, eds., *Alban Berg: Historical and Analytical Perspectives* (Oxford, 1989).

5. Karl Kraus, *Literatur und Lüge* (Munich, 1958), pp. 9–21.

6. Ibid., p. 12.

7. See Douglas Jarman's essay "Dr. Schön's Five-Strophe Aria," in his book *The Music of Alban Berg* (Berkeley, Calif., 1979).

8. Friedrich Rothe, *Frank Wedekinds Dramen: Jugendstil und Lebensphilosophie* (Stuttgart, 1968), p. 57.

9. The first three pitches of Schön's and Alwa's rows in their untransposed and prime positions constitute A major and minor triads, respectively, in the second inversion—they are differentiated by C-sharp and C-natural.

10. Unpublished essay by Judy Lochhead, "*Lulu: Structural Principles.*"

11. Perle, *Lulu,* p. 34.

12. Jan Kott, "Ionesco, or a Pregnant Death," in *The Theater of Essence* (Evanston, Il., 1984), p. 99; also the essay "Witkiewicz, or the Dialectic of Anachronism" in the same collection, where Kott writes "a time is coming in which only farce will have the appearance of tragedy" (pp. 80–81).

13. Paul Fechter, *Frank Wedekind: Der Mensch und das Werk* (Jena, 1920), pp. 56, 58–59.

14. Berg's decision to make the orchestral voice in the D-minor interlude of *Wozzeck* suddenly his own is questioned by Joseph Kerman and Igor Stravinsky. The suggestion from both is that the interjection of a direct expression of the composer's own feelings for the first and only time so late in the opera radically disrupts and thereby weakens the dramatic transaction. Should we not read in Berg's musical commentaries on the deaths of both his leading ladies expressions not only of compassion but also of remorse? And are they not further signs of his ambivalence? Kerman's comment is in *Opera and Drama* (New York, 1956), pp. 230–33. Stravinsky's critique is quoted by Robert Craft in *Stravinsky: Chronicle of a Friendship* (New York, 1972), pp. 32–34. I am grateful to David Gable for calling my attention to those passages.

15. Jarman, *The Music of Alban Berg,* p. 234.

16. Quoted from the translation by Richard Howard (Boston, 1982), pp. 5–6.

17. Program booklet (see note 2), p. 15.

18. Cited in M. L. von Franz, "The Process of Individuation," in Carl G. Jung, ed., *Man and his Symbols* (New York, 1964), p. 180.

19. Tilly Wedekind, "Lulu—The Role of My Life," *Theater Quarterly,* 1 (1971), 3–7.

20. Goethe, *Wilhelm Meister,* trans. Thomas Carlyle, 2nd ed. (Boston, 1839), p. ix.

21. See Jacques Bril, *Lilith, ou la mére obscure* (Paris 1981), and Barbara Black Koltuv, *The Book of Lilith* (York Beach, Me. 1986). Jewish tradition regarding the origins of Lilith and Eve is reported in Susan Weidman Schneider, *Jewish and Female* (New York, 1984). I am obliged to Professor Joseph Strauss for calling my attention to the latter source.

22. Clive Bennett, "Maschinist Hopkins: A Father for Lulu?" in *Musical Times,* September 1986, pp. 481–84.

23. The classic treatment of this subject is in Mario Praz, *The Romantic Agony* (Oxford, 1970), chap. 4, "La Belle Dame Sans Merci." See also Martha Kingsbury, "The Femme Fatale and her Sisters," in Thomas B. Hess and Linda Nochlin, eds., *Woman as Sex Object: Studies in Erotic Art 1730–1970* (New York, 1972), pp. 182–205.

24. Helen of Troy is prominent in Praz's gallery of fatal women. In a letter to his wife Helene (17 June 1928) Berg characterized John Erskine's novel *The*

Private Life of Helen of Troy as "a delightful book: the only possible interpretation of Helen, as Lulu." Now, Nelly is a common nickname for Helen, but it was of course already in Wedekind's text—yet another odd coincidence. The letter is cited by Perle (*Lulu,* p. 40), who takes no notice of this connection between Erskine's and Berg's heroines.

25. Throwing caution to the winds, Perle identifies Don Giovanni as Lulu's "male counterpart," then moves on to characterize Lulu with the language Kierkegaard used in his famous interpretation of the Don, in *Either/Or.*

26. See von Franz, "The Process of Individuation," pp. 177–88.

27. A very rich interpretation of the Pierrot figure is given by Jean Starobinski in *Portrait de l'artiste en saltimbanque* (Geneva, 1970).

28. Tilly Wedekind, "Lulu—The Role of My Life," p. 7.

Credits

The essays in this volume originally appeared as follows:

1. "History, Criticism, and Beethoven's Ninth Symphony," *19th Century Music,* 3 (1980).
2. "'To Worship That Celestial Sound': Motives for Analysis," *Journal of Musicology,* 1 (1982).
3. "Music Analysis in an Historical Context," *College Music Symposium,* 6 (1966).
4. "On Historical Criticism," *The Musical Quarterly,* 53 (1967).
5. "The Present as History," *Perspectives of New Music,* 7 (1969).
6. "What Kind of Story Is History?" *19th Century Music,* 7 (1984).
7. "Absolut Mozart," paper given at symposium on "Biography and the Work of Art: The Case of Mozart," Rutgers University, 1984. Published in H. Danuser, H. de la Motte-Haber, S. Leopold, and N. Miller, eds., *Das Musikalische Kunstwerk: Festschrift Carl Dahlhaus* (Laaber, 1988).
8. "Dufay the Progressive," in Allan W. Atlas, ed., *Dufay Quincentenary Conference* (Brooklyn, N.Y., 1976).
9. "*Wozzeck* and the Apocalypse: An Essay in Historical Criticism," *Critical Inquiry* (Winter 1976).
10. First appearance of this essay.

For permission to reproduce illustrations or musical examples I am grateful to the following:

The Art Institute of Chicago, John H. Wrenn Memorial Collection, 1947.689 (Fig. 10.5) and Clarence Buckingham Collection, 1963.284 (Fig. 10.9), © 1987 The Art Institute of Chicago, all rights reserved.

The Epstein Collections, Washington, D.C. (Figs. 10.6 and 10.8).

Index